World ...

SPAIN

WORLD FOOD Spain
1st edition

Published by
Lonely Planet Publications Pty Ltd A.C.N. 005 607 983
192 Burwood Rd, Hawthorn, Victoria 3122, Australia

Lonely Planet Offices
Australia PO Box 617, Hawthorn, Victoria 3122
USA 150 Linden Street, Oakland CA 94607
UK 10a Spring Place, London NW5 3BH
France 1 rue du Dahomey, 75011 Paris

Photography
All of the images in this guide are available
for licensing from Lonely Planet Images.
email: lpi@lonelyplanet.com.au

Published
March 2000

Although the author and publisher have tried to make the information as accurate as possible, they accept no responsibility for any loss, injury or inconvenience sustained by any person using this book

ISBN 1 86450 025 5

text & maps © Lonely Planet Publications Pty Ltd, 2000
photos © photographers as indicated 2000

Printed by
The Bookmaker Pty. Ltd.
Printed in China.

About the Author

Richard Sterling is known as the Indiana Jones of Gastronomy for his willingness to go anywhere and court any danger for the sake of a good meal. His other books include *Dining with Headhunters; The Fearless Diner;* and the award winning *Travelers' Tales: A Taste of the Road.* He has been honoured by the James Beard Foundation for his food writing, and by the Lowell Thomas awards for his travel literature. His lifestyle column 'The Best Revenge' appears monthly in *Code* magazine. Though he lives in Berkeley, California, he is very often politically incorrect.

About the Photographer

Oliver Strewe is a Sydney-based food & travel photographer. This is his first food guide although he has photographed for many food and wine books, and is a regular contributor to a number of Australian and international magazines. At any given time, along with his wife Tina, his ambition is to visit a new country. Spain is his favourite destination: San Sebastián for the best pub food in the world, Barcelona for the architecture, Madrid for the bars and Sevilla for romance.

About the Linguist

The language sections were compiled by Allison Jones, UK, author of the Lonely Planet *Spanish* phrasebook.

From the Publisher

This first edition of *World Food Spain* was edited by Patrick Witton and designed by Brendan Dempsey of Lonely Planet's Melbourne office. Natasha Vellelley mapped with finishing touches provided by Paul Clifton. Lara Morcombe indexed. Valerie Tellini, Lonely Planet Images, co-ordinated the supply of photographs. Dora Chai assisted with production. Sally Steward and Peter D'Onghia oversaw the production of the language section.

Sally Steward, publisher, developed the series and Martin Hughes, series editor, nurtured each book from the seeds of ideas through to fruition, with inimitable flair.

Acknowledgements

The publisher wishes to thank Allison Jones, London, who made helpful suggestions, and Guy Mirabella for design concepts. Warm thanks to Richard Sterling who entertained, provided and was delightfully inefficient when it didn't matter and a gun when it did.

From the author: special thanks to Pilar Vico of the Commercial Office Embassy of Spain for her advice and secret knowledge. To Brett Allen King for aiding and abetting us. Thanks also to Louis Irízar of San

Sebastián for guiding us through new territory. And to the nuns of Convento de Corpus Cristi, Madrid. And to the beautiful mime on La Rambla, whose name we shall sadly never know, who made our last tapeo in Barcelona a time of magic.

From the photographer: I would like to thank Tina, Halley and Billy; Eduardo Gonzalez and Juan Manual Osorio of the Commercial Office Embassy of Spain; Nicole Lawless of Kodak; Luis Irízar of the San Sebastián Cooking School; Maria Luisa Albacar, Turisme De Barcelona; all my friends at Bar Pinotxo; Rick Jefferies; all the people at Restaurant Los Caracoles ; Elisabeth Thallwitz; Paco Vilas of Restaurant Vilas, Santiago; Rosa Purificacion Romani Suarez and Mike Lilly.

From the linguist: thanks to Izaskun Arretxe for her work on the Lonely Planet *Spanish* Phrasebook, on which the phrases used here are based, to Mar and Santi for inspiration and calçots at Cal Petrarch, to Paul Matthews, Stewart King and everyone else who offered ideas, food and help with the language section.

Warning & Request

Things change; markets give way to supermarkets, prices go up, good places go bad and not much stays the same. Please tell us if you've discovered changes and help make the next edition even more useful. We value all your feedback, and strive to improve our books accordingly. We have a well-travelled, well-fed team that reads and acknowledges every letter, postcard and email and ensures that every morsel of information finds its way to the appropriate people.

Each correspondent will receive the latest issue of Planet Talk, our quarterly printed newsletter, or Comet, our monthly email newsletter. Subscriptions to both are free. The newsletters might even feature your letter so let us know if you don't want it published.

If you have an interesting anecdote or story to do with your culinary travels, we'd love to hear it. If we publish it in the next edition, we'll send you a free Lonely Planet book of your choice.

Send your correspondence to the nearest Lonely Planet office:
Australia: PO Box 617, Hawthorn, Victoria 3122
UK: 10a Spring Place, London NW5 3BH
USA: 150 Linden St, Oakland CA 94607
France: 1 rue du Dahomey, Paris 75011

Or email us at: talk2us@lonelyplanet.com

Contents

Introduction 8

**The Culture of
Spanish Cuisine** 9
History 15

Staples & Specialities 23
Pan (Bread) 24
Queso (Cheese) 26
Huevos (Eggs) 27
Pescados & Mariscos
(Fish & Seafood) 29
Fruto y Verduras
(Fruit & Vegetables) 32
Jamón (Ham) 34
Sausages 40
Cecina (Cured Meat) 42
Caza (Game) 43
Vaca (Beef) 44
Ave de Corral (Fowl) 44
Hierbas y Especias
(Herbs & Spices) 46
Aceite de Oliva (Olive Oil) 49
Arroz (Rice) 57
Salsas (Sauces) 63
Sopas (Soups) 67
Postres (Desserts) 70
Tapas (Hors d'Oeuvres) 73

Drinks 77
Wine 79
Sherry 93
Other Alcohol 97
Non-Alcoholic Drinks 105

Home Cooking & Traditions 109
The Spanish Kitchen & Utensils 112

Celebrating with Food 117

127 **Regional Variations**
128 The Heart of Spain
143 Atlantic Spain
155 Mediterranean Spain
164 The Pyrenees

175 **Shopping & Markets**
177 Mercado (Market)
183 Speciality Shops
187 Things to Take Home

189 **Where to Eat & Drink**
192 Where to Eat
205 Where to Drink

209 **Understanding the Menu**
211 Menú del Día (Day's Set Menu)
215 Menú la Carta (A la Carte Menu)
216 Carta de Vinos (Wine List)

217 **A Spanish Banquet**

225 **Fit & Healthy**

233 **Recommended Reading**

234 **Photo Credits**

235 **Eat Your Words – Language Guide**
236 Pronunciation Guide
237 Useful Phrases
245 English – Spanish Glossary
259 Spanish Culinary Dictionary

297 **Index**

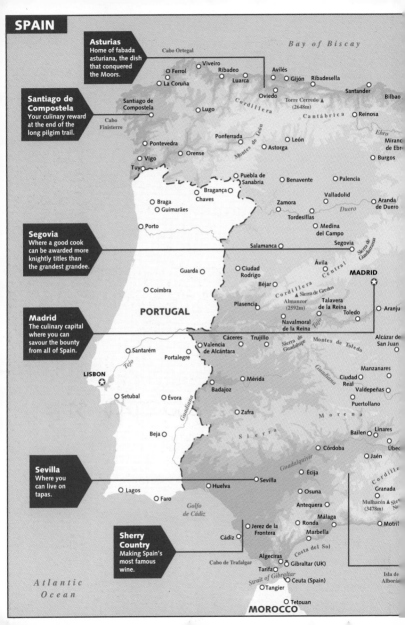

SPAIN

Asturias
Home of fabada asturiana, the dish that conquered the Moors.

Santiago de Compostela
Your culinary reward at the end of the long pilgrim trail.

Segovia
Where a good cook can be awarded more knightly titles than the grandest grandee.

Madrid
The culinary capital where you can savour the bounty from all of Spain.

Sevilla
Where you can live on tapas.

Sherry Country
Making Spain's most famous wine.

Bay of Biscay

Cabo Ortegal
O Viveiro
O Ferrol   Ribadeo   Avilés
O La Coruña   Luarca   O Gijón   Ribadesella   O Santander   Bilbao
                          Oviedo   O
Santiago de   *Cordillera*   Torre Cerredo ▲   O Reinosa
Compostela   O Lugo   (2648m)   *Cantábrica*
Cabo   *Ebro*
Finisterre   Miranc
                      Ponferrada   O León   de Ebr
O Pontevedra   *Montes de León*   O Astorga   O Burgos
O Orense
O Vigo
O Tuy   O Puebla de   O Benavente   O Palencia
                  Sanabria   Valladolid   O Aranda
O Braga   Bragança O   Zamora   O   O   de Duero
O Guimarães Chaves   *Duero*
                                    Tordesillas
O Porto   O Medina
                                   del Campo
                    Salamanca O   Segovia O   *Sierra de Guadarrama*

Guarda O   O Ciudad   Ávila O   **MADRID** ★
               Rodrigo
                                          Cordillera   Central
O Coimbra   Béjar O   ▲ Sierra de Gredos
                 Plasencia   Almanzor
PORTUGAL   O   (2592m) Talavera   O Aranju
                 Navalmoral   de la Reina Toledo
                 de la Reina   *Tajo*

                 Cáceres Trujillo *Sierra de*   *Montes de Toledo*   Alcázar de
O Santarém   Valencia O   O   *Guadalupe*   San Juan
              de Alcántara   O
O Portalegre   O Manzanares
LISBON ★   Ciudad
                    O Mérida   Real O
O Setubal   Badajoz   Valdepeñas O
              O   Puertollano O
O Évora   M o r e n a
           O Zafra
                                                        S i e r r a   Bailén O Linares
Beja O   O Úbec
                              Guadalquivir   O Córdoba
                                                                             O Jaén
                         O Écija   *Cordille*
O Lagos   O Huelva   Sevilla O   Granada O
  O Faro   O Osuna   Mulhacén ▲ Sie
  Golfo   Antequera O   (3478m)   Ne
  de Cádiz   Málaga   O Motril
                              O Jerez de la Ronda O
                  Cádiz   Frontera   Marbella   *Costa del Sol*
Atlantic   Algeciras
                              Tarifa Gibraltar (UK)   Isla de
                      Cabo de Trafalgar   Alborán
Ocean   Tangier O *Strait of Gibraltar* Ceuta (Spain)
                              O Tetouan
                          MOROCCO

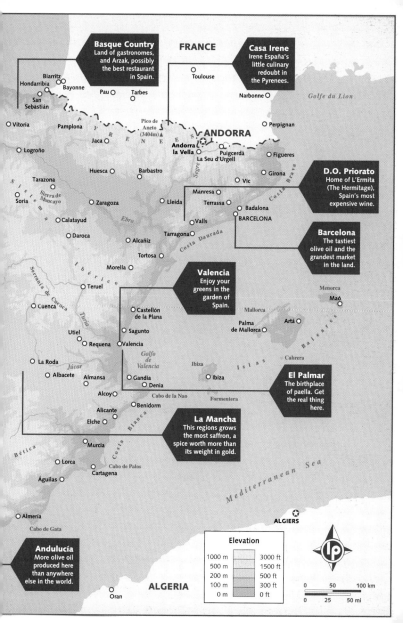

Basque Country
Land of gastronomes, and Arzak, possibly the best restaurant in Spain.

Casa Irene
Irene España's little culinary redoubt in the Pyrenees.

D.O. Priorato
Home of L'Ermita (The Hermitage), Spain's most expensive wine.

Barcelona
The tastiest olive oil and the grandest market in the land.

Valencia
Enjoy your greens in the garden of Spain.

El Palmar
The birthplace of paella. Get the real thing here.

La Mancha
This regions grows the most saffron, a spice worth more than its weight in gold.

Andalucía
More olive oil produced here than anywhere else in the world.

FRANCE

Toulouse
Narbonne
Golfe du Lion

Biarritz
Hondarribia
Bayonne
Pau
Tarbes
San Sebastián
Vitoria
Pamplona
Jaca
Pico de Aneto (3404m)
ANDORRA
Perpignan
Andorra la Vella
Puigcerdà
Logroño
La Seu d'Urgell
Figueres
Tarazona
Huesca
Barbastro
Vic
Girona
Soria
Sierra de Moncayo
Manresa
Costa Brava
Calatayud
Zaragoza
Lleida
Terrassa
Badalona
Daroca
Alcañiz
Valls
BARCELONA
Morella
Tarragona
Costa Daurada
Tortosa
Teruel
Cuenca
Serranía de Cuenca
Turia
Castellón de la Plana
Menorca
Maó
Mallorca
Sagunto
Palma de Mallorca
Artá
Utiel
Requena
Valencia
Baleares
La Roda
Golfo de Valencia
Albacete
Almansa
Ibiza
Islas
Cabrera
Gandia
Ibiza
Alcoy
Denia
Alicante
Benidorm
Cabo de la Nao
Elche
Formentera
Costa Blanca
Murcia
Lorca
Cabo de Palos
Águilas
Cartagena
Mediterranean Sea
Almería
Cabo de Gata
ALGIERS

Elevation

1000 m	3000 ft
500 m	1500 ft
200 m	500 ft
100 m	300 ft
0 m	0 ft

0   50   100 km
0   25   50 mi

ALGERIA
Oran

PYRENEES
Sistema Ibérico
Ebro
Segre
Júcar
Bética

 The popular images of Spain include Gypsies and paella, bullfights and sherry, Gaudí and sangría. Food goes hand in hand with history, architecture and the everyday, and all these elements you will find both in Spain, and within these pages.

In Spain, a cuisine is served that vividly reflects and celebrates its culture and colourful history. Dining Spanish style means dining with the memories and influences of Romans, Moors, Aztecs, Basque fishermen, La Manchan peasants, Spanish grandees and French tourists. You will encounter a confusion of styles, sensuality balanced by simplicity, culinary routine punctuated by indulgence, and an unerringly constant kitchen philosophy. Spanish cuisine will surprise and intrigue; exhaust and delight – it will fill you up, make you cry for mercy, and then beg for more.

You will soon discover that there is no single Spanish cuisine. Geographically, culturally, emotionally, and gastronomically, Spain is a proud and adaptive melange. It's a shape-shifter, in the best mythological style. Politically, Spain is divided into 17 regions. Gastronomically, you should add one more: the kitchen of every Spaniard that you meet. But within these pages you will find Spain divided into its four greater geographic zones: the Heart of Spain; Atlantic Spain; Mediterranean Spain; and the Pyrenees. These divisions, we believe, make the Iberian peninsula accessible to the traveller and to the reader. Among these terrains, and this book's descriptions of culture, history and appetites, you will find the Spain that best suits you. Here you will discover your own tastes and your own hungers. Here you will discover your own personal Spain.

the
culture
of spanish cuisine

History, religion and love have all influenced the way the Spanish eat. In fact, the elements that make up an authentic Spanish meal do not rest solely on the table: they are found in the atmosphere, the appreciation of the food, and the friends that dine with you.

Church door in Sevilla, Andalucía

It is hard to speak of the 'cuisine' of Spain, for Spanish cuisine has no single form. There are many threads of tradition and influence running through the Spanish kitchen. Romans, Moors, Aztecs, French and Italians have all woven themselves into the tapestry of culinary Spain. In certain corners the colours are predominantly Moorish, in others Roman. The shapes shift in the picture as you change your angle of view, the American here, the Latin there. And each time you look at it a different weave reveals itself. The vision will never be captured, so there is no 'final shape' of Spain's cuisine. The Iberian kitchen gods are full of mischief. They surely have names like Puck, Eros and Coyote.

But even if we cannot fully grip this beautiful trickster, there are certain traits that we can tease out. Spanish cooking is straightforward. There is never any mistaking what you are eating. 'It should taste of what it is' goes the mantra. To disguise a food or to hide its true nature is sacrilege. Herbs and spices are used sparingly. The cook will seldom alter, mash, puree or mould a food beyond recognition, for it must also look of what it is. To these ends simplicity is prized. And simplicity can be a very difficult thing to achieve. It takes concentration and kitchen alchemy to draw out a delicate flavour by means of fire and oil and little else. It is an easy thing, on the other hand, to destroy it. A dish of Spain is generous. You will never have to lift up a sprig of parsley to find your portion of meat. And Spanish cookery is unpretentious. Your food will not be tarted up and made to look cute, or grand, or rare and costly, or more colourful. There is no over-reliance on sauces. There is no confusion of tastes.

Vineyard and winery, Galicia

So much for what it is not. Now take a seat at any table in Spain. Almost without exception you will face what we call the Holy Trinity of Spanish cuisine: bread, oil and wine. This triumvirate is the cornerstone of Spain's culinary history.

The legacy of Rome is both gastronomic and religious. And it was Rome that gave Spain the Trinity of Father, Son and Holy Ghost; and the Trinity of Wheat, Olive and the Vine. All three have been cultivated here for at least as long as records have been kept, and that goes back to Phoenician times. But it was under the influence of Rome that we first see them coalescing into a culinary tradition in which bread, oil and wine are not sufficient unto themselves, but rather the three parts of the larger whole. A meal without these three is mere feeding. When all are present we cross from simple sustenance into the art of cuisine, an essential of the art of living.

Chimney pots on the La Pedrera building, designed by Gaudí, Barcelona, Catalunya

Tomatoes, garlic and bread from Los Caracoles Restaurante, Barcelona, Catalunya

Other cultures rely to greater or lesser degree on bread, oil and wine, but none, we think, as much as Spain. To this Holy Trinity we add a trio of touchstones. We know when we are at the Spanish table there will be garlic, religion and conviviality. Spanish fare has been described by better writers to be 'thick with garlic and religion'. And indeed garlic is infused in almost everything. We have garlic soup, bread rubbed with raw garlic and garlic sauces such as **alioli** (garlic mayonnaise). The list goes on and on. And as for conviviality, the very purpose of Spanish dining is to nourish the soul as well as the body. The Latin verb, *convivire* (to live together) is the only essential sauce at the Spanish table. Dining is the time to strengthen ties between family, community and religion. So many recipes have been brought into being by religious observance or proscription: **tarta de Santiago** (Saint James' cake), **huessos santos** (saint's bones), to name just two. When the Spanish take communion in church, and consume the body and blood of Christ, they really mean it. When they lift their glass to you and say 'Salud', they really mean it.

CULTURE

History

Spain has the Romans to thank for the basis of their cuisine, upon which other cultures, armies and importers have placed their own tastes. Following the Romans came the Visigoths, whose sorry legacy includes some simple architecture and nothing good to eat. But then came the Moors from North Africa. To the fields they brought the almond groves, oranges and other fruits. Sugar cane was an important Moorish import, and the reduction and distillation of sugar syrups led to the development of perfumes, liqueurs, and medicinal tinctures. Moorish trade provided artichokes, eggplants, spinach, rice, the reintroduction of saffron and sophisticated agricultural techniques. To the kitchen they brought the characteristic combination of finely chopped ingredients that eventually led to dishes like paella. They also introduced spiced casseroles, stews, nut sauces and fruit syrups.

The Spanish, having gradually adopted Moorish cuisine, soon met with another rich tradition, the highly developed imperial cookery of the Aztecs. Montezuma's kitchens had developed complex nut sauces, and they made skilful use of such ingredients as chilli, chocolate and tomato. Spanish cooks readily adopted these foods into their own culinary canon, and a wonderful early fusion cuisine arose. An inspired cook could take the best of all, creating new flavours. For a simple example, taste a cup of Spanish chocolate: chocolate from the Aztecs, cinnamon from the Moors. It's the taste of crossroads (see the recipe on the next page).

DENOMINATIONS OF ORIGIN AND SPECIFICITY

One of the most important aspects of Spanish food and beverages is the system of **Denominación de Origen (DO)** (Denomination of Origin). This is a government designation classifying products whose raw materials are produced and manufactured within a specified geographical area, and possess distinctive qualities and characteristics, mainly due to climate, soil, methods of manufacture, ageing and amelioration. This system applies to most agricultural products, but not to fish, game or imports.

A related designation is the **Denominación Especifica (DE)** (Specific Denomination). This applies to products characterised by a relationship to a given geographical setting, with the use of specified raw materials *or* method of manufacture. It differs from a DO in that both factors do not have to be present. To be considered under this denomination, the producers must submit a list of criteria under which they intend their products to be processed. This may include geographical delimitation, raw materials used, proofs of origin and description of processes. Both DO and DE are managed by regulators called Consejo Regulador.

The fishing port in San Sebastián, Basque Country

CULTURE

Churros con Chocolate
(Fried Doughnut Strips with Chocolate)

Churros

1	cup water
½	cup margarine or butter
¼	teaspoon salt
1	cup all-purpose flour
3	eggs
¼	cup sugar
1	teaspoon cinnamon
	vegetable or olive oil

Prepare to fry the churros by heating 3cm of oil in a pan.

To make the churro dough, put the water, margarine and salt in a 3-litre saucepan and heat to a rolling boil. Stir in the flour and keep stirring over low heat until the mixture forms a ball (about 1 minute). Remove from the heat. Beat the eggs until smooth then stir them into the mixture.

Spoon mixture into a cake decorators' tube with a large star tip. Squeeze 10cm strips of dough into hot oil. Fry three or four strips at a time until golden brown, turning once (about 2 minutes on each side). Drain on paper towels. Mix the sugar and cinnamon; roll churros in the mixture or dump it on the pile of churros (like the pros). That churro taste will take you right back to the days of walking the paseos of Spain.

Chocolate for Churro Dunking

110g dark chocolate, chopped
850ml milk

1	tablespoon cornflour
4	tablespoon sugar
1	pinch cinnamon

Heat the chocolate and half the milk in a pan, stirring until the chocolate has melted. Dissolve the cornflour in the remaining milk and whisk into the chocolate along with the sugar. Cook on low heat, whisking until the chocolate thickens (about 5 minutes). Remove and dust with cinnamon. Pour into cups or bowls for dunking churros.

All these ingredients have come together on the Iberian peninsula. And in the Iberian school of cookery they must maintain their natural integrity. They can be combined, mixed and matched, but they must not lose their essential character. For the sum of Spanish cuisine is in the nature of its parts. It is more in the bricks than in the final edifice, that we define the food of Cervantes and Gaudí. The greatest effort of the Spanish culture to nourish itself goes not into the making of sauces or complex preparations. It goes into the making of the raw materials. As you shall see throughout this book. It is in the methods of curing meats, secrets of making cheese, using the right type of rice, whether a fish is taken by net or hook. Spanish agriculture is dedicated to the production of raw materials of the highest quality and reputation. The elements of Spanish cookery are so firmly rooted in the soil and traditions of Spain that this cuisine simply will not travel. This cuisine is literally the taste of Spain itself. A good Spanish cook knows this, and knows that if the raw materials are not unduly interfered with, a good meal will be had.

Scallops and bread

CULTURE

FACES OF GASTRONOMY – Jose Grimaldi

It's one of those hot afternoons in Cádiz when the sun is so bright it hurts your eyes. Sensible folk have retreated indoors, businesses are closed until evening. We stagger down the Calle Libertad trying desperately to stay in the shade. That's when we encounter Jose Grimaldi sitting outside his restaurant. "Señores, you look like you will die. Stop and join me for a nice cool glass of wine. I have natural air-conditioning" he says with a grin, referring to the sea breeze. Who could argue?

Jose has been owner and chef of Restaurante Grimaldi since 1994. Before that he was a fisherman, like his father and his grandfather. His father still goes out in the mornings for a few hours and brings his son to his catch. Sherry is poured and we talk cookery. "I learned to cook on the fishing boat and I learned from my parents. Fishermen make good cooks. We love fish and we know how to treat it. The trick is to get the freshest fish and other natural ingredients and then use your imagination. I'll show you." He presents a plate with what look like home-baked biscuits studded with chopped nuts. But they smell of the sea. The 'nuts', we discover, are chopped shrimp. And the 'biscuits' have been fried in olive oil and are marbled with what appear to be flakes of parsley. They are beguilingly tasty. The flavours and aromas sing of the sea. The texture is crumbly and soft yet offers something to the teeth. It tastes of purity. Almost of innocence. It's like eating virtue.

"These are **tortillas de camarones** (shrimp fritters). They're very simple. Anybody can cook them. The shrimp were alive when I bought them, so I know they are good. The flour and the oil are the best. But I wanted a little more taste of the sea, so I used my imagination. I put a little bit of chopped seaweed in my batter. Such simple things, but all good things. That's our only secret here in Spain. And olive oil, of course."

Tortillas de Camarones (Shrimp Fritters)

½	cup white flour	1	cup water
½	cup chickpea flour	1	teaspoon salt
	(or ⅓ cup more white flour)	¼	cup onion, finely chopped
2	tablespoons parsley	250g	tiny shrimp or chopped
1.5cm depth of olive oil for frying			larger shrimp

Whisk all the ingredients except the oil in a bowl to make a batter. Let it stand for 2-3 hours. If it becomes too thick, thin it with water to a slightly pourable consistency. Pour oil into a heavy pan and heat to smoking. Pour the batter into the oil a tablespoon at a time, spreading it around in circles to form a biscuit shape. Brown on both sides.

Makes about 24

How Spaniards Eat

The Spanish begin their day simply enough. Coffee and a bit of bread or biscuit with a little butter or jam. And perhaps a glass of sherry or a gin & tonic. Yes, yes, you read correctly. The morning tipple is an institution in Spain. Stay here long enough and you will adjust your sleeping schedule to 5 hours (2-7am) then 3 hours (4-7pm). At 8am on such a schedule you will find a noggin of gin or a glass of **fino** (dry sherry) just the thing. Admittedly, this is more the custom among retired folks and writers than among people who must drive or operate heavy machinery for a living, but there are a lot of retired folks and writers in Spain.

The midday meal is the big one. It won't start earlier than 2pm. Everyone in Spain except waiters and cooks set aside their tasks and turn to the table. For the next couple of hours their world will revolve around the table and each other. Nothing else will matter. Lovers will feast their eyes upon each other, grandparents will dote upon their progeny, children will look to their parents for love and validation. Life happens in Spain at the table. Adults will drink and laugh. Kids will play and shout. Oh how they will shout. And all will be right with the world for a while. We of the Anglophone world might think this naive or sentimental, but then we live with migraines and stress. The Spanish feed their children ice cream and sleep soundly through their afternoon siesta.

Locals relaxing in Plaça Major, Olot, Catalunya

After 7pm people rise, bathe, read the paper and call relatives. At 9pm the streets come to life. Young women, all of whom are the soul of Carmen, meet on corners dressed in their flimsy finest. When enough of them have gathered, they begin a slow progress down the street to the centre of town, singing. They clap out Flamenco rhythms and intone old songs. They are young yet sing ancient songs, not the pop charts. They pass men strumming soulfully on guitars. Families, gangs of young men, groups of old ladies, and legions of old men follow the music to the places of feasting.

As you sit at your table with your **aperitivo** (aperitif), perfect strangers will pass you on the way to their tables. They will look at you squarely and smilingly say '**Buen provecho!**' (enjoy your meal). The clatter of crystal and china offer counterpoint to the music wafting through the streets. The wine is heady. The dinner is light, the midday meal having been so substantial. But the conviviality is as thick as the garlic in the alioli. Welcome to Spain. Buen provecho.

Etiquette

Spanish table manners and settings are studies in simplicity. Unless you are in a very smart restaurant you will keep the same knife and fork throughout the meal. You might also have a spoon and that will be that for your implements of destruction. No need for highly specialised surgical instruments. You will have one wine glass and one water glass, unless you also order **cava** (sparkling wine). Then you might be given a flute or a tulip for the bubbly. Your water glass will be larger than your wine glass. The message of this should be clear. The only bit of arcana to remember at the Spanish table is that you should always keep your hands in view, never let them be hidden in the folds of napery or under the table. We don't know the reason for this, but perhaps it goes back to days of blood feuds and hidden daggers.

Cafe, Bilbao, Basque Country

One word of warning: among the basic food groups, the Spanish would seem to include tobacco. Men smoke, women smoke, teenagers smoke. It is almost a rite of passage to arrive at adolescence and select your favourite brand of coffin nail and air pollution. Wherever you go you'll soon be enveloped in a thick blue haze of cigarette smoke. If you are at a table with six Spaniards, three of them will be smoking at any given time. If you are next to a table of Spanish gentlemen who have just finished a convivial repast, you may find yourself befogged by the effluent of several monstrous cigars. Great fat rolls of tobacco, big enough to double as torches. And they seem not to have the faintest notion that this could be distressing to anyone.

Restaurant in Barcelona, Catalunya

There is no use in protesting to the smoker next to you. You'll only be met with befuddlement. And there is no use in asking to be seated in the non-smoking section of the restaurant, it is non existent. And while the railways provide many non-smoking cars, the dining cars are not among them, so that's where everyone goes to smoke. The air in a flamenco bar can be so thick that visibility is reduced. We have had to stagger out of such places gasping, eyes stinging, before we could even drink our beer.

So what to do? Take up smoking? Hold your breath? Eschew flamenco? Luckily, many restaurants are outdoors. You need only take a table upwind. If no upwind tables are available, there is always another restaurant in Spain. When in one of the many deep and narrow cafes, never ever sit in the back of the room. Never. Sit as close as possible to the door. In the warm Spanish weather a door or a window will usually be left open. Air conditioning is the exception rather than the norm; the Spanish don't care much for it. Inside a proper sit-down restaurant in the evening with all the doors and windows closed, select a table near the air-conditioner if there is one, or a table off to the side, and wear your stiff upper lip.

staples
& specialities

Beyond the Holy Trinity of bread, oil and wine, Spanish cuisine boasts a cornucopia of diversity. Plentiful seafood dishes, regional breads and a selection of garden produce represent a small corner of what is available to the Spanish diner. And prepare yourself for the ham onslaught, as nowhere else in the world is a pig so admired.

Pan (Bread)

The first branch of the Holy Trinity of Spanish food is bread. Suffusing every aspect of the county's cuisine, bread is a symbol of continuity, prosperity, and security. While France expresses herself with cheeses and Italy with pasta, Spain does so with bread, not only by holding an astounding variety, but also by knowing so many ways to enjoy it. Perhaps those other countries did similarly in times past, but Spain in many ways *is* times past.

Bread is the basis of any meal. It might be as simple as bread dipped in milk, drizzled with olive oil for breakfast, or part of a soup such as in **salmorejo** (thick cold tomato soup). The Andalucían farmer's breakfast, **migas canas**, is emblematic of the most basic, minimalist cookery using bread. The hungry campesino soaks a dry loaf in salted water. He peels a few cloves of garlic and fries them in oil. When they are brown he adds the bread and stirs, cooking and browning until it resolves itself into toasty crumbs. He adds hot milk, and cooks it to a rich and savoury porridge.

Empanada, essentially bread with a filling, constitutes the culinary 'great leap forward' from bread mixed or taken with something, to bread cooked with something. In Spain this is the beginning of cuisine and the

advancement of human happiness. At its simplest an empanada is a layer of bread dough, something spread atop it, and another layer of dough laid down on that. Baked golden you will see this ancient dish served in **tascas** (tapas bars) and **sidrerías** (cider bars). Empanadas are commonly filled with tuna. In Extremadura the mixture is simple, in Catalunya it is spiced and enriched with tomato. In Andalucía it may contain chopped olives.

No meal in Spain is complete without bread. Though the diner may only nibble at it, if the bread isn't served there will be complaints. Sadly people *don't* complain when the bread isn't up to scratch. In recent years the Spanish have learned how to make insubstantial aerated bread that costs little. This is what you will be served at most restaurants. The better restaurants will still give you better bread. And you can buy superb breads at shops called **panadería artesana**. You will see them in every city in Spain. And that is generally where you must go for decent bread, such as **baguette** (the regular old French variety) as well as **pan decebolla** (onion bread) and **pan de chorizo** (bread with a sausage baked into it). The exception is in Galicia, where all bread is glorious (see Atlantic Spain in the Regional Variations chapter).

Early morning fresh bread delivery, San Sebastián, Basque Country

Queso (Cheese)

Unlike its near neighbours, France and Italy, Spain is not widely known for cheese. Although in regions such as Asturias, where **cabrales** (blue vein mountain cheese) comes from, it seems that there are as many different cheeses as cheese makers. In recent years the most well-known Spanish cheeses such as **Manchego** (hard sheep's milk cheese from the region of La Mancha in the Heart of Spain) have come under DO control and so a reliable and consistent product reaches the market.

> **Uvas y queso, saben a beso.**
> Grapes with cheese, like a kiss are these.
> —Spanish proverb

Cheese is commonly eaten but Spaniards tend to take it for granted rather than wax rhapsodic about it. They like to eat it as a snack, or as a **tapa** (hors d'oeuvre), rather than after a meal as the French would do. Also unlike the French, the Spanish tend not to cook with cheese. They eat it plain, or with their ham and a piece of bread. A shepherd's lunch has for millennia been just that and little more. When they do eat cheese after a meal, it's usually with grapes or quince jelly. The sweet tartness is a fine balance to the salt and pungency of the cheese. (For more on specific cheeses see the Regional Variations chapter.)

Homemade cheese and single flower honey at market, Santiago de Compostela, Galicia

Huevos (Eggs)

Eggs have for a long time been an important feature of the Spanish table, less for breakfast than other times of the day. Not the least important form of egg consumption is in mayonnaise. The oil and egg emulsion is the very meaning of life for some people in Spain.

Another popular egg appearance is in **tortilla española**. This is often described as a potato omelette, but it's more of a frittata. It is made by boiling potatoes, then dicing them rather fine. Olive oil and chopped onions go into a 30-40cm pan, followed by the potatoes. When they are heated through, enough beaten eggs are poured on top to cover the mixture. The heat is reduced to low and the dish allowed to cook until the bottom starts to brown. It is then flipped over and slowly cooked through. It is cut into wedges and eaten at room temperature. Satisfyingly simple.

It would be bland were it not for the quality of Spanish eggs. While the industrial world has turned to producing eggs by industrial means, Spain has continued mostly in the old time honoured way of letting the hen take care of the business the way she sees fit. You can even see the difference in the result. It is larger for starters. Break it open and see that the colour of the yolk is no mere yellow, but a vivid gold. It even smells good. Raw even. An egg like this is delicious cooked plain. It makes a mayonnaise that is, well, the meaning of life. And it makes that disarmingly simple dish, the tortilla española, a sense memory that you will carry forever.

Pescados & Mariscos (Fish & Seafood)

With the possible exception of the Japanese there are no keener seafood aficionados than the Spanish. They will eat any creature that emerges from the depths. When it comes to fin fish their favourites are **bonito** (tuna), **bacalao** (cod), **sardinas** (sardines) and **anchoas** (anchovies). All fresh. As for shellfish, it's difficult to say that they have a favourite. If it lives in a shell they love it. They will forego weekends in the country for a dinner of shellfish. If it's a question of gasoline in the tank of the car or a belly full of **gambas** (prawns), the belly wins.

The Iberians have an abiding relationship with the sea and its creatures. They have always ventured seaward in search of food, adventure, trade, and more food. The distribution of seafood within Spain is admirable. While each region has its traditional specialities, there is hardly a thing you cannot find in any major city. What with all the roads converging on Madrid, so much of the sea's harvest arrives here daily that this landlocked city is often called the best seaport in Spain.

Bacalao (Cod)

The Spanish may lust for seafood. They may chase after meals of fried sardines, and pursue dishes of tuna with single-minded devotion. But nothing holds a place in the Spanish heart, soul and belly like dry salted **bacalao** (cod). Even those who rarely eat bacalao still revere it, and this has been so for centuries. So much of Spanish history is bound up in it, fuelled by it. As an Englishman might never see a football game yet he knows Manchester United well, the Spaniard is intensely aware of bacalao, even if it is seldom found on the table. Bacalao is at the forefront of Spanish culinary consciousness.

This is remarkable when you consider that bacalao has never been seen, let alone caught, off the coasts of Spain. Bacalao lives in the cold waters of the northern Atlantic, off Newfoundland, Iceland, the British Isles and Scandinavia. But for centuries it has been a mainstay of the Spanish diet. Nobody really knows exactly for how long. But we do know that medieval fishermen followed whales into the Atlantic, harvesting them as well as smaller creatures that lived in their wake. At some point we know that Basque fishermen began to take bacalao, pack them in salt, and live off them while they were at sea. Eventually they discovered great shoals of them and began bringing home the salted catch. Serious scholars have postulated that these same Basque fishermen, in their pursuit of bacalao, discovered Newfoundland centuries before Columbus' voyage, yet kept their secret lest their fishing grounds be compromised.

Fisherman on the wharf at Cala Figuera, Mallorca, Balearic Islands

STAPLES

Cod shop sign, Santiago de Compostela, Galicia

Dates aside, bacalao came into the diet by two paths: as food for the poor and food for the pious. Landing on the docks of Spain, bacalao was cheap enough to be purchased in quantity by muleteers who led long pack trains deep into the interior. Over the centuries these men, with whom Cervantes shared a few meals in his travels, became victuallers to shepherds of La Mancha, to swordsmiths of Toledo, and to Gypsies and winemakers of Andalucía. There is hardly a corner of Spain that has not been touched by the Basque fishermen and the itinerant muleteers.

And in this most Catholic of Catholic countries people practised their religion in the eating of bacalao. At times there were as many as 150 days in the Spanish calendar when eating meat wasn't allowed. As well as meatless Fridays there were a pageant of saints to be honoured, victories over the Moors to be commemorated, long days of Lent and any number of solemn observances. All marked by meatless meals. Were it not for bacalao, Spain might have gone vegetarian or Protestant! For the Spanish, bacalao kept God and protein in the kitchen.

Bacalao is not merely historic and imbued with saintly sacrifice. It is delicious too. Though you would not know that to look at it in its preserved state. Encrusted with salt crystals, and having a whitish-grey appearance it looks more like a geological object than foodstuff. But soaked overnight it comes magically back to life. And for its time in suspended animation it has undergone the most remarkable changes. It is somehow both firmer and yet more tender than it was when it went into its salty sleep. It barely tastes of salt, and it tastes richly but not pungently of the sea. The flesh separates easily yet does not disintegrate into a mash between the teeth.

Today bacalao is a food of irony. Firstly, it is no longer a food of the poor; it has become an expensive luxury food. Offshore economic zones keep native fishing fleets from much of their traditional shoals. Nowadays the greater part of bacalao comes from foreign fishermen working the grand banks. The preferred varieties come from Scotland and Norway where local fleets bring in the catch and send it to Spain via the Low Countries. And the other irony? This revered food of good Catholics is now so much less so because, as any Spaniard will tell you, speaking of their neighbours, there are so few good Catholics left.

You can enjoy bacalao in any city in Spain. But perhaps the best place is in the Basque country where it still holds its sway just as strongly as ever. Even Basque atheists, all half dozen or so, love it. And everyone will pay the price necessary, regardless how high. One of the best introductions to bacalao is in **esqueixada**, a salad of raw desalted bacalao with crushed tomatoes, olives and onions. The acid in the tomatoes takes the raw edge off the bacalao, revealing its flavour. **Bacalao al pil-pil** is an ancient preparation with garlic and oil, and **bacalao a la vizcaína** combines cod with chillies and capsicums. Taste the bacalao, and taste the soul and history of Spain.

STAPLES

ANGUILAS (EELS)

For centuries people thought that anguilas (whose immature form is the **angula**) appeared spontaneously from the muck and mire of the river bottom. There was no other explanation as the females were never observed carrying roe. Folklore aside, the truth of the eel is just as astonishing as the myth.

The life of the eel is the reverse of the salmon. The adult lives in the river, and goes to the ocean to spawn and die. When spawning time arrives, they descend the northern rivers in great schools, heading out to sea. They swim all the way across the Atlantic Ocean to the Sargasso Sea, on the edge of the Bermuda Triangle. There they are met by their like-minded American cousins, though they will not interbreed.

They spawn and the females die, leaving their fertilised eggs behind. When they hatch, the elvers (as the fry are known) are no bigger than short bits of thread. Those descended from the Americas head west, and their European counterparts begin the 5000km swim east to the rivers of northern Spain. So arduous is the journey that they hardly grow during the crossing, arriving no bigger than matchsticks. Those that survive and escape the fishermen's nets will reach up to a meter in length. However, millions are scooped up into gossamer nets, parboiled, then rushed off to tascas and restaurants all over Spain, where eager diners pay dearly for the travel-weary catch.

STAPLES

Fruto y Verduras (Fruit & Vegetables)

In many ways Spain is the garden of Europe. It produces and exports more fruit and vegetables than most other nations of the EU, grows more grapes and olives than any nation in the world, and has almost every climate and microclimate with the exception of tropical rainforest. The range of fruit and vegetables available to the average Spanish cook or housewife is enviable (they really don't have any househusbands to speak of, more's the pity – tsk tsk). And so envy them you will when you travel to Spain. Unless you take up housekeeping and cook for yourself, or get invited home to dinner by people who don't want to overly impress you, you are going to be living chiefly on animal protein and fried potatoes. And mayonnaise, of course.

Woman arranging mushrooms at La Boquería Market, Barcelona, Catalunya

DRESS YOUR SALAD

Salad will be served to you undressed. You will be given decanters of vinegar and oil to accomplish the job to your taste. Show your Spanish salad savvy by dressing it like a Spaniard. First, salt it. If you are Spanish this will mean a lot of salt. Then the oil. And now more oil. And yes even more. A true Spanish salad is swimming in olive oil. This also helps to dissolve the grains of salt and distribute them evenly throughout the salad. Now shake on about a teaspoon of red wine vinegar. Do this now because if you add the vinegar before the oil it can chemically 'scorch' the delicate greens. Now lightly toss with your fork and enjoy. "What?" you say. "No fresh ground pepper from a grinder the size of a baseball bat?" No, señor. They don't do that here.

STAPLES

The Spanish do like their vegetables, oh yes. Do not be misled on this account. You'll see shoppers in the market expertly probing Brussels sprouts, squeezing squashes, caressing cauliflower. Eggplant they'll buy by the dozen and scurry home with them to create **berenjenas salteadas** (sauteed eggplant). Broccoli they'll braise and dress with garlic and oil. With **judías** (green beans) they'll make a dish so fine it will cause you to sigh for those who will never taste it. And in most restaurants you will probably never taste it.

When the Spanish go out to dine they understandably want what they don't have at home. And it happens that, unlike in most of the Anglophone world, the Spanish diet at home is heavily vegetarian. Not that your average Spaniard would ever call themselves vegetarian. Far from it. In Spain vegetarians are thought mainly to be foreigners. Or anarchists. So restaurants are places to eat meat, fish, fowl and ham (a food group unto itself).

Keeping fruit & vegetables in your diet can be done, although it can take some diligence. Seek and without doubt you shall find enough garden produce to keep you in good shape. Among our favourite vegetables are the onions. You'll find them everywhere. They are so sweet and mild they can almost be eaten like apples. At the Mercado Central in Cádiz look for the sweet and flavourful vine-ripened tomatoes. If all you are used to is the industrial products called tomatoes sold in supermarkets, these will be your epiphany. Small **fruterías** (fruit shops) are common throughout the land. You'll even find them in the middle of downtown Madrid, so you'll never want for a good fruit feast. Spain is famous, of course, for its oranges. Pick up a bag in Sevilla and enjoy them fresh. Use them in sangría (see the recipe in the Drinks chapter) or have them cooked with duck, the local speciality.

Jamón (Ham)

Ham is the great culinary constant. This is what unites the Spanish. They speak different languages and belong to different political parties. Some revere the crown and others would abolish it. Some are Celts, some are Iberians, others are Gypsies, Basques or Catalans. But 99.9% of them are eaters of cured ham. Strapped into a cradle-like frame called a **jamónera**, every bar, restaurant and tasca in the Kingdom of Spain has at least one ham a' carving at any given time. More often the establishment has several hams, the skins and hooves still attached, hanging from the walls or ceilings. Stuck into the bottom of each ham is a little plastic cup resembling an upside-down umbrella to catch the slow drippings. Even your average Spanish home has a jamónera in the kitchen. It might not have a cookie jar, but a Spanish kid can always have ham.

The best ham is that of the acorn-fed black Ibérico pig, Andalucía

TEST YOUR HAM KNOWLEDGE

jamón ibérico	a general term for any ham from black-coate ibérico pigs
jamón real ibérico	ham from ibérico pigs whose feeding in the wild is supplemented with fodder
jamón ibérico de bellota	the king of hams, from ibérico pigs that have fed on acorns in the wild during the season before slaughter
pata negra	literally, black hoof; another term for ibérico. Spanish hams are normally shipped and hung with the hoof attached. A black hoof is an indication, though not a guarantee, that it's ibérico ham.
jamón serrano	any cured ham made from white coated, non-ibérico pigs
serrano consorcio	certified as having been cured for a minimum of 36 weeks
Jabugo	a town in Huelva province with a long ham-producing tradition. Contrary to popular belief, it is not a Denomination of Origin (DO)
DO Dehesa de Extremadura	from the free range of Extremadura. Hams from pure-bred ibérico pigs, or cross breeds that are at least 75% Iberian bloodstock.
DO Guijuelo	province of Salamanca in western Spain, close to the Portuguese border. Hams from this DO are made either from pure-bred Iberian pigs, or crossbreeds that are at least 75% ibérico bloodstock.
DO Teruel	province of Teruel (northeast Spain). The hams from this denomination are air cured at more than 800 metres above sea level. The are all serrano, being from white-coated, non-ibérico pigs.
DO Huelva	hams from ibérico pigs in the Sierra de Huelva (northern Huelva province).
jamón York/ jamón dulce	boiled ham, as you might find in a delicatessen. It is used mainly in sandwiches.

STAPLES

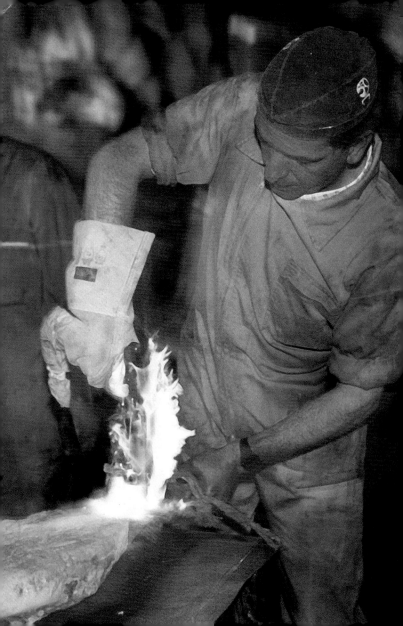

Salted and semi-dried by the cold dry winds of the Spanish sierra, Spanish ham is like no other in the world. It's closest relative is the Italian prosciutto. But if we could say that the Italian version is feminine, then the Spanish is pure male. The Italian is delicate and pink. Sliced paper thin and arranged in ruffles and curls on a plate, often with chunks of fruit lying within its folds, it presents a coy appearance, it's aroma slightly flowery and its taste of a gentle come-hither kind. It's very tender.

But a Spanish ham is a bold, deep red, sometimes even the colour of wine. It's well marbled with buttery fat streaking through the lean like a rainbow. It smells like meat, forest and field, and of the mushrooms, acorns and herbs that the beast has fed upon. Perhaps the most remarkable feature is its texture. It is neither tough nor tender. It offers something to the teeth, yet yields easily. It is rarely fibrous, and seems to dissolve upon the tongue like rich fat chocolate. One does not swallow a masticated mass, but a succession of liquefied reductions of robust flavour and nourishment. People don't serve fruit with Spanish ham. They serve caviar, cheese, peasant bread, nuts, beer, glasses of port, and more ham. Aficionados will gather for ham tastings in the same way that others will attend wine tastings. They select hams from the various regions and styles of Spain, of various ages and methods of ageing. They will discuss the subtleties, complexities and other virtues of the artisan that comes from a small village in Extremadura, and compare them to the scientifically produced ham of a larger enterprise. They will make notes. And they will eat more ham.

So know your ham, reader. Let's bone up on it now. Spanish hams are of two principal types: **ibérico** and **serrano**. The ibérico is from a pig indigenous to the Iberian peninsula and believed to be a descendant of *sus mediterraneus*, a wild boar. The animal has evolved entirely in response to its native habitat and so is distinguished from other breeds. It has a black coat and usually black trotters. Gastronomically one important distinction is its ability to infiltrate fat into the muscle tissue, thus producing an exceedingly well-marbled meat. Its habitat is known as **dehesa** (loosely translated as 'free range') well populated with acorn-bearing oak trees. After weaning they are brought up to a weight of at least 80kg on a diet of fodder, cereals and other tasty pig treats. Then begins a period known as the **montera**. It starts when the acorns appear and ends when they are gone. During this time the pigs eat acorns and little else, which makes them very fat and happy. If they gain at least 50% of their pre-montera weight they will be classified as **ibérico de bellota**, acorn fed. This is the creme de la creme of Spanish ham. If they fail to make weight on acorns alone they will be given supplemental fodder and classified as **ibérico**.

Branding the pig, Andalucía

HAM IN MONTEFRIO

Most of the commercially sold hams are currently made in factories with special cold rooms for the curing process; but in the villages where each family makes its own, things are still done the natural way, with vastly superior results. To begin with, the pigs used for commercial ham are raised to be lean, because all of their meat except the hind legs will be sold in butcher shops and eaten fresh; whereas, as every self-respecting Andaluz knows, the best ham is always the one which has the thickest layer of fat. Every farmhouse has its **cámara**, a room in the attic with barred, unglazed windows that let the cold winter air blow through; the hams are rolled in salt on a table called the **saladero** and left there for several weeks. Then all the salt is washed away and the hams are hung from the rafters to cure. The whole objective is to cure them with the minimum amount of salt, since the meat should be sweet in taste. About one in every five hams are lost this way, although this is only discovered when the curing process is over and the leathery crust around them is pierced for the final examination, with a long splinter of cow-bone. A quick whiff of the bone after removal is enough to tell if the ham has cured or spoiled.

When I rebuilt my farmhouse I turned my cámara into a bedroom and the saladero into a double bed, but every year in December I am invited to my neighbour's down the path, to take part in the year's most joyous – and perhaps most useful – event, evocatively known as La Matanza. Surely, only in Spain could a party be called 'the killing', although I always get there well after the execution of the pigs, which occurs at dawn. All the neighbours and relatives take part, and a special man is assigned the solemn task of pinchar-ing, or 'sticking' the pig. In fact, no one ever says "Tomorrow we're going to kill the pig", but "Mañana vamos a pinchar el marrano", which, to my ear, sounds more like teasing the pig rather than putting it to death.

By the time I arrive the carcasses are hanging from an oak tree and the women are busy stuffing sausage. With their sleeves rolled up and their arms coated in blood, they knead the mash of onions, flesh and blood until it is ready to be stuffed into a large syringe-like device called the **maquina**. One of them braces the maquina against her shoulder and pumps, while another holds the empty intestine over the nozzle to receive the filling. What with the red flesh slithering into the transparent sheath of the intestine, the vigorous pumping and the women's grins and cackles, there is something unmistakably sexual about the whole scene. Indeed this process is the subject of many raucous jokes.

Lorenzo Bohme

Slaughter takes place in winter and is followed by a fortnight in which the hams are packed deeply in salt so as to draw off excess moisture. The hams are then hung in sheds called **secaderos** where the cold, dry winds flow through and slowly 'cure' or dry them. Over the course of the year the mean temperature gradually rises, and as it does so, the fat demonstrates its unique ability to infiltrate the muscle tissue and impregnate it with its rich aroma. In autumn the hams are transferred to ageing cellars where they will begin to acquire their unique taste and flavour characteristics. They can be ready for market after 15 months, but they may spend as much as 24 months in the cure. As this entire process is a natural one, ibérico ham is an artisan product. It is also addictively delicious and can be ruinously expensive. Indeed, in villages where small family operations produce jamón ibérico de bellota the hams can actually be the target of burglars who eschew the family jewels and heist the hams instead!

Serrano means 'of the sierra' or the mountains. It used to designate any cured ham from Spain. Now it refers to hams made from white-coated pigs that were introduced into Spain from northern Europe in the 1950s. It was customary for ham producers to set up shop in mountainous areas to take advantage of the cool dry air for curing. Nowadays, most serrano hams are cured in climate-controlled sheds and cellars for 9-14 months. They are raised on farms where they live in sheds or pig pens and are fed on fodder if it's a big operation, and on a mix of fodder and kitchen slops if on a small farm. Both the **jamón** (hindquarter) and the **paleta** (foreleg) are used for curing. Serrano accounts for over 90% of the cured ham production of Spain. If the very expensive ibérico is heaven in your mouth, the reasonably priced serrano is at least knocking on the Pearly Gates.

How best to enjoy Spanish ham? In great quantity! But start out with the ham at room temperature (about 25°C). This is when its taste and smell constituents are at optimum volatility. It's warm enough to release them, but not warm enough to dissipate them. Cut it as thin as you can into bite-size pieces just before serving – this stuff dries out quickly when exposed to air so always cover it with plastic wrap when not in use. Serve it as an appetiser with Manchego cheese. Eat it with a cold beer or some deep red wine, or a glass of sherry. Though a Spaniard would not do this, would be aghast even, we find a well shaken Martini straight up with an olive to be the perfect foil to el jamón.

The Spanish love to cook with ham as well as eat it plain. **Rehogado con jamón**, which might be translated as 'hash' is popular: lightly fry diced ham in olive oil, then saute blanched vegetables in the mixture. Try it with artichokes, or green beans. Throw in some garlic. Or chop up the ham and add it to spaghetti sauce or an omelette. Fry slices of jamón and eat it on toast. Put a dollop of caviar on it. Yum!

Sausages

Of course not everything in the Spanish world of cured meats is ham. But a lot of it is still pork. Since the Moorish conquest the eating of pork has been a Christian credential. It was a public proclamation that even the inarticulate could make. After the reconquista, converted Jews and Muslims took it out onto the streets to eat on Muslim and Jewish Sabbaths (Friday and Saturday) to let all the world see their fealty to their new faith. Many were expelled anyway, but that's grist for another kind of mill.

Fresh pork is not a very common item of diet, other than suckling pig (see Heart of Spain in the Regional Variations chapter) and plain chops, but pork sausage is a staple food. In your travels you will see it, like ham, literally every day. No tasca is without it. Few restaurants or homes don't use it in the kitchen. Not only is it popular by itself, it's a favourite flavouring agent in beans, stews and casseroles. It's commonly used in sandwiches, tapas and omelettes. And there are so many kinds, and each region has its own variations, that it would be either meaningless or ponderous to attempt to describe them all.

But we can divide them into their general types: the raw and the cooked. And under the category of raw we have the red and the white; and under the cooked we have the black and the white.

Of the raw, or cured, sausages the most common is called **chorizo**, a red. While sausages have been made here since Roman times, the chorizo is the newest member of the family, dating back only to the 17th century. This is a post Colombian sausage, incorporating New World crops, not

Market stalls in Santiago de Compostela, Galicia

heretofore available. Chief among them is **pimentón** (paprika), the dried powder of the ground sweet red capsicum. This along with salt, garlic and black pepper, is used to season a ground mixture of pork and pork fat. Chorizo can be stuffed into large or small intestine, and smoked or air cured. It will likely be the most common sausage you see in Spain. It has a bright red colour, a chewy texture, and an assertive, spicy taste reminiscent of salami. It is usually cylindrical, but it can also be made spherical by stuffing it into a casing made of caecum, the widest part of the large intestine.

Salchichón is a cured white sausage, as is **longaniza**, a lengthier variety. These are all similar to chorizo but made without paprika. Some variations are spiced with oregano or nutmeg. Others are more delicate, yet very aromatic with a hearty meaty smell. They are usually cylindrical, and can be very long and thin. In this shape the sausage is called **fuet**, and presents a wrinkled appearance and a hard texture. **Sobrasada de Mallorca** is a gourmet version of a raw sausage. The meat is very finely chopped, combined with lard and spices, then stuffed into a spherical casing. After air curing for up to a year the filling resolves itself into such a smooth texture that it is almost like pâté.

Among the cooked sausages, **morcilla** is like a Spanish black pudding, a blood sausage. This is made immediately after slaughter, as the blood is the most perishable ingredient. It is simmered in cauldrons, usually at the slaughter site, until it turns black and coagulates. Also in the morcilla recipe are pork fat, salt, and often a few spices, onion or chopped nuts. A very common addition to the morcilla is cooked rice. You will often see it displayed at the market or tasca, attractively sliced to reveal the white grains embedded like clusters of stars in a dark sky.

Morcilla is an essential ingredient in one of Spain's most popular dishes, a stew called **fabada asturiana**. It is also folded into omelettes, served sliced on bread, cut up into soup. There are even morcillas that are made sweet, and are taken as either appetiser or dessert. Sweet or savoury, its flavour is deep but not assertive. And with its pudding-like texture, is so tender it hardly needs chewing.

In the white cooked sausages department there is a very wide range of **butifarras**. They are most popular in Catalunya, but you will see them everywhere. Like morcillas, they are made right after slaughter, cooked plain or with spices and other ingredients, and stuffed into casings large and small. Generally the meat is finely chopped but the recipe might also include larger bits of meat, or trimmings of cooked rind, or head cheese, or bread crumbs. Butifarra can be made spicy, but is usually mild. In the north of Spain it might be smoked, but elsewhere it is not. It's usually eaten by itself or with a piece of cheese, and goes well with a glass of beer. Being among the milder sausages it is not widely used in cookery.

Cecina (Cured Meat)

In the days of sailing ships American seamen were fed a diet consisting largely of salt pork. Dry and hard stuff, they derisively called it 'old horse'. At the same time in Spain it really was, literally, old horse. When a draught animal reached the end of its working life it was slaughtered, salted, smoked and air dried following a recipe for cured ham laid down 2000 years ago by no less a personage than Cato the Elder in his *De Res Rustica*. The finished product was called **cecina**, after the Latin *siccina* (cured meat). One wonders what the noble Roman would have thought of his Epicurean recipe being turned horseward.

For centuries in Spain cecina was survival fare, travel food, defence against the lean times and winter, and the soldiers' iron ration. Food fit for warriors with little time for anything but fighting. Or as others have described it, 'a chewy piece of wood'. It was sliced thin and eaten plain on the march or in the field, gnawed on for a snack, or chunks of it added to the bean pot. It could keep indefinitely.

After refrigeration came to Spain, cecina began to disappear from the menu. But not entirely. Nowadays cecina is being made with top quality beef. It's still Cato's recipe, but the raw material is the finest available. Well marbled, tender beef is used to produce what is often called 'beef ham', and this stuff bears comparison to the best jamón ibérico. Its texture is very similar, dissolving on the tongue, but its taste is the richest and beefiest with a tang of oak smoke. It is delicious plain or drizzled with olive oil. Taken with bread, robust cheese and a jug of Asturian cider, it makes a fine lunch.

Cecina is not as widely available as ham, but you can find it on the bone in speciality shops, vacuum packed at the airport duty free, and served in the smarter tascas of Madrid. Cecina also comes as **cecina de castron** (made from goat), **cecina de cabra** (kid) and **cecina de venado** (venison). And yes, you still can find **cecina de caballo**. The old horse still serves. Look for it at La Boquería market in Barcelona. Hi-ho, Silver! Away!

These are happier days for draught horses, Montras, Catalunya

Caza (Game)

Hunting has always been a popular sport in Spain, and it's becoming more so with increasing numbers of German, French, Italian and British tourists eager to bag their limit. The most common species taken are hare, deer and partridge.

One of the most popular ways of preparing game is **en escabeche**: marinated in vinegar and spices, cooked in the marinade, and served in the marinade. This process helps to tenderise the meat, which is tougher than that of a farm animal. And it attenuates the 'gamey' taste that some people object to.

Unfortunately for game lovers most game ends up on the tables of the hunters' families. However, when the game is in season you can get it at speciality restaurants. The best bet in cities like Madrid and Barcelona is to find an eastern European restaurant, as German, Polish and Czech chefs make more use of it. Of course it won't be the taste of Spain, but you got game.

What with the growth in hunting as a sport, there is a nascent industry providing forest food products. In Salamanca a whole game delicatessen industry is burgeoning around the local hunting territories. You can buy venison chorizo. It has a deeper and more assertive taste than the pork variety. Also available are pâtés of wild boar and pheasant. Certain game parks are sending partridge to meat processors for ultimate sale to domestic and restaurant customers. And if you like you can go hunting in Spain in just such a game park through a hunting agency.

Lastly, there is one sort of game that is available somewhere in most Spanish cities when in season, and that is the meat of the bulls killed in the ring, often called **carne de lidia**. Doesn't sound like game to you? Remember that the fighting bull is a wild animal. He spends his days like any other wild animal, roaming freely on the range, chasing females, and fighting over them and his turf. And he dies face to face, by the sword, in single combat. The odds are stacked against the bull but it's a lot more game than bringing down a deer at 100m with a scope-mounted rifle while sitting in a hunting blind with a cup of coffee.

Watch for restaurants sporting colourful posters that look like they are announcing bull fights. Read more closely and you will see that the fight has already been won and a memorial banquet is in the offing. The sirloins are excellent, and a ragout of fighting bull is a delicious dish. A speciality in the Andalucían town of Córdoba is **estofado de rabo de toro**, a stew made with the tails of the fallen. Traditionally, the testicles were reserved for the matadors, battered (no pun intended) and fried. But now you can have them too. Toro!

STAPLES

Vaca (Beef)

With the exception of the fighting bulls, beef has never been a great feature of the Spanish table. Galicia has always produced fine beef, much of it for export, but Galicia has always marched to a different beat. With the rising prosperity of post-Franco Spain, beef is becoming more common. Whether it's because of rising incomes or the view of beefsteak as a status symbol, or both, we can't say. But we can say that one of the best T-bone steaks we've ever eaten was in Hondarribia in the Basque Country. They called it a 'beef chop'. More frequently on the menu you will find **ternera**. This is often translated as 'veal', but it is not quite correct. Ternera is more mature than veal, more robust, giving thicker cuts and deeper flavour. It has barely developed a beefy red colour, yet when cooked turns white.

In a restaurant, ternera is usually prepared, like most meats, simply: on a grill, or in a pan, with a little olive oil and salt. Potatoes on the side as a rule. You'll find other common meats done the same, such as **chuletas de cordero** (lamb chops), **chuletas de cerdo** (pork chops) and **conejo** (rabbit). Don't look for meats to be done up a' la mode, cordon bleu, stroganoff or rossini. To the Spanish such preparations are a French idea and so worthy of criticism. When the Spaniard wants the taste of flesh in his mouth he doesn't want the taste of cheese, cream, or truffles getting in the way. No tarted up dishes, please, just honest meat and potatoes. Gracias.

Ave de Corral (Fowl)

Perhaps the most admired feathered food is the **codorniz** (quail). But **pichón** (pigeon) and **perdiz** (partridge) are popular too. You will find them roasted, braised, stewed and stuffed. **Pato** (duck) is a good dish to try. In Atlantic Spain they enjoy it roasted with **nabos** (turnips). Along the Mediterranean look for it with **higos** (figs). The most famous preparation for duck would be **a la sevillana**, with bitter oranges in the style of Sevilla. Some French claim this dish as theirs, but they are not suffered to enter the city of Sevilla. The genius of this dish is that the acidity and bitterness of Sevilla oranges, and the tang of Andalucían olives cuts through the fat of the fowl, or at least makes it taste better.

Unless you are shopping at the market to cook for yourself, don't look for chicken. You will find it at KFC, but real restaurants rarely offer it. And if you do come across it, don't bother asking for white meat. They just don't have it. The Spanish would seem to regard chicken as a vegetable. It's cheap, abundant, one of those things they eat at home. But when they go to a restaurant, they want something special. The exception is in **cocido**. Here you cannot escape chicken. Every serving will include a drumstick, and perhaps a thigh. But still no white meat.

FOR THE LOVE OF GUTS

Do you like beef heart? Does tripe hold no dread for you? Veal brains sound good? Ahh, how about a dish of kid's lungs, known in English as 'lights'. Or, on the other hand, does your stomach turn when you think of chitterlings, fried rings of pig's intestine? (They look a bit like calamari rings.) If you were confronted with the grinning skull of a baby lamb, its skin removed, would your skin crawl? Do you blanche at the thought of eating a hoof or a tail, a cow's udder or a calf's head? Blood doesn't float your boat? Welcome to Spain.

Waste not, want not is the proud motto here. When an animal is slaughtered for food, then food it shall be and no part shall go uneaten. The English prefer not to eat ribs (probably because they have to eat them with their hands, and get all messy) and the North Americans don't care much for blood (black pudding, ooh yucky) and the Aussies are quite unpredictable. But the Spanish can stand up and be counted. When it comes to making food of a pig, a cow, or a sheep they will eat everything but the oink, the moo, and the baa baa baa. And they cannot for the life of them understand why those unfathomable Anglophones don't do the same.

Bulls' testicles

When you go to the market, whether to a traditional farmers' market or to a supermercado, be prepared. A lot of dead animals are going to be looking you square in the eye and saying "take me home for supper". Their entrails will be hung from hooks, their organs piled high, their brains arranged in pretty patterns and their little disembodied feet resting daintily on the counter. And the average Spanish shopper will look at them and start salivating.

Even at the restaurant you will encounter this blood and guts gusto. Today's special organ meat will be described to you in minute detail by a waiter who has just eaten two of them. "They come from here" he will say, and he will indicate on his own body with a cutting motion. It gives the meal a downright cannibal aspect. Or why don't you order a **cabeza de ternera** (calf's head). It will come to you, boiled, skinned and split down the middle, exposing both hemispheres of the brain. Are you a right brain person, or a left brain person?

Don't be put off by all this. Just be prepared. All these things are really quite delicious, and very wholesome. If they weren't the Spanish wouldn't eat them. So don't be afraid. Or if you are, just don't ever let 'em see you sweat.

Hierbas y Especias (Herbs & Spices)

Walk into the Corte Ingles, or any other large supermarket. Visit La Bouquería. Stop in a family-run grocery store. And look for the spice rack. You may have trouble finding it. And when you do, you'll be surprised at how small it is. This is not a land of curries. Despite the common language with Mexico, this is not a land of chillies. Here you'll find sugar and nice, but very little spice. To the Spaniard a food should taste of what it is, and it should not burn the tongue. You may find yourself longing for a little hint of spice now and then, and hope to satisfy it by stepping into one of the foreign restaurants in the major cities. And when you do you'll find the Mexican fare doused of its characteristic flame; the Indian reduced to blandness; the Chinese robbed of its Chineseness. Spicy barbecue? Nah. Your average Spanish recipe doesn't even call for black pepper, and you won't normally see it in restaurants.

If you are staying in a home in Barcelona and want to cook Chinese, betake yourself quickly to La Boquería before the three or four bottles of soy sauce available are snapped up by Chinese flower sellers. Don't even look for fish sauce. You can find Tabasco and Worcestershire because any bar worth its beer will have them. They may not use them, but they will have them. There is some sort of international convention to this effect. Perhaps Anglo-American pressure is brought to bear. You might want to buy some and carry it with you for emergencies. Really. No joke.

The spice rack in the Spanish home or restaurant will have the following and little else: saffron, garlic, parsley, salt, paprika, vinegar, oregano (maybe), thyme (possibly), pepper (old and unused) and, in small amounts, cumin or cinnamon (Moorish influence).

In addition to these flavourings the Spanish cook employs lots of ham, often diced and added to vegetables. Sausages go into all sorts of dishes including beans and soups. More than spices the Spanish use vegetables to flavour foods. Salt is used liberally, both in the kitchen and at the table.

By far the most common flavourer is **ajo** (garlic). It works its way into nearly everything. It's even used raw on the Catalan speciality **pá amb tomáquet** (tomato bread), a thick slice of toasted bread rubbed vigorously with a cut clove of garlic, then with a cut tomato, sprinkled with salt and drizzled with the fruity arbequina olive oil of Catalunya. Simplicity itself and one of the most delicious things you'll ever eat.

The herb par excellence is **perejil** (parsley), no contest. This is the base of **salsa verde** (green sauce) in which a dozen different fish dishes are cooked. In fact it can be used anywhere, anytime in anything. It can be added to salad; minced and sprinkled on roasts or sauteed fish; even chewed plain to freshen the breath or prepare the palate for the next course.

Salt is a major seasoning. We tend to think of high salt usage as unhealthy, causing high blood pressure. But in Spain we perspire a lot, what with the long hot summers purging our bodies of at least some salt. And in Spain we find that life has very little stress, that other major cause of high blood pressure, ulcers, heart attacks, hate and discontent. Maybe salt isn't so bad for you as long as you stay in Spain.

Herbs like oregano and thyme are occasionally used, in small amounts. Sometimes these herbs are rubbed on meats before roasting. But ideally the cook has found a meat supplier whose animals have been feeding on herbs, thus deeply infusing their flesh with extra flavour. Subtlety is a highly prized quality in a dish, and the ability of the diner to detect such nuances is a much admired talent. Dishes of Moorish origin do tend to be a bit more spiced than those of European Spain. It was the Moors, after all, who brought so many of the common spices into the Iberian peninsula. Those dishes are more commonly found in the south, especially in Andalucía. Look for dishes such as **garbanzos con espinacas** (chickpeas with spinach) or **cebollas con miel** (onions cooked in honey).

STAPLES

NO TABASCO

Sarah and I were really loving the food in Spain. Everything was so fresh, and so appealing to the eye. But I always had to ask for black pepper. It was never on the table next to the salt like at home. Sometimes when I asked for it the waiter would advise against it, saying it would spoil the taste of the food. But I would insist and they would bring it. Slowly.

As we sat at a bar in Valencia one fine afternoon, Sarah asked the barman to make her one of the house's special **bocadillos**, a roll filled with grilled meats and vegetables. He was one of those handsome Spanish men who just can't help exuding sex appeal. He wasn't trying to be magnetic, he just was. So I watched as he worked. He grilled the meats, turning them one by one. He added this and he added that. Then I noticed a bottle of Tabasco on the counter next to him. I nudged Sarah and pointed, knowing she likes it. "Oh" she said as he put the finishing touches on her bocadillo. "Please add some of that Tabasco for me."

"No" the man said.

"Pardon?" said Sarah.

"No" the deity of the kitchen repeated. He wasn't nasty or rude. He wasn't snobbish or hostile. He was matter of fact. As though she had simply asked him if he liked Tabasco. As he brought it to her, all she could say was, "Tabasco?" The man set it down before her, smiled wanly, and said, "No." Then he turned and went back to his work. Sarah says the bocadillo was still good.

Stella Pike

Aceite de Oliva (Olive Oil)

Spain grows 262 varieties of olive, 90% of the produce of which is sent to the presses for their oil. At an annual production of over 600,000 metric tons Spain is the world's largest producer, and consumer, of olive oil.

Olive groves, Baeza, Andalucía

Indeed it is anointed, saturated, awash and delightfully drowning in the most flavourful golden fluid under the Mediterranean sun. Olive oil isn't just salad dressing. It doesn't stop at the saute pan. In Spain this is the cooking medium *par excellence*. The Spanish use it to make desserts; to cook **patatas fritas** (potato chips); to keep their skin smooth; and we will leave you to imagine its more romantic applications.

Hojiblanco tasting, Sevilla

Olive oil is a food unto itself, taken for its nutritive as well as gustatory value. It is arguably the chief flavouring agent of Spanish cuisine. In doubt about how to prepare something in the Spanish manner? Just cook it how you will and then drizzle it liberally with olive oil. No Spaniard will fault you. None will protest "here now, this is not the Spanish way with fish, meat, fowl, rutabagas, calabashes, tofu!" (well, there really is *no* Spanish way with tofu). If it just *tastes* of olive oil you're half way to gastronomic Spain. This stuff is the *sine qua non*. Without olive oil Spanish cookery as we know it would not exist. It would be sorely lacking without bread. It would be impoverished without wine. But without the blood of the olive it would not exist. A Spaniard could huddle by a small fire on a bitter Castillian night, but feel nourished with nothing but a crust and the green-gold expression of the olive. Minimalist cookery, to be sure, but it's where mere feeding ends and cuisine, the soul of the hearth, begins.

So if you would navigate the culinary landscape of Spain you must do so upon the rivers of oil that course through it. For your gastronomic voyage we offer you a few landmarks to guide you, and a few shoals and shallows to avoid. But first the lay of the land.

Olive press, Baeza, Andalucía

OLIVE OILS

Spanish health regulations define three grades of olive oil

Aceite de oliva virgen	(virgin olive oil) is oil expressed from olives by methods that do not modify it's basic properties. Within the 'virgin' classification there are three quality levels:
extra	oil exhibiting the best taste characteristics and an acidity level no higher than 1%.
corriente	(average) oil with a good taste and an acidity level no higher than 3.3%
lampante	(strong) oil that possesses little taste or has an acidity level above 3.3%
Aceite de Oliva Refinado	(Refined Olive Oil) is virgin oil whose taste or acidity levels make it unsatisfactory, but having been refined it results in marked improvement. While still a healthy and usable product, it lacks the full taste of virgin olive oil.
Aceite de Oliva	(Olive Oil) is a blend of both refined and virgin olive oil. This is the overall market standard.

Spain, as we have said, is the world's largest producer of olives and oil, and Andalucía is Spain's largest olive growing area. The province of Jaén alone produces more oil than all of Greece, to put things into perspective. Andalucía lies under the leafy shade of some 165 million olive trees, half of which are in Jaén, a third in Córdoba, and the remainder spread across Sevilla, Málaga, Granada, Huelva, Almería and Cádiz. Other important growing areas in Spain include Castilla-La Mancha, the Ebro Valley and Catalunya. As with wine, climate and soil have as much influence on the taste and smell of the final product as the variety grown. And also as with wine, mechanisation and modern methods of production are increasing, but traditions and techniques as old as Rome are still much in evidence. Harvesting is still done largely by hand. Harvesting teams go into the orchards bearing longs sticks with which they shake the high branches to loosen the heavy fruit until it falls on canvas drop cloths spread beneath the trees. And yet again as with wine, for highly prized delicacy oils, workers climb into the trees and select only the ripest, most perfect fruit on the branch. These are the kinds of oils that find their way to the tables of kings.

THE ESSENTIAL OIL

As with the finest French wines, the finest Spanish olive oils are most often blends. By law, a virgin oil must meet 40 criteria for quality and purity, and to be classified as extra virgin its acidity level can be no higher than 1%. And under the laws of consumer demand the product must be consistent over the years. The oil must have a predictable taste, smell and texture, and a predictable flash point. The blending room of a larger producer will have as many as a dozen tasters working at one time, mixing, tasting and smelling, to create the signature oil. The oils are tasted at about 38°C for that is the temperature of optimum volatility. The oil's colour has no bearing on its taste and smell, but colour can influence a human taster so the oils are presented in coloured glasses so they will appear as the same colour. Between sips of oil the tasters chew slices of green apple to clear the palate. When the proper balance is achieved the 'coupage' (final recipe) is sent to the blending vats. The blended oil is then transferred to large earthenware vats to age, and acquire richness and depth of flavour. Salud!

150-year-old budegows, Sevilla, Andalucía

STAPLES

Green olives, Baeza, Andalucía

CERTIFIED OLIVE OIL AREAS

The four chief DO certified olive oil producing areas are:

Les Garrigues Province of Lérida in northeast Spain. The principal olive type is Arbequina constituting 90% of production. Also grown is the Verdiel.

Siurana Province of Tarragona, in northeast Spain just south of Les Garrigues. Arbequina makes up most of the crop (90%). Also grown are Royal and Morrut.

Sierra del Segura Province of Jaén in southern Spain. The most common olive type is Picual. Other olives grown include Verdala, Royal, and Manzanillo de Jaén.

Baena Province of Córdoba in southern Spain. Picuda, Lechín, Chorrío, Pajarero, Hojiblanco, and Picual are all grown here.

Green Olives, Baeza, Andalucía

Some of the more important varieties of olive include the **Picual**. This is grown in Andalucía, chiefly in Jaén province, and accounts for 50% of all Spanish olive production. It takes its name from its shape, as it has a pointed **pico** (tip). It yields a good cooking and general purpose oil as it contains a high vegetable fat content as well as a good amount of natural antioxidants. Due to its high polyphenol content this oil keeps well and is stable over a fire. When grown in lowland areas the oil tends to be full bodied and full flavoured. That grown in mountainous regions is sweeter and fruitier. It's the most popular oil for frying, but works well enough in salads, and often finds its way into gazpacho.

From the area around Sevilla and Málaga the **Hojiblanco** is named for the silvery underside of its leaves. It's a big olive, dark and spherical. Its oil is extremely well balanced and has a complex taste and aroma, reminiscent of fruits, grasses and nuts. However, it is unstable. It should be kept in a cool, dark place and used fairly quickly. While it is often used to fry delicate fish, it is an ideal oil for making breads and pastries.

In the northern part of Spain the most important olive is the **Arbequina**, named for its place of origin, Arbeca, in Lérida. Ideally it is harvested right after a seasonal rain, as it has the effect of 'washing' the olives and carrying away bitterness. The oil is sweet and golden, light and fruity. Catalan cooks don't cook much with this oil. Cooking tends to boil away its good qualities. It is the preferred oil for **pá amb tomáquet** (tomato bread), salads, raw or lightly cooked vegetables, and is delicious mixed with honey and poured on egg bread. It is delicate and unstable, so should be used as quickly as possible and kept in a cool, dark place.

From the heart of Spain comes the **Cornicabra**. It comes from a very ancient stock, originating near Toledo. The olive goes through several colour changes as it ripens. The oil has greenish tints, and if expressed from mature fruit will often present a deep aroma of tropical flowers. It is well balanced and has plenty of the fatty acids that help to reduce blood cholesterol. It's very good for basting roasts, and for making mayonnaise and marinades.

Poppies growing in an olive grove

ACEITUNAS ALIÑADAS (Marinated Olives)

Not every olive goes to oil. About 10% are preserved and eaten as tapas, in salads, or even used in sauces. Sometimes they are marinated in simple brines, often with the addition of herbs such as oregano and thyme, or with lemon zest or even crushed red capsicum. In these iterations they are called **aceitunas aliñadas**. You'll see them in bars all over Spain, as common as you'd see crisps at home. Watch for these favourite varieties.

Arbequina	not only does this produce some of the best oils, it's a tasty snacking olive. Watch for its dark greenish-purple colour. Taste its bitter mildness. It's common in Barcelona bars.
Cuquillo	you'll recognise this one by its common preparation: mixed with chopped onions and crushed red capsicum. With its bold flavour and spicy presentation, Cuquillo is an excellent accompaniment to a cold beer.
Manzanilla	the most popular snacking olive in the land. In colour and shape it looks like a tiny pear. These with a few almonds make the a perfect accompaniment to dry Sherry.
Negral	native of Aragón it is treated in many ways. It might be pickled, it might be spiced, it might even be dried. It has a deep flavour that makes for a good pairing with red wine.

Marinated Arbequina olives for tapas

Arroz (Rice)

Paella, paella, paella. Blast paella! At least for now. Banish it from your thoughts until we have broadened your mind with the wide universe of Spanish rice recipes. Long before paella was put in a pan the people of the Iberian peninsula were preparing rice dishes of ethereal quality and gustatory delight. Pilavs with almonds, raisins or dates; rice stews of slurp-it-up goodness such as **arroz marinera** (rice with seafood); baked casseroles of rice and legumes made fragrant with garlic, enriched with potatoes and blessed with the tang of ripe tomatoes; rice and black beans combined to make the holiday dish, **Moros y Cristianos** (Moors & Christians); dishes for Lent and dishes that would nourish and please a vegetarian; rice for holidays and rice for work days; and rice for dessert. In the vaulting firmament of Spanish rice dishes, paella is simply its most visible star.

Rice came to Spain in the seed bags of Arab farmers. To this day many of the water courses they constructed for growing rice are still in use. The principal rice growing areas are along the Mediterranean coast in the district called El Levante, southern Andalucía, and in smaller areas such as Mallorca and Gerona. After the reconquista and the subsequent expulsion of the Moors, much rice growing expertise was lost and crops shrank. Worse still was the occurrence of marsh malaria in the rice fields.

WATER RIGHTS

In the town of Pego, the inhabitants recently began farming rice again, primarily because the state was going to declare their ancestral rice lands a natural preserve – and not compensate the people. The boundaries of the preserve were to stretch (conveniently) to the edge of a zone marked for housing development.

The water that supplies those fields comes from a formidable spring that, according to 13th century royal decree, belongs to the town of Pego. More recently a nearby town has punched into the same acquifer to provide water to the growing number of resort homes. So the big money (and thus the regional government) is opposed to rice culture happening in that area due to the competition for water it creates. The day Pego farmers were clearing the cane away to plant rice, the Spanish federal police came out to put a stop to it. The mayor of Pego ordered the local police to block the feds, which they did. Then a group of farmers grabbed the government representative and threw him in the river. That was three years – and crops – ago.

Brian King

It became so serious at times that planting would be banned by royal decree. When the farmers were faced with malaria or starvation, however, the decrees went unheeded. It wasn't until 1860 that rice cultivation was officially and finally legalised and licensed. Still, until the cause of malaria was discovered around the turn of the 20th century, as many as 90% of the inhabitants of the rice regions had marsh malaria. El Levante was known as **terra de arros, terra de plos** (land of rice, land of tears). But the hard life of the rice growers forged a strong community bond, for they shared not only the hardship but the work, the land, and the everyday task of making a living (see Blessed Rice in the Celebrations chapter).

Now here is the fundamental, guiding principal of Spanish rice cookery: each and every little grain must become like a little sponge and soak up the flavouring agents in which it is cooked. The grain is the vehicle for the taste and smell of all the other ingredients. It is the messenger to your mouth. This is what dictates the grain variety and the cooking method. It isn't unknown for the Spanish to eat plain rice, but it's damn rare. This has been the rule for rice since the Moors taught the Spanish to eat it. The high and the mighty liked to eat their rice infused with rich and sweet concoctions. They used almond milk, sugar or honey, and heavy cream to infuse a finely polished white rice. Some of those recipes are popular still in the form of **arroz con leche** (rice pudding). The peasantry ate their rice with whatever the forest and field provided: water rats, snails, eels, fish, the odd jack rabbit. And they cooked it over an open fire of vine cuttings and sat in a circle to eat together from the one pan.

So how many rice recipes are there? In Valencia they tell a tale from the War of Independence, the struggle against Napoleon. A certain French general had taken many Spanish prisoners, and one Spanish cook. Smitten by her first few offerings of rice the general told her that he would free one of her countrymen for each new dish she prepared. 176 Spaniards, so they say, had been freed by the time the general was relieved of his command. The suggestion here is that the cook could have gone on forever, for rice cookery, more than any other aspect of Spanish cuisine, is improvisational. Its chief ingredients are rice, imagination and opportunity. Here the kitchen muse extemporises with whatever is to hand, and can easily go beyond 176.

And there is one more that is not exactly rice, but it doesn't fit anywhere else in the canon, and it is always displayed with rice dishes. This is **fideua**. At first glance it looks like a dish of paella. But this is made not with rice, but with a kind of pasta made to look like rice. It is cooked by the same process that is used to make paella. It's 'pasta pallea'. We don't know many Spaniards who eat this stuff. But we are told by a chef that it was recently developed because "Italian tourists must have their pasta".

Paella

So alright. Now we'll talk about paella. What exactly is it? It depends on who you ask. Put two Spanish cooks together and you'll likely get three paellas. All will agree that a paella contains short grain rice, garlic, parsley, olive oil and saffron. The popular image of paella is a pan of saffron-coloured rice bursting with shellfish, known as **paella de mariscos**. Most people will agree that the original came from the field in the mid to late 19th century and was made with such things as snails, rabbit and chicken. You won't see such paellas very often in restaurants. Rice is cheap, rabbit is cheap. They just can't charge you very much for the dish. But throw in those red jewels called lobsters and crayfish, and they can really make you pay. And then they can save themselves a good bit of money by skipping the saffron and using yellow dye number 2. And since they are giving you a bastardised dish it's no big deal to cook it too fast or insufficiently, giving you grains of rice that go 'crunch' when you bite them or that turn into a mush in your mouth.

Food from Restaurante Los Caracoles, Barcelona, Catalunya

Paella, a national dish

Hmmm. Detecting a theme? We are no honest book if we do not warn you that restaurant paella is generally a sad affair. The reasons for this are many and varied, not the least of which was government interference in the development of mass tourism. The state has shown itself to be a decent hotelier, but it's a lousy cook.

Most visitors to Spain have never had paella, or nothing worth the name, and so don't know when to howl in protest, and how to justify the noise with a detailed, nit-picking analysis. But you will. First, learn how to sniff out a fraud. If you take our advice, you're going to buy some saffron while in Spain, so buy it on your first day. Smell it. Its delicate yet pervasive aroma is unmistakable and unforgettable. If that aroma isn't wafting up at you from the pan, you've been served a counterfeit (see Things To Buy in the Shopping chapter). It should not be 'bursting' with shellfish, or bursting with anything else. The rice is the chief player in this little gastro-drama and nothing should be upstaging it. One piece of meat per diner is about right. The grains of rice should be dry, plump and tender. There are many varieties of rice, but ideally the paella should be made with **bomba** rice. Its distinctive starch structure causes it to open out accordion fashion when cooked, allowing for maximum absorption while remaining firm. The cooking dish should be shallow, allowing for optimum cooking of the short grain rice and for maximum contact with the bottom of the pan, where most of the flavour resides. And for the final touch of authenticity, the cook should turn up the heat in the final minutes of cooking so as to brown the bottom into a crunchy, savoury crust called the **socarrat**. You will hear people telling you, and read it in books, that their paella was perfectly cooked because the grains of rice had a 'crunch'. Poor little innocents abroad. The grains had a crunch because in the centre they were *raw*! The crunch must come from the socarrat – tsk tsk. The paella should be served in one pan, out of which all the diners eat. Ah, conviviality. (See the recipe Paella de La Huerta in the Spanish Banquet Chapter.)

PAELLA MAN

My job in the food importation business often took me to Valencia. Scouting for olive oils one day I found myself in the nearby village of Benissano. And that's where I met Don Rafael Vidal, possibly the greatest paella maker in Spain. In his plain little restaurant called El Levante he serves nothing but paella. And that's because he can't cook anything else. He doesn't know how. He'll tell you himself that he couldn't even boil potatoes properly. But does he ever make a fine paella.

He started out as a mechanic and he had a little garage where he did auto repairs, all on his own. One day when he was working on a man's car it came to be lunchtime. Since the car wasn't ready and the man couldn't go anywhere, Rafael invited him to lunch. He killed a chicken and cooked it with some rice and white beans and a bit of this and that, and sat the man down to what he thought was a very humble meal. The man thought differently. So differently that he told others about it. Soon Rafael didn't have many customers except at lunch time. "No hay remedio" he said to himself. There was nothing else for it but convert the garage to a roadhouse. That was a long time ago, and since then Don Rafael has made a lot of people happy with his paella. Famous cooks, wealthy travellers, not so wealthy travellers, actors and singers. Even the king of Spain.

Rod Johnson

Salsas (Sauces)

If you pick up your average European cookery book you'll find a whole section on sauces; sauces with grand sounding names like Grand Veneur, or Chantilly. You might even see Sauce Espagnole. So named because when tomato is added to basic brown sauce it takes on a deeper colour, giving it a swarthy hue. Hmmm. But you won't find such a section in the Spanish cookery book for the Spanish take quite a different view of sauce and sauce-making. Let it be noted that the word for sauce is **salsa**, but this has nothing to do with salsa Mexicana or salsa picante.

There are four basic principles to Spanish sauce making. Firstly, Spanish sauces are based on olive oil. Indeed, olive oil *is* a sauce. It is the most basic sauce and condiment in the Spanish pantry. All other sauces are olive oil with something added; olive oil dressed for the fair. Galicia produces excellent sweet butter but Spaniards don't use it for sauce. Secondly, Spanish sauces are not thickened with flour or roux. When they require thickening, it is done with ground nuts or bread crumbs. Thirdly, sauces begin in the mortar with pestle. Nowadays people will use food processors when they are pressed for time, but there is really no substitute for mortar and pestle to adequately emulsify. Lastly, for the most part, sauce is not a discreet ingredient, not something prepared separately by a sous chef. In Spain a sauce is usually the liquid in which the food is cooked, or the liquid the food expresses during cooking. Or both. With few, and one great and singular, exceptions which we shall see later, sauce is an integral part of the dish, not something to be poured on later to gild the lily. We can divide Spanish sauces into eight distinct varieties.

Salsa Romesco

Ingredients

2	tablespoons paprika	3	tomatoes
½	teaspoon cayenne	1	head of garlic
1	tablespoon parsley, chopped	1	slice toasted bread
1	tablespoon olive oil	1	teaspoon salt
24	hazelnuts, skinned	1	tablespoon vinegar
12	almonds, blanched and peeled		

In a hot oven or over an open flame sear the tomatoes and garlic until the skins of the tomatoes split. Remove the skins from tomatoes and garlic. Squeeze out the seeds from the tomatoes. Reduce all the ingredients to a paste with a mortar and pestle (or in a food processor). It should be like heavy cream, ready to be used as a cooking ingredient or condiment. Or store it in the refrigerator with a layer of olive oil on top.

Boquerones en vinagre (anchovies in vinaigrette) with Manzanilla Olives

Ajo (Garlic)

These sauces came to Spain with the Romans. Soldiers, peasants, fishermen and farmers combined olive oil with chopped garlic and parsley, maybe a squeeze of lemon juice or dash of vinegar. In this guise it's called **aliño**. It basically amounts to salad dressing, and of course is used as such. It is also used to baste fish and meats, or to drizzle on bread. A more sophisticated version is **alioli**. In its original and still popular form this is made by pounding much garlic with a mortar and pestle, then adding olive oil. Sometimes bread crumbs are added to stabilise the mixture. It is often stirred into soups, or added to rice dishes.

Sofrito (Fried Tomato Sauce)

This is Spanish tomato sauce, very quick and simple. Chopped tomato, onion, green capsicum, a little garlic are cooked in olive oil until the liquid is cooked away (10-15 minutes). It's now ready to be used in cooking or stored for later. It's an essential in paella, but almost anything can be cooked in it. Usually it's made liquid again by the addition of wine, or vinegar and water. Braised chicken, shellfish and stews of lamb are commonly prepared with sofrito.

Pimentón (Paprika)

In this category we find what many say is the queen of Spanish sauces, the Catalan **salsa romesco** (see recipe on previous page). These sauces are flavoured with, indeed are vehicles for, red capsicums. Most often this is in the form of paprika. In Spain paprika is sweet but not mild. It asserts itself upon the tongue but does not burn. A small amount of chilli may be added. Other vegetables find their way into the sauce, chiefly onion, tomato and garlic. And of course the finest olive oil available. A thick romesco can be used as a condiment. In parts of Catalunya spring onions are grilled over wood fires then dipped in thick romesco. Thinned with water and vinegar it becomes a salad dressing. Vegetables, meats, fish or fowl can be cooked in the sauce.

Variations of the paprika sauce include **salsa a la vizcaína**, from the Basque country, made with dried **choricero** pepper and used in preparations of **bacalao** (cod). The signature dish of Galicia, **pulpo gallego** (spicy boiled octopus) is dressed with **ajada**, a sauce of garlic browned in olive oil, sprinkled with paprika and moistened with vinegar. When you have your paella in Valencia you will likely also be served **ali-pebre**, a garlic and paprika sauce for the local eels.

Nueces (Nuts)

Almonds

Almonds blanket huge swathes of Spain. Galicia is covered with chestnuts, the Basque country with walnuts, Catalunya with hazelnuts. The sauces made with these nuts have been around for centuries. The nuts are finely ground with such things as garlic, bread, saffron, wine and, of course, olive oil. The resulting mixture, **picada**, is cooked into meats and poultry. It can be folded into ground meat for **albóndigas** (meatballs) or used as a gravy base. Perhaps the most famous Spanish nut sauce was made far away from Spain, in Puebla, Mexico. Spanish nuns, long known for cookery, were visited by the viceroy in the 16th century. For his dinner they prepared a nut sauce using traditional ingredients plus a few local additions such as chilli and chocolate. The result was the now famous **mole poblano**. Today Catalan picada reflects that development with the use of small amounts of chocolate.

Adobos (Marinades)

Marinades are the spiciest of Spanish sauces. They employ strong vinegar, garlic and oregano, bay leaf and sometimes chilli. Their original purpose was not so much gustatory but preservative. Marinades are still popular, especially for cooking game and heavy meats.

Wine Sauce

Wine is so integral to Spanish cookery that to consider it a sauce would be like considering water or salt as sauce. Any Spanish cook will have an open bottle of wine nearby and when inspiration seizes, add it to the dish. Add some to the cook for good measure. It might serve to baste a roast or grill, add character to a soup, or moisture to a too dry fish or chicken. And it is always useful to de-glaze a pan and pour the resulting liquid over the food cooked therein. A common and popular dish cooked with wine is **riñones al jerez**, kidneys cooked with sherry. In Andalucía it's a standard tapa. And very good with a glass of sherry.

Salsa Verde (Green Sauce)

The most popular herb in Spain, by far, is **perejil** (parsley). Spaniards love its subtle earthy taste and palate-cleansing freshness. Other herbs they use very discreetly, if they use them at all. But they use parsley with abandon. Thus, **salsa verde** (green sauce), made with olive oil, garlic and bunches of minced parsley.

Almost every restaurant in Spain will have something cooked in this, usually fish and most often the cheeks of hake. The ingredients are added to the pan as the fish cooks, a little wine or stock added if it's too dry. The hake cheeks contain a lot of natural gelatine that is expressed when cooked. This combines with the oil, and with a constant gentle swirl of the pan the mixture emulsifies, producing the rich, silky consistency the Spanish are so fond of.

Mayonesa (Mayonnaise)

And that search for emulsion brings us to the undisputed king of sauce on the Iberian peninsula. Unless you hide out in your room and shun the company of humanity entirely, you are going to see mayonnaise every day that you are in Spain. Gobs of it.

You will see tapas seemingly made of it. You will see potatoes smothered in it. You will see what at first glance appear to be cakes covered in white frosting, replete with florets and garlands. Do not be fooled. It's mayo. That 'cake' is layers of fish and potato, with mayo deposited thickly between the strata. Order a paella de mariscos (seafood paella) and you will get mayonnaise on the side with which to further enrich the dish. Not a little plastic packet of mayonnaise. Not a dollop or a teaspoon. You will get an ice-cream scoop of mayonnaise! If you see anything on the menu 'con dos salsas' it means two ice-cream scoops of mayonnaise, one of which was coloured with paprika. We can't tell you the way to a Spaniard's heart, but we can tell you that once you get there you'll find a lot of mayonnaise.

The origin of mayonnaise is hotly disputed. It seems every Mediterranean country claims it, each with its own creation myth. Even the British Isles weighs in on this one. Pious Scots will tell you that it was created by a Glaswegian cook by the name of Mahon. He is said to have been in the employ of a French nobleman of the late middle ages. So taken was His Grace with the wonderful new sauce that he named it for its creator. 'Mahonaise' in a French accent being rendered 'mayonnaise'. They say this with a straight face. The Spanish will tell you that it comes from Mahón on the island of Menorca. Wherever it came from, it's in Spain to stay.

Sopas (Soups)

Soups in Spain are normally straightforward, honest, wholesome and tasty. For the most part. They can be bland. **Caldo gallego** (broth with beans, ham and sausage) at its meaty best is as good as anything your own grandmother made, but sometimes it's just a bowl of dishwater with a few ragged greens in it, or a suggestion of something that once walked on four legs. **Sopa de ajo** (garlic soup) can be shockingly bland or gloriously garlicky, billowing with clouds of aromatic *allium sativum*. Soup in Spain is, shall we say, pot luck.

But one thing you may always count on, it will be right for the climate. In the Pyrenees or the Atlantic coast, or the central high plateau where the winters are brutally cold, the soup will give you renewal. On those bitter days it will come to you in a heavy earthenware bowl that retains the heat while you eat. The broth will carry its warm, invigorating message of sustenance throughout your body. Those three terrible months of Spanish winter will be well fended off with soups such as **sopa aragonesa**, which looks a little like French onion soup. It's a beef stock, full of calf's liver. It's topped with bread and cheese and finished in a hot oven.

Bean & chorizo soup

And for those nine months of hell that follow the winter, a plethora of chilled soups to cool you. They are all just variations on a theme, making use of what is good locally, and of what might be left over in the kitchen. Of course the most famous soup from Spain is gazpacho, and when done well the taste will stay in your heart forever.

STAPLES

Gazpacho

Gazpacho is emblematic of Spanish cookery. It is a dish that says "I am Spain". It is not simply a cool bowl of tomato juice. It isn't always made from tomatoes. It isn't always chilled. It isn't always a soup; sometimes it's a cool refreshing drink. It isn't even always called gazpacho. In places like Córdoba it sometimes goes by the older name of **salmorejo**, or is said to be a descendant of salmorejo, a sauce base. It was often prepared in a vessel called a **gazpachero**, hence its name.

Gazpacho is a whole family of soups, and not easy to pin down and define precisely. But there are three common threads that together make gazpacho a quintessence of gastronomic Spain. The first is that Holy Trinity of Spanish cuisine: bread, oil and garlic. The next is the presence of New World crops such as tomatoes, capsicums, even potatoes, without which Spain would be a very different place. And the last thread is that persistent Moorish ghost that flickers and shimmers in the undercurrents of Arabian spices, nuts, and in smooth and soft textures. All in all, this is liquid Spain.

Gazpacho Andaluz (Andalucían Gazpacho)

Ingredients

2	slices white bread, crusts removed
1kg	ripe tomatoes, peeled, seeded, chopped
2	cloves garlic
6	tablespoons olive oil
3	tablespoons sherry vinegar
1	tablespoon salt
3	tablespoons ice water

Soak the bread in cold water for one hour, then squeeze it dry. Blend all ingredients with 1 tablespoon of the ice water in a mortar with pestle, or in a food processor. Strain through a sieve. Refrigerate for 2 hours. Stir in enough of the remaining ice water to obtain a soupy consistency.

NOTE: When serving gazpacho on the patio in midsummer heat, it will quickly lose its cool. To combat this, it is perfectly acceptable to place a cube of ice in each diner's bowl.

Ajo Blanco (White Gazpacho)

Ingredients

6 slices white bread, crusts removed	1 cup almonds, peeled
2 tablespoons sherry vinegar	6 tablespoons olive oil
2 cloves garlic	1 litre ice water
salt to taste	

Soak the bread in cold water for one hour, then squeeze it dry. Blend all ingredients with half a cup of the ice water in a mortar with pestle, or in a food processor. Refrigerate for 2 hours. Stir in enough of the remaining ice water to obtain a gravy-like consistency.
Serves 6

STAPLES

Gazpacho originated, as did so many European dishes, as a way of using bread gone dry after a day or two on the shelf. There are many ways to make use of dry bread, and the poor even went so far as to use the crumbs. And peasant fare often percolates its way up through the social strata, expanding and evolving in its uses. Crumbs became the thickening agent for sauces and soups, and remained so until Antonin Careme championed the use of roux (flour and fat cooked together as a separate ingredient) in the early 19th century. Gazpacho would seem to be the only holdout against Careme. A bowl of gazpacho, then, is a culinary time capsule. A taste of centuries past.

Nowadays, like paella, gazpacho is offered in many bastardised forms. In restaurants outside Spain it doesn't even contain crumbs. It's doused with Italian vinegar, and made with canned tomato juice. Tourist restaurants in Spain haven't sunk that low, but they have learned that in California so called 'Spanish' restaurants serve it laden with chopped raw vegetables such as onion and cucumber, and dollops of sour cream. Some even add avocado and corn chips, perpetuating a common belief that it's a Mexican dish.

Don't let this happen to you. Eschew such offerings. They have also taken to serving it as a first course, just like any hot soup would be. But traditionally gazpacho is offered at the end of a meal. Just as the French like to serve the salad at the end of the meal to scour the maw after heavy meats and sauces, so gazpacho has a cleansing effect on the palate, and aids in digestion. Tell your Spanish waiter you'll have none of his foreign ways. Tell him that you want your gazpacho in true Spanish style. Salud!

Postres (Desserts)

For a people with a sweet tooth the Spanish are short on sweets. Or at least variety in sweets. You won't find much in the way of Bavarian flights of sugary fancy, or French panache in pastry. The Italians surpass the Spanish in confectionery. Even the English are more imaginative with their traditional sweet trolley. You will see candy shops every few blocks in the major cities, and they all handle the same wares: mostly hard candies individually wrapped and stacked with bricklayer's symmetry in display cases. They almost look like building materials. But the candies are for kids, for the most part. And their doting parents buy them far too much. In upmarket neighbourhoods and cities closer to France and Italy you'll find more confections, and pastry shops are increasing in number as Spain enters the European mainstream. But these are not representative of the culture as a whole, and little in part.

Bundelos, Andalucía

One bit of pastry that does seem to speak good Spanish is the **Tarta de Santiago.** You will see this every day in the town of Santiago de Compostela, and all over the country on Saint James' day. It is a flat, dense cake of flour, eggs, cinnamon, sugar and ground almonds. And it is the taste of Spain's religious and historical dichotomy. What with its ground almonds this is a Moorish hand-me-down, yet it is a food to commemorate the defeat of those same people. On its surface, dusted in powdered sugar, is a stencil of the cross of the monastic and military order, sometimes called the cross of Saint James. Look at it with one eye and you see a crucifix. Look with the other and see a sword. Muslim and Christian, peace and war, sacred and profane, sweet but not too sweet. That is the taste of Spain.

Oranges for dessert, Sevilla, Andalucía

STAPLES

In the nation that wrested chocolate from the New World and carried it off to the old, chocolate is most often a disappointment. Especially if you have just come from Switzerland or Austria. The hot chocolate that people drink from early morning to midday in the **chocolaterías** is good although it's not what you would expect. It's thick, more of a chocolate porridge than a drink. But it is good with churros or other not-too-sweet pastries. Adults get much of their sugar ration from their coffee. It's not unusual to see a Spanish lady or gentleman add three teaspoons of sugar to a single demitasse, stir it for what seems an age while it cools just a bit, then down it in three sweet gulps. Sugar shock! For a sweet after dinner they might have a custard dessert, such as **crema catalana** (creme brulee). A very rich, sweet custard, usually flavoured with lemon zest or cinnamon or both. A top coating of sugar is caramelised before serving. There are many similar desserts, some incorporating rice, such as **arroz con leche** (rice pudding). All these concoctions are variations on a theme. While they are tasty, they can get monotonous. More often adults will have fruit, if anything.

The Spanish, like just about everybody in the world, like **helado** (ice cream). You'll see **helado Italiano** shops in all major cities. The ice cream is good, but only just. If you are anywhere along the Santiago pilgrimage trail watch for **frigo pies** (frozen foot). This is ice cream on a stick, but it's moulded into the shape of a footprint. When you've hiked for days along the Santiago trail, all you can think about is your tired, hot feet. The very sight of that cold, sweet footprint of tastiness is enough to lift the spirits of the most dispirited pilgrim on the trail.

One area where you can count on the Spanish to provide an abundance and variety of good sweets is in their holiday fare (see the Celebrating with Food chapter). Aside from holidays you will find one true constant, the fixed star in the sugary sky. Follow this, ye wise men and women, and be led to the Bethlehem of biscuits, cakes and buns. Behind cloistered walls seek your sweets, and ye shall find.

For centuries, religious communities such as convents have supported themselves, indeed some have grown rich, by making and selling sweets. One wonders why they chose such a seemingly frivolous means of labouring in the vineyards of the Lord. Why not good honest shoe-making, or bricklaying, or school teaching instead? Why not nursing the sick? In part it is because these are mostly cloistered orders. They cannot have unwarranted contact with those outside their walls. And perhaps it is in part because they take to heart the words of Saint Theresa of Avila who said that "God walks among the stewpots" (see The Unseen Hand in the Shopping chapter).

The St James cake, baked by nuns, Santiago de Compostela, Galicia

Tapas (Hors d'Oeuvres)

In trendy restaurants from Perth to Los Angeles they are serving little dishes they call tapas, and telling their patrons that they are Spanish specialities. Tailored gentlemen with expensive wristwatches and young women dressed to kill pick at them daintily in the satisfied delusion that they really are eating Spanish food. But they are mistaken. They are eating no such thing. They are being fed little more than reduced rations without the correspondingly reduced prices. But then, one must pay to be trendy.

> The tapa, invented in an age less obsessed with productivity, is a trick for spinning out your drinks without getting drunk.
>
> *Pedro Soleras,*
> *El País newspaper, Madrid*

Tapas, the true tapas of Spain, are not merely things to eat. And they do not travel well. Like so much of Spanish gastronomy, tapas are indissolubly knit to the culture and soil of Spain. Tapas are not a collection of recipes, or the shape or size of a morsel. They are an expression of a people and their unique way of living. They are not things to eat, but a way to eat them. And yet they are even more. They are a way of visiting, and talking and enjoying. They are a way of being part of the community. A way of staying in touch and of staying sober. They are both symbol and substance of Spanish conviviality. They are intimate.

The word tapa means lid, or top. The verb form, **tapar**, means to top or to cover. You might encounter a dish with a name like **carne tapada con queso** (meat topped with cheese). While there is some argument as to the origin of the tapa, most people agree that it harks back to the 18th century. Tavern keepers would place a slice of ham or cheese or bread on the mouth of a glass of sherry or other wine to keep out the dust and flies. The salt or dryness of the 'top' created thirst. And thirst created profits. And a grand custom was born. That may be true as far as it goes, but it doesn't go far enough.

The tapa came about not just as a matter of serendipity. It was a matter of necessity. The Spaniard has a deep sense of unease about alcohol being consumed without something else to digest. The Spanish have traditionally regarded public intoxication as an unpardonable breach of decorum. And a Spaniard is nothing if not decorous. Often loudly decorous, but decorous nonetheless. Taking food with drink is the Spanish way of staying sober. Indeed for as long as writers have been writing about Spain they have been unanimous about her lack of drunkards. We ourselves, in all our Spanish days, have never seen a falling-down-drunk Spaniard. We once did see a man holding forth in a bar in Jerez de la Frontera, and he obviously had a

lot of wind in his sails, but we were discreetly informed that the poor old chap had misspent his youth and learned his habits in England.

Tapas were also necessary because the Spanish do little of their drinking at home and rarely solo. For a drink they must go to the bar where they will find company. And if they go to the bar and have drink they must have a bite to eat. And if they stay at one bar all night long life will be dull, and what's the sense of drinking if it's going to be dull. Thus, the **tapeo**, the tapas crawl. You do not stay at one tasca very long. You have one, maybe two drinks and tapas at each of several. You might go with a small group of friends, or you might go alone and visit several like-minded friends along the way. The tapeo might serve as prelude to dinner, or it might be dinner, or breakfast or lunch, or it might even be a fourth meal of the day.

What constitutes a tapa? Aside from the circumstances of its consumption, anything can be a tapa, as long as it is small, easy to eat (preferably by hand or toothpick), and thirst provoking or alcohol absorbing. A scoop of paella on a saucer can be a tapa. A hunk of bread drizzled with olive oil, a few slices of chorizo, a hard boiled egg, a piece of cheese, all can be tapas. Theoretically, last night's leftover roast beef cut into little bits and slathered with mustard can be a tapa. Theoretically. But commonly you will find **pulpo gallego** (spicy boiled octopus), **garbanzos con espinacas** (chickpeas with spinach), **anchoas fritas a la catalana** (deep-fried anchovies); **gambas al ajillo** (garlic shrimps). When sheep give birth their tails often fall off. Watch for them in spring, served in a sauce of tomatoes, crushed almonds and green peppercorns. The **tortilla española** (Spanish omelette) and **boquerones** (fresh anchovies marinated in wine vinegar) are universal. In Madrid try **callos** (tripe, see the Regional Variations chapter). In Andalucía go for **caracoles** (snails). In the Basque Country everything conceivable is made with **bacalao** (cod).

You'll find tascas in every city in Spain, though they are less common in the northern Mediterranean region. Visit a tasca and you'll be astounded by the variety set before you: shellfish on sticks, cheese and ham, slices of bread topped with whatever is to hand, individual little earthenware dishes filled with hot casseroles of clams, cod or vegetables, and lovely mayonnaise-laden morsels. And the tapas are made in-house. They are not bought from some 'fabrica de tapas'. When supplies are running low a tasca may send out to a brother tasca with which it has a prearranged agreement to support one another in times of extra revelry. But by and large, what you see is what they make. And so many tastes, so little time. And the simple visual impact of the display is often stunning. The tasca men (for they are almost always men) live and work in a still-life painting.

A bar of tapas, Barcelona, Catalunya

TASCAS AND KIDS

My family and I lived in Franco's Madrid when I was between the ages of 8 and 11, and one of the things we'd do for kicks was to go out at night and eat tapas with friends. We'd head down toward Plaza Mayor or the Paseo del Prado, where there were clusters of tascas, those friendly bars found all over Spain that specialise in the little plates of food called tapas. We used to call it tasca hopping, and what fun it was! We'd go into the most promising looking place and sit at a thick wooden table, sawdust underfoot, while the adults ordered red wine, and for my little sister and me, lemon Fanta. Then came the tapas, which seemed to me to be proportioned just right for a kid. We'd eat shrimp grilled in the shell, garlicky onions, red capsicums, and always tortilla española.

I vividly remember the wonderfully mingled scents of cigarette smoke, sawdust, olive oil and wine, and the comforting dim-yellow light that illuminated these places. I also remember that there were always plenty of kids running around – and I remember that at the smallest tables sat ancient men in dark work clothes, elbows planted on either side of their plates, chewing with their mouths open. My sister and I would watch them surreptitiously as they broke all the rules of etiquette that had been drummed into us. Later we'd stroll out into the night and down a couple of doors to the next most appealing looking tasca. The adults, as I see them now, were always laughing eyes and teeth gleaming in the street lights, and it was wonderful to be part of their adventure. Eventually, Julie and I would fall asleep and be gently carried home.

Those tasca evenings let adults be adults – let them drink and talk – but we were able to run amok, as kids should. Whenever I walk into a regular bar in the states and see the signs reading 21 and older, I think how lucky Spanish kids are – and how lucky we were.

Margo True (editor, Gourmet Magazine)

The tasca is an egalitarian institution. There are restaurants where only the wealthy may go. And there are restaurants where the wealthy would not be seen. We know of restaurants that only Gypsies and communists patronise. Sadly, we know of old peasants who would enter a restaurant and not order the better cuts of meat not because they lack the funds, but because those are only for the wealthy. But all class distinctions are left at the door of the tasca. No man may enter with his vanities. No woman is too fine a lady to drink deeply and laugh loudly. The fisherman rubs elbows with the banker, the shady lady with the housewife. All and sundry are just people thirsty for a drink and company, hungering for food and conversation. God might not have made persons equal, but the tasca does.

drinks

The Spanish are very protective of their wine production, and like to make sure what is on the label is what you are drinking. Calling any wine a 'Rioja' would be misleading, confusing it with a French drop would be heresy. This is also the birthplace of sherry. And along with alcoholic drinks there are also warming beverages and mineral-rich waters to put back what the summer sun takes out.

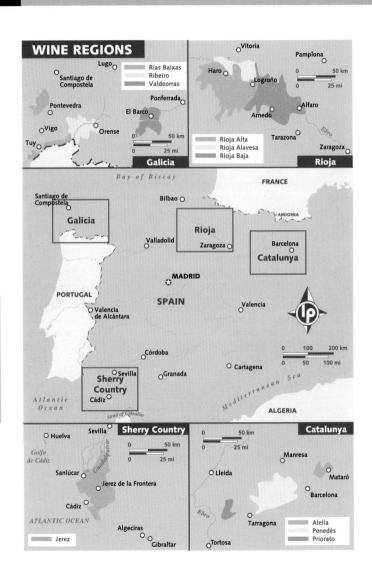

WINE REGIONS

Galicia

- Lugo
- Santiago de Compostela
- Pontevedra
- Ponferrada
- El Barco
- Vigo
- Orense
- Tuy

Legend:
- Rías Baixas
- Ribeiro
- Valdeorras

0 50 km
0 25 mi

Rioja

- Vitoria
- Pamplona
- Haro
- Logroño
- Arnedo
- Alfaro
- Tarazona
- Zaragoza
- Ebro

0 50 km
0 25 mi

Legend:
- Rioja Alta
- Rioja Alavesa
- Rioja Baja

Bay of Biscay

FRANCE

- Santiago de Compostela
- **Galicia**
- Bilbao
- ANDORRA
- **Rioja**
- Valladolid
- Zaragoza
- Barcelona
- **Catalunya**
- MADRID
- PORTUGAL
- Valencia de Alcántara
- SPAIN
- Valencia
- Córdoba
- Cartagena
- Sevilla
- **Sherry Country**
- Granada
- Cádiz
- Atlantic Ocean
- Strait of Gibraltar
- Mediterranean Sea
- ALGERIA

0 100 200 km
0 50 100 mi

LP

Sherry Country

- Huelva
- Sevilla
- Golfo de Cádiz
- Sanlúcar
- Jerez de la Frontera
- Guadalquivir
- Cádiz
- ATLANTIC OCEAN
- Algeciras
- Gibraltar

Legend:
- Jerez

0 50 km
0 25 mi

Catalunya

- Manresa
- Lleida
- Mataró
- Barcelona
- Ebro
- Tarragona
- Tortosa

Legend:
- Alella
- Penedès
- Priorato

0 50 km
0 25 mi

Wine

Welcome to Spain. Now let's drink some wine. The Spanish do. Every day. One chamber of the Spanish heart is reserved for olive oil and the other for wine. Wine is present at every lunch and dinner, and it isn't uncommon to have a nip of dry sherry after breakfast or on the way to work. Spain has more acreage under vines than any other nation although, due to methods in use, it does not have the greatest wine production. But never fear, you won't run dry. Wine runs through the nation like blood.

For as often as the Spanish drink wine you would think them a nation of drunkards. But the opposite is the truth. The Spanish are people of moderation and consistency; they regularly drink wine moderately. Sometimes they'll mix it with water, especially when giving it to drinkers of a youngish age. Eighteen is the age of consent, but generally Spaniards are ready to drink wine when they start to ask for it. They grow up with responsible attitudes towards drink, and they keep them for life. So don't look for a piss-up or Bacchanalian revel. Here wine is a food, not a drug.

Wine has been grown in Spain for at least as long as records have been kept. And during Roman times it was said to produce pretty good stuff. Then came the fall of Rome, and those pesky Visigoths made a mess of most things and reduced the common denominator in all things but pillage. Wine quality went down. Then came those abstemious Moors and their tiresome ways about food and drink. Both quality and quantity went down. By the time the Spanish had reclaimed all of Spain it seemed everyone was a soldier and satisfied with dried meat, hard cheese and rough wine. Quantity rose dramatically, but not so quality.

And with the exception of sherry, for which the British can be credited, things stayed that way for a long time. Then in the 19th century, certain Francophiles in Catalunya began to make sparkling wine imitations of Champagne. In the early 20th century a number of French vintners moved to Spain, bringing with them superior grape varieties and refined techniques. But it wasn't until the second half of the 20th century that wine quality in Spain began to really take off. And in post-Franco Spain with so many gusts, nay storms, of fresh air blowing in, Spanish wines have come to compete admirably in the world market.

Perhaps your first encounter with a Spanish wine import was with Freixenet **cava** (sparkling wine) in its trademark black bottle. Or it might have been a burlap-wrapped bottle of a rich red Rioja. Maybe you came of age sipping sherry. And of course you were always delighted with the price of Spanish imports. Well the prices have gone up, but they are still very competitive. And the variety has exploded! And when you get to Spain you'll find even more.

You'll find the wine to be 'user friendly'. It's easy to understand both on the label and in the bottle. Like their solid food, the Spaniards' liquid nourishment is straightforward and unpretentious. They do not like fussy wine any more than fussy food. They like it to taste good, smell good, and feel good going down. They do not require it to have infinite complexity over which one may linger and chat about for an hour. This is largely because they do not take wine by itself. It's part of a meal. So eat, drink and enjoy. Comprende? You'll never hear a bent pinkie Spaniard say something prissy like "it's just a minor little Ribeiro del Duero, but I think you'll be amused by its presumptuousness". The Spanish don't even say we 'make' wine. Nature makes wine, by a very simple process. We simply 'elaborate' it.

Almost all areas of Spain grow wine. And while we think none of it is bad, a great deal of it, especially from central Spain, is grown for blending. It's pumped into railroad tank cars and shipped off to France where dealers mix it with their own common stuff and sell it as cheap *vin ordinaire*. A fitting end. Many areas known mainly for bulk wines are improving, and in the next edition of this book we hope to include some of them. But for now we'll focus on what we think will please you most: the regions of Rioja, where the best in bold reds is to be found; Catalunya, where cava comes from; Galicia, known for its excellent white wines; and Andalucía whence comes the unique and transcendental sherry. (For an understanding of Spanish wine designations, see Denominations of Origin and Specificity in the Culture of Spanish Cuisine chapter.)

The barrel room at Bodega de Sarria, Navarra

White grapes, Galicia

Catalunya

The Catalans have divvied up their corner of Spain into more DOs than any other region of the country. At the time of writing there were 10, and you may watch for a few more to develop in the future. While Catalan wines are among the highest in quality, not every DO can take credit. Some pretty ordinary stuff also comes from here, but it goes mainly into blending vats. So you won't be in much danger of being blindsided by plonk dressed in a fancy label or curvaceous bottle.

Penedès

West of Barcelona, Penedès is one of the most important wine regions of Spain. This is due not only to volume and variety, but also to it being a hotbed of experimentation and development. In many ways Penedès is less Spanish and more French. And even more Californian. Here you'll find many 'new' wines. They aren't necessarily young wines, they are newly developed. One of the most popular new wines is **Viña Sol**. It is a pure varietal, being made exclusively of **Parellada**, a native Spanish grape. But it is cold fermented in stainless steel and bottled very young. A traditional Spanish wine would have been naturally fermented and aged in wood, then bottled partially oxidised. Such a seriously Spanish wine would be full in the mouth and somewhat austere in the nose. It would speak of musty old wine cellars, and dour dons and doñas. But the Catalan iconoclasts make of Viña Sol a wine that is intensely fruity and cheerfully tart. It makes us think of lemonade with a touch of pineapple. It says 'fiesta' in your mouth. It has a huge following, especially among younger drinkers, and you will find it in almost every bar.

DRINKS

The Catalans are smitten by the international varieties so popular in France, California and Australia, and they plant them here as nowhere else in Spain. They are crazy for Cabernet Sauvignon, mad for Merlot, potty over Pinot Noir, and they also like Chardonnay. And if that isn't enough to raise the grapey hackles of the old guard, even Zinfandel is cropping up. Wines here are grown with creative agronomy and made with innovative technologies. It is almost as though Catalunya has issued a declaration of oenological independence.

CREATING CAVA

There are many criteria to be met for a wine to be called cava, but the most important is that it be made by the method known as *Methode Champanoise*. In this process, the original for Champagne, a still wine is fermented in vats per the usual custom. It is then bottled, but before corking a dosage of yeast is added. This feeds on the residual sugars, causing a secondary fermentation.

One product of fermentation is carbon dioxide, hence the bubbles. The discovery of this is credited, at least in France, to Saint Remi. Upon tasting it for the first time he is said to have called out to his brethren, "Come quickly! I am drinking Stars!"

In Spain the cava stars began in 1872 as an imitation of Champagne. Señor Jose Raventós, owner of Codorníu was so enamoured of the bubbly that he created his own. Now his descendants, who still own Codorníu, claim to be the largest makers of sparkling wine in the world. Ah, but what would Spanish gastronomy be without a heated dispute? Freixenet, the makers of that famous wine in the black bottle, claim that they are the biggest! Who is really the biggest? Quien sabe? And who cares anyway? As long as they keep making it.

Barcelona, Catalunya

Wine taster, Bodega de Sarria, Navarra

Penedès also produces a very fine dessert wine made from the Malvasia grape. This comes from the area around Stiges. There isn't much of this seductive grape left in the world, and what is labelled Malvasia is often a base counterfeit made with Muscat. Not that Muscat is a bad grape, but it's not one to sing 'hosanna' over either. Get the genuine DO article here.

Above all, Penedès is the cava capital. Cava used to refer to any sparkling wine made in Spain. Now it is held to rigid accountability, and is highly specific to an area that is almost all within Catalunya. Small areas of Rioja and Aragón produce cava, but nowhere near as much. Cava is a blend of the white grapes **Parellada**, **Xarel-lo**, and **Macabeo**. These three make an ideal balance of acidity, body and colour. Some producers also experiment with Chardonnay in the mix.

Alella

There was a time when a drive up the coast of Alella, north of Barcelona, was an unfolding scene of vineyards. Sadly, production here has been decreasing due to urban and tourism development displacing vineyards and driving up the price of real estate. Grape varieties include the whites, **Xarel-lo**, **Pansá Blanca**, **Garnacha Blanca**, the pink **Pansá Rosada**, and the red **Tempranillo**. Little red wine is made here, though. Interesting dessert wines are often made by adding sweet must to existing dry white wine. It doesn't sound very hopeful, but it is tasty. And you'll find small amounts of cava made here too.

Priorato

We have a special place in our heart for pitiful Priorato, located in the region of the Rio Siurana. This is another area where wine production has declined in recent years. And for special Spanish reasons beyond our ken it does not enjoy as high a reputation as Penedès, although much of its wine is bought by Penedès vintners for blending with their own stuff. The wines are generally deep red and flavourful. We find them admirable but, searching the shop shelf, we find them only with difficulty. But here is an opportunity for you to mount a Dionysian quest. Betake yourself on a tour of the restaurants of Barcelona and Tarragona. Those are the best places to find them. And then you may also seek out Priorato's greatest distinction. Though overshadowed by Penedès, Priorato produces the most expensive wine in Spain, **L'Ermita** (The Hermitage). It is a surprising wine in that it is made of **Garnacha**, not ordinarily thought of as a 'noble' grape, and often going into unremarkable rosés. Also surprising is the 14% alcohol content. Of course it is a very limited production wine, aged 20 months in barrels, and selling for about US$150 per bottle. And it's not a bad deal!

Galicia

Galicia is the opposite of Rioja in that where Rioja is one DO that straddling three areas, Galicia has three DOs to the one area. And, to further confuse things, two of them are geographically defined and one is defined by the **Albariño** grape, wherever it might be grown. People have grown wine in Galicia since time out of mind. But only since the 1980s has the world been aware of it.

Picking grapes, Galicia

E haberá vino ne Gloria?
Coló, coló! Cousa boa!
Cólase como xarabe!
Meu compadre, o que ben sabe corre sin trigo nin broa.

And would there be wine in Heaven?
Drink, drink! What a beautiful thing!
It's as smooth as syrup!
Oh, how it slips down, my friend, with neither wheat nor corn bread.

Rosalia de Castro (1837-1885) Galicia's greatest poet

Wine production in this area has long been a small, family affair. People often grew enough for their own use, and maybe a little for sale or barter. They did not normally bottle it, preferring casks or jugs, as bottled wine was suspect among the Gallegos. "You don't know what they put in it", went their complaint. And there was a widely accepted calumny that wines from Galicia did not travel well. We often wonder, what with a poet like Rosalia de Castro singing the wine's praises, how this kind of fuzzy logic ever started. But at least now it has faded, and vineyard production is up dramatically, hundreds of people getting into the act. Rosalia would be proud to know that the thin white wines of the Celtic north are growing into respectable members of the Spanish wine family.

Dempóis de Dios, viva o vino!
After God, praise wine!
Rosalia de Castro

Barrelmaker, Galicia

Rías Baixas

The DO Rías Baixas covers three geographically separate subzones, but they all grow the **Albariño** grape. And while you might refer to a 'red Rioja' or a 'Jerez', you don't want to say "give me a Rías Baixas". Always ask for an Albariño. And ask often. You'll find it usually a dry, rich, flavourful, and very crisp white wine. It can be highly aromatic. People that we trust have said that they have been able to smell a glass of it from a distance of three metres. But we don't recommend staying three metres away from a good glass of wine. Get close, and you'll find that the aroma is of fresh or green fruits. Albariño is good wine to accompany the local seafood. It is very much like a Riesling in character, and has the same range of possibility. It can be made sweet or dry, Bordeaux or Moselle style. The great controversy, and controversy is an essential ingredient in Spanish cuisine, is in what style and with what characteristics the wine should be produced. Unlike Californian wine makers who are wedded to variety, the Spanish insist that wine be identified with the place of production. Watch for the range of the Albariño's expression to narrow over the years as it gains definition.

That eventual definition will not reduce to less than the DO's three subzones. Two of them (O Rosal and Condado de Tea) are along the banks of the Rio Miño at the border with Portugal. Here the weather is warmer and drier than in the northern subzone of Val do Salnes. The wine made here tends to be lower in alcohol and higher in acid than its southern counterparts. In O Rosal, the wine makers apply the blender's art, using such varieties as **Loureira** and **Treixadura** to produce wines of greater complexity and subtlety.

Harvest time in Orense, Galicia

Ribeiro

Ribeiro is the Gallego word for river-bank, and the wine of that name is grown along the banks of the Miño to the west of the DO Rías Baixas. The DO Ribeiro produces the best known Gallego wines. Most are blends of the varieties **Lado**, **Torrontés**, **Treixadura**, **Albariño** and **Loureira**. They are pale, straw coloured, light and refreshing. The bouquet is typically full of flowers and mint. In the mouth they are very flavourful and have a long finish. They are very susceptible to the weather. A lack of sun, a frequent condition in Galicia, can mean a lack of alcohol and a rather flat wine. In buying vintage wines you take your chances. Have a glass in the bar before investing in the bottle.

Grapes, Galicia

Valdeorras

The valley of the river Sil from El Barco to La Rua delimits the DO Valdeorras. This is an area in which production of wine, and especially of native wines, almost died out due to a combination of bad luck and bad taste. The phylloxera (a root-feeding aphid) was especially virulent in 1911 and brought the bad luck. The bad taste was provided by a foolish and damnable prejudice for non-local varieties. These two scourges had reduced the plantings of the native **Godello** to a fraction of total production. In 1976 a few well-educated, clear-thinking wine makers began to produce new clones and pruning methods that rehabilitated this indigenous white grape. New plantings are now increasing and people are coming to once again recognise the Godello as the taste of this region. It is clean and fruity, with a bitter finish reminiscent of Gewürztraminer.

Valdeorras also grows some decent if not spectacular red grapes. Chief among them is the **Mencía**. It is thought to be a mutant or a relative of the Cabernet Franc. Some wine makers use a little Cabernet Sauvignon in their blends on the strength of that relationship. The unblended wine is sometimes a little flat, being low in acid, but it is usually very fragrant with smells of liquorice and fruit. It goes very well with bread and cheese, and is a fine picnic wine.

WISDOM IN WINE

Wine is so firmly established in the Spanish consciousness that it often enters daily conversation in the guise of idioms and proverbs.

Quen bebe, vive.
He who drinks, lives.

El agua hace mal, el vino cantar.
Water makes you sick, but wine makes you sing.

Vino de Illana todo mal sana.
The wine of Illana cures all ills.

Por la manana puro, por la tarde sin agua.
Take wine pure in the morning and unwatered in the afternoon.

Antes de comer, dos vasos has de beber. En comiendo, otros vasos seguias bebiendo. Mas despues de haber comido, tampoco te sentaran mal mas vasos.
Two glasses before eating. Two more while you eat. And after you have eaten, a few more won't do you any harm.

Comer sin vino, comer mosquino.
A meal without wine is a stingy one.

Pan de antedia, vino de ano, y carne de ese dia.
Day-old bread, wine a year old, and fresh meat.

Al buen amigo, tu pan y tu vino. Al malo, tu perro y tu palo.
For a good friend, your bread and your wine. For a false friend, your dog and a stick.

El vino, para que sepa a vino, bebelo con un amigo.
For wine to taste of wine, you must drink it with a friend.

Vino y amigo que se torvieron, nunca a ser buena volvieron.
Wine or friendship gone sour will never be restored.

Viejo que vino no bebe, cerca esta de la muerte.
And old man who drinks no wine is near death.

Rioja

Rioja is the DO given to wines grown in the area lying between the Cantabrian mountain range in the north and the Demanda range in the south. It lies along the valley of the Ebro river and takes its name from one of its tributaries, the Río Oja. Its boundaries reflect only geographical, not political considerations, as it straddles the areas of La Rioja, Navarra, Castilla y León and the Basque Country.

DRINKS

DRINKS

Harvest time in Orense, Galicia

Vineyards have flourished in Rioja since ancient times. Excavations have turned up wineries capable of producing 30,000 gallons per year. Even with the Moorish conquest wine did not cease. The Moors were happy to collect taxes on the Christian wine. And the Christians reaffirmed their identity by drinking wine, in their religious ceremonies as well as in daily life. Monasteries became major producers, and believed they were doing God's work, or were at least working towards God's ends. As the Moors were driven back, wine became even more important. As the Santiago pilgrim trail, which goes through the heart of Rioja, carried more and more faithful, the wine makers sold more and more wine.

France has had a lot of influence in the wines of Rioja, although you should not say so to a Spaniard. However, it is undeniable that when the phylloxera blight struck France many Bordeaux wine makers came to Rioja for a generation or two and taught the locals a few tricks. Many oenologists believe that the **Tempranillo** grape originally came from France. But advancing this point of view is the surest way to open unpleasantries anywhere in Spain, and to start a fistfight in Rioja. Cabernet Sauvignon is another case in point. This grape, with a few highly restricted exceptions, may not be used in any wine bearing the Rioja DO, yet many quietly experiment with it – sshhhh.

When hunting down vino in Rioja, it pays to be familiar with a few terms. **Sin Crianza** refers to young wines, even less than a year old. One such wine, **Vi Novell**, is made by carbonic maceration rather than by crushing. This wine is ready to drink as soon as it is bottled, in fact it should be drunk within three months. Don't buy it if it's more than a year old. **Crianza** refers to red wine at least two years old, having spent at least one year in the barrel, and some months in the bottle. White or rosé crianza need only age for one year. **Reserva** is the name given to selected red wines that have the right characteristics for long ageing. They require at least one year in the barrel, and must be at least three years old before sale. Wines of truly exceptional vintage are known as **Gran Reserva**. If red, they are aged for a minimum of two years in the barrel and three years in the bottle. One year less for whites. **Castillo** is chateau-bottled wine, wherein all the grapes used are grown on the estate. Castillo wines are a rarity here, and not necessarily an indication of quality.

GRAPE VARIETIES OF RIOJA	
Tempranillo	The most common grape, red or white. It is widely believed to be a mutant form of the Pinot Noir. Its wine is smooth and fruity, seldom as dry as its supposed French counterpart.
Garnacha	Much of the Garnacha crop goes to the making of rosados. It is intensely aromatic, making it a good addition to the Tempranillo, which can sometimes be a bit austere.
Graciano	Good aroma and a beautiful ruby hue, but highly acidic. Used mainly for blending.
Manzuelo	Very tannic, highly acidic, with good fruit aromas. Commonly blended with Tempranillo.
Viura	The region's most commonly used white grape. High acidity makes for a very crisp, refreshing wine. It can be dry or semi-dry and can also be used in blending, even with reds.
Malvasia	Yields a luscious, very fruity white wine. It can be bottled as itself or blended with Viura.
Garnacha Blanca	Yields a light, dry wine good for picnics. Best drunk young.

DRINKS

Sherry

Were it not for the English taste, nay, insatiable thirst, for sherry it would likely be an obscure Spanish anomaly pooh-poohed by Frenchmen and laughed at by Italians. The Greeks would sniff at it too, but their love of retsina (wine spiked with pine resin) gives them no room to talk. To this day sherry is a staple of the English bar and parlour. Some people even think it's English. And, indeed, some sherries are brought to England in cask where they are blended and bottled according to local taste. The English even gave it its name. Though it is known in Spain as **Jerez**, the rest of the world knows it as the anglicised version of the Arab name for its place of origin, Sheris.

> Prince Harry is valiant, for the cold blood he did naturally inherit of his father he hath, like lean, sterile and bare land, manured, husbanded and tilled with excellent endeavour of drinking good store of fertile sherry that he has become very hot and valiant. If I had a thousand sons the first humane principle I would teach them should be to forswear thin potations, and to addict themselves to sack (sherry).
>
> Sir John Falstaff, *Henry IV* Pt II, iv:iv:135

Nobody knows how this taste began, but we do know that the first written record of the English-Spanish sherry trade was penned in the reign of Henry I. Seven Henries later Catherine of Aragón, wife to Hefty Harry, complained that "the king, my husband, keeps all the best wines from the Canaries and Jerez for himself". When Drake's fleet raided Cádiz in 1587 they carried off 3000 butts of sherry. Queen Elizabeth described it as "the ideal wine". Even the lower classes liked it and many of Shakespeare's characters are seen quaffing it and singing its praises. Maybe it was just a cheap drink. Brandy was expensive, and beer impractical to carry in a hip flask. With an alcohol strength of 15-20% sherry was no thin potation.

In order to ensure their supplies against wars, revolutions and financial ups and downs, British businessmen began investing in sherry concerns, buying their own vineyards and **bodegas** (wineries). Hence, famous sherry names like Byass, Sandeman and Osborne were established. In order to ensure a consistent product, they and their Spanish counterparts began experimenting with what would become the solera system (see the boxed text The Solera System later in this chapter).

Sherry barrels, Jerez de la Frontera, Andalucía

Most wines occur by a completely natural process. If a grape were to fall into a stony depression and break its skin and bleed out its juice, the yeast spores in the air and soil would feed on its sugars and make wine, completely without human involvement. Sherry, however, is a human invention, the product of great artificers. It begins with the chalky **albariza** soil in southern Andalucía, bounded by Cádiz, Jerez de la Frontera and Sanlúcar. Also in Andalucía is the small district of Montilla with that same soil and producing a similar kind of wine. This soil is the first of many factors in the creation of sherry that are the opposite to any other wine. Things that would destroy other wines are what make sherry. Most wine grapes require well-drained soil, so that the roots can strike deep, bringing in a wider variety of nutrients. The albariza soil, however, is like a sponge in its ability to retain rainwater. Without this soil, little would grow in this semi-arid region. The hot weather would also reduce any other wine to a 'thin potation', but here the sherry grapes thrive.

Bottles of sherry, Jerez de la Frontera, Andalucía

The principal grape for sherry is the **Palomino**, indigenous to this region. White and juicy Palomino is also good to eat, unlike so many other wine grapes. **Pedro Ximénez** is also grown. Legend says that it is a type of Riesling brought to the region in the 16th century by a German soldier named Peter Seimens (hence the name). It yields a full-bodied and intensely sweet wine used almost exclusively for blending. To enhance sweetness and deepen flavour, the Pedro Ximénez grapes are spread out on rush mats. Under the sun their moisture quickly evaporates, and when they are nearly raisins they are gathered up and crushed, expressing a thick, sweet, golden must.

During the harvest, both grape varieties collect a certain amount of dust called **pruina**. No attempt is made to remove this dust, as it contains a yeast which sparks a fermentation process. At the end of this process a dry white wine of little distinction is obtained. This is racked off from the several fermentation vats into butts of American white oak, a type of wood chosen for its optimum porosity. The new wines are now classified and the butts marked with specific chalk strokes.

One stroke indicates wine that is well formed and clean to the nose. It will develop into one of three styles of sherry. **Fino** is pale, straw, or golden coloured with a sharp aroma of almonds. It is very dry and refreshing, and probably the most common tapa tipple in southern Spain. Spaniards also enjoy it as a table wine, and serve it with seafood and soups. **Manzanilla** is almost the same as fino, but with characteristics imparted by the area in which it is produced, the seaside town of Sanlúcar de Barrameda. Manzanilla has an almost salty finish said to be an endowment of the local sea breezes. **Amontillado** is amber in colour with a nutty aroma reminiscent of hazelnuts and raisins. It goes well with strong cheeses and oily fish.

Jerez de la Frontera, Andalucia

DRINKS

One stroke and a dot on the butt identifies a full-bodied wine that will become **Oloroso**. This is often blended with Pedro Ximénez wine to make cream sherry: full bodied, dark, rich and sweet. Oloroso goes well with strong meats and game, or with walnuts and cheese.

Two strokes means the wine is not yet classifiable and will need to be revisited later. Three strokes is for wines not up to snuff. These will be sent to the distillery.

In another one of the vinous opposites that distinguish sherry, the wine is aged aerobically (in contact with air). The butts are filled to only about four fifths capacity. Contact with air turns other wines to vinegar, but in the case of Fino, Manzanilla and Amontillado, a unique yeast called **flor** (*mycoderma vini*) appears on the surface of the wine and protects it from the air. It resembles a layer of bread crumbs, and indeed smells like bread dough. This will remain throughout the ageing process and help to give the wine its essential character. Oloroso is the exception, as its high alcohol content means the flor can't survive.

THE SOLERA SYSTEM

In the solera system of ageing, barrels are stacked in rows at least three high. The row at the bottom is called the solera, from the word **suelo** (floor). The rows above are **criaderos** (nurseries). The oldest wine is at the bottom, the wine of the previous year is in the next row up, and the wine of the current year is at the top. Each year about one third of the wine is drawn from the solera and bottled. The missing wine is replaced with wine from the next criadero. That wine is then immediately replaced with wine from the top criadero. And that is replaced by the new wine of the year. In this resulting blending of vintages over the years a fairly consistent product is obtained. Wine from the solera can contain minute amounts of a vintage 100 years old. Most bodegas have the one solera and two criaderos, but there are some producers of top quality wines that have four and even five levels. When old barrels are replaced, they are transported to Scotland where they are used for ageing whisky.

Buying sherry, remember that all the ageing is done in the barrel. It will not improve in the bottle. Once opened, it will last longer than ordinary wine, but should be consumed within 48 hours. Keep it cool and serve chilled. Excellent for cooking, add sherry to cream sauces, a bowl of beef soup, or stew fruit in the stuff for a delicious dessert.

Other Alcohol
Sidra (Cider)

Atlantic Spain grows vines and has for centuries, but not in great quantity.
What it does grow in great quantity is apples. More apples than people
could possibly want to eat. And so people ferment apple must in chestnut
barrels and drink their apples in the form of sidra, the tangy, light, and
mildly effervescent drink, known by Asturians as zythos.

The common form of cider is **sidra gasificada**, mass produced and
available in dry and semi-dry varieties. The other form, **sidra natural** is
more of a 'home brew', made on a smaller scale with no additives. Unlike
sidra gasificada, this brew is cloudier, fruitier and must be drunk young.

Cider is a splendid accompaniment to seafood and pork, but it's also
good by itself on a hot day. It is also used for cooking, going into sauces,
soups, pastries and breads; it makes admirable demi-glace, and can be used
as a marinade. In Madrid and other cities you will find it bottled and
widely available in restaurants. It's almost as common as beer, though
while every bar has beer, they don't all have cider (see Sidrería in the
Where to Eat & Drink chapter).

Cerveza (Beer)

Beer is not generally what people think of when they think of Spain. They
think of wine, sherry and sangría. Sometimes they erroneously think of
tequila. But suds just don't seem to speak Español to most people. Get
ready for a shock: Spain's sales of beer surpassed sales of wine in the early
1990s. There are many reasons or this seemingly mad state of affairs, not
the least of which is the long presence of British tourists in the land. And
now Germans as well. And most of the time it is very hot in Spain. After
walking even short distances you can raise a powerful thirst. Then there
are tapas, many of them made with vinegar and salt. Wine on top of a
mouthful of anchovies is just not the ideal thing. Beer is!

Mostly it is a generational change. People who came to adulthood in
the waning years of Franco's Spain were looking for new things, new ways
to live, new habits and customs. The addition of beer to the table is just
one manifestation of many from this trend. And if you are a beer lover, it's
a fine manifestation indeed!

Cruzcampo was started in 1904 by the sherry makers, Roberto and Tomas
Osborne. Their British lineage is obvious in their name, and perhaps that is
the beginning of their interest in beer. The Osbornes studied brewing in
Germany, then returned to Seville to start their company. They built their
brewery just outside the entrance to the city, and delivered their wares to
dealers as well as selling retail from the premises. Soon it became a place to

stop after a night of revelry, and often the partying would continue into the wee hours. Presiding over all this was a shrine with a stone cross known as the **cruz del campo** (cross of the country), hence the beer's name.

Cruzcampo is the closest you'll get to light beer without asking for it. It is a light and dry brew with a somewhat sour flavour. It is pale and bubbly but has virtually no head. Once you pour it in the glass, the bubbles keep rising and what little head there is immediately disappears. The beer is hoppy and has a simple aroma slightly reminiscent of rising bread dough. Other beers brewed by Cruzcampo include Alcázar, Calatrava and Keler. The brewery is now owned by Guinness.

Beers on tap, Barcelona, Catalunya

Mahou is not a Spanish name. Casimiro Mahou was from the French city of Metz, home of much good beer. He moved to Madrid, operated a number of businesses, and in 1890 opened a brewery in the centre of the city. It included a tasting room where customers could sample what was for most a very foreign item. Not wanting to drink without eating, customers would buy cooked crabs from a nearby shop and take them to the tasting room. Eventually the tasting room became a bar, known as El Cangrejero (The Crab Fisher).

Mahou Classic is a mellow, slightly malty beer with a good deal of body. It is darker than Cruzcampo, somewhat saturated in colour. It doesn't have much head on it, but more than Cruzcampo. The beer smells sweet and goes down smoothly. The taste is slightly honey-like, without being too sweet.

San Miguel was originally brewed by Spanish monks in the San Miguel district of Manila, while the Philippines was still a Spanish colony. In the mid 20th century a Spanish businessman, Andres Soriano, took a liking to the beer. He thought it might do well in Spain, so he travelled to Lérida in Catalunya where he took samples of the water in the Segre River. Back in Manila the monks of San Miguel pronounced the water to be perfect for their beer. In 1956 the first bottles of San Miguel beer made in Spain were ready for sale.

San Miguel Premium is quite strong (5.4%) but has a light, slightly sweet, almost fruity taste to it. The beer has a complex and flowery aroma. San Miguel's other brew, Nostrum de San Miguel, is stronger (6.2%) with a full and smooth body.

Damm brewery's history began when Auguste Kuentzmann Damm left Alsace for Spain to escape the Franco-Prussian war of 1870. He settled in Barcelona and began his brewery in 1876. So successful was Damm that he spawned a host of imitators. Soon Barcelona was rich with what we could kindly call 'microbreweries'. In order to maintain quality and a hold on the market, three of the better operations merged in 1910 to form the present day company.

Damm's all-malt beer, Edel, is rich, mellow and has a smell reminiscent of molasses or corn syrup. The taste is also honey-like (more so than Mahou) without being especially sweet. The head is creamy. Damm brew a number of other beers including the Estrella Damn Pilsner, which is perfect for the Spanish summer. It also comes in a light version (3.2%). At the other end is Voll-Damm (7.2%), a hoppy, creamy lager that plays honour to Damm's Germanic background.

Sangría

The wines of Spain were not always of the high quality we have come to expect these days. When they were good, of course, they were very, very good. But when they were bad – Diablos! But instead of wasting it, the Spanish would take the bad wine and put something into it to mitigate the taste. Sometimes it was just water, sometimes it was other wine, often it was spices or fruit juice. Over time a few recipes came into being that pleased most and offended none. To this day sangría is an idea, not a chemical formula. Some people might use apple juice, or pineapple juice. Others might use nutmeg, or cloves. But a fairly standard recipe calls for citrus and cinnamon. How much of this or that to add to the wine depends on the wine: how good, how bad, how sweet, how dry. The final product should be refreshing and quaffable. Unfortunately, when served in tourist restaurants it is usually cloyingly sweet.

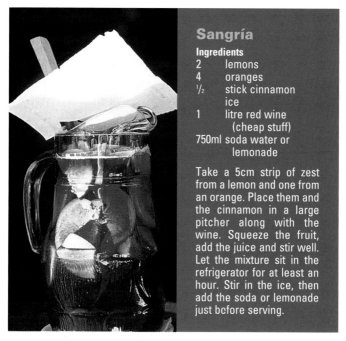

Sangría

Ingredients

2	lemons
4	oranges
$1/2$	stick cinnamon
	ice
1	litre red wine (cheap stuff)
750ml	soda water or lemonade

Take a 5cm strip of zest from a lemon and one from an orange. Place them and the cinnamon in a large pitcher along with the wine. Squeeze the fruit, add the juice and stir well. Let the mixture sit in the refrigerator for at least an hour. Stir in the ice, then add the soda or lemonade just before serving.

DRINKS

Pouring cider in San Sebastián, Basque Country

Drinks at the Margarita Blue Bar, Barcelona, Catalunya

Aguardiente (Spirits)

Brandy and other distillates have been made in Spain for at least as long as sherry. Sherry would not exist without brandy. And brandy made of sherry is a fine and noble drink of its own. But there is a whole tribe of liqueurs and spirits all known by the catch-all term of **aguardientes**.

One of the oldest liqueurs in Spain is **anís**. Originally brought to Europe by the Dutch, the liquorice-flavoured seeds of the anise plant found instant popularity among the Spanish. They turned it into a drink almost immediately and by the 1700s it was the national tipple. Today anís is a common last note to a fine meal. Or sometimes a first note. Or a note at any time. The chief area of production is around the city of Chinchón. And the only DO for anís is Chinchón. The makers there only use pure ingredients, whereas other anís makers often substitute other plants for the hard-to-grow anise plant. Look for the DO seal on the Chinchón label.

In the area around Pamplona grows a sorry little excuse for a very sour plum. It is in fact the sloe fruit, and when added to anís it is the basis of one of Spain's most popular liqueurs, **pacharán**. This aguardiente tastes a bit like sloe gin with a dose of five-spice powder. It's best drunk by itself or with nuts. Try it in the early evening, before your **paseo** (stroll). The most common brand is Zoco, accounting for more than half the national sales.

Extremadura is famous for cherries. It is also famous for one of the newer members of the aguardiente tribe. Throughout Europe cherry-flavoured liqueur is called kirsch. And if you say kirsch, people in Spain will know what you are talking about. But if you want to sound like you know what you are talking about, ask for **aguardiente valle del jerte**.

In France people make an apple brandy called Calvados. In Spain they make a similar drink called **aguardiente de sidra** (cider brandy). It is a luscious product, redolent of apples and the oak casks in which it is made. Production is rather small, being limited to the north. It is sold mainly in Asturias and in the better restaurants of major cities.

In wine-growing countries it has long been a custom to turn the pulp of the crushed grapes to good use. Many viticulturists spread it on the earth of the vineyard as fertiliser. Others make liqueur with it. In French it's called *marc*, in Italian it's *grappa*, and in Spain it's **orujo**. Not everybody does this, but it is the practice in Galicia. For centuries making orujo was illegal, done on small isolated farmsteads, unreported and untaxed. It was Gallego moonshine. Nowadays distillation plants produce this fruity, wood-flavoured drop and there is now a DE for Galicia's orujo. There are 20 orujo makers, including Zirall, Pazo and Lauro. Another spirit, **queimada**, is made by burning orujo and adding lemon, sugar and coffee.

The historical record shows that when the Romans expelled the Carthaginians from Spain they found people in the southeast making an alcoholic drink which came to be known as Licor Mirabilis. The recipe calls for 43 different ingredients, mainly citrus juices and aromatic plants. About one hundred years ago a distiller in Cartcgena took that recipe and converted it into an aguardiente. As homage to its ancient Iberian inventors it was christened **Licor 43**. Today the herb and fruit-flavoured spirit is consumed all over Spain and exported to 60 countries. It can be taken neat or mixed with juice, soft drinks, milk or coffee.

Aguardientes, Galicia

But the granddaddy of all Spanish liqueurs is **Ponche Caballero**. Not only is it number one in Spain, it is number eight in sales across the globe, exceeding such liqueurs as Drambuie and Tia Maria. Its name comes from two sources. The first is a Persian drink called panch, meaning five. The name refers to the drink's five key ingredients, which include alcohol, sugar and spices. In English the name is rendered as punch, and in Spanish, ponche. The second source is attributed to Luis Caballero, who moved to Jerez from Galicia where he drank much sherry brandy. In 1917 while playing with the recipe for panch, he came up with the sweet-and-spicy combination that is so popular today.

DRINKS

Non-Alcoholic Drinks
Horchata

A girl in a little town offered a drink to the visiting King of Catalunya and Aragón. After tasting the drink, the King asked, "Que es aixo?" (What is this?). The girl answered, "Es leche de chufa" (It's chufa milk), to which the King replied, "Aixo no es llet, aixo es or, xata" (This is not milk, this is gold, pretty child). The word 'xata' in Catalan, which the King spoke, is a term of endearment to a child. The story spread throughout the country and the name of the drink became known as 'orchata'. Later, the 'h' was added.

Chufa (tiger nut) is the main ingredient in horchata. It is the small, tuberous root of a sedge plant. Chufa's origin dates back to ancient Egypt, and it has been found in vases within the tombs of pharaohs. The Moors introduced it to Spain, with the province of Valencia proving to be best area for cultivation. These days it is here that horchata is most popular. It is said to also be rich in minerals and vitamins, with high levels of iron and potassium. If you're feeling sluggish, horchata is good for an energy boost. It can be bought in bottles but it's better when fresh. In Valencia it can be found in places called **horchaterías**, served with cakes and pastries.

Chocolate

Along with coffee, the most common hot beverage in Spain is **chocolate caliente** (hot chocolate). This is not the hot cocoa you are used to from childhood. This stuff is thick like porridge, barely pourable from the urn. Popular in the morning, most Spaniards stop drinking it by midday. It is traditionally taken with **churros** (fried doughnut strips – see the recipe in the Culture of Spanish Cuisine chapter).

Té (Tea) & Infusiónes (Herbal Teas)

Tea, as in a nice cup of tea, is not so nice in Spain. It simply is not a very important part of the culture. It's available, in teabags containing leaves of doubtful parentage. If you ask for it you'll get one of them and a cup of water that might be hot enough. There are simply very few people in this country who care enough about a proper pot of tea. You'll see proper tea most often in Catalunya, especially in Barcelona where you can actually find little tea boutiques.

Infusiónes (herbal teas) on the other hand are quite traditional in Spain. **Manzanilla** (not to be confused with the sherry of the same name) is made of chamomile and is the most common. Mint tea is also popular, as is verbena. And every mother and grandmother living on the Iberian peninsula has a secret recipe for herbal teas to cure whatever ails you. Most often what seems to ail folks here is 'los nerviosos'. Complain of it publicly and be prepared to hear of the sure cure.

The Four Cats Cafe, once a favourite of Pablo Picasso, Madrid

Café (Coffee)

Coffee is as essential to the Spanish as tea is to the English. But the Spanish don't make a to-do over it. There is little or no ceremony involved. Add a pound of sugar to a cup of coffee, stir and gulp. Brewed coffee is what people often have at home. In the restaurant or bar it is always made espresso style. Don't go looking for 'gourmet' coffee. Again the exception is in Catalunya, where coffee can be sipped several ways. Try your coffee **solo** (black), **cordato** (small coffee with milk) or **con leche** (with more milk). For a real buzz ask for **café doble** (long black coffee).

Coffee and water

CHOOSE YOUR BREW

café con leche	coffee with milk
café cortado	small coffee with milk
café descafeinado	decaffeinated coffee
café doble	long black coffee
café escocés	coffee with Scotch whisky
café exprés	espresso
café instantáneo	instant coffee
café irlandés	coffee with Irish whiskey
café solo	black coffee
café vienés	coffee with whipped cream

Refescos (Soft Drinks)

There is little to say about soft drinks in Spain except that everything you are used to is available here. And then some of local origin. Perhaps the most popular local stuff is **limonada**, a carbonated soda rather than lemonade as we know it. Otherwise, you can anticipate all the usual suspects.

Mineral water, juice and carbonated drinks

Agua (Water)

The tap water in Spain is excellent, and conforms to the highest standards for purity. The **Madrileños** (people of Madrid) are especially proud of their tap water. They will happily discuss it with you, and be sure that you understand that it is the best in Europe, and then they'll drink bottled water. **Agua mineral** (mineral water) is almost a staple food in Spain. Many people are connoisseurs of the stuff. At the bullfights and other public events you'll see vendors of beer, soda, wine. But doing the most business is that guy singing "Agua Fria!" at the top of his lungs. Admittedly during the Spanish summer everyone needs frequent rehydration, but fluid necessity does not alone account for the high Spanish consumption of H2O. The truth is they just like it. They even put it in their wine. No table is properly set without a bottle of water, either sparkling or still.

As any Spaniard will tell you, the country's geology is extremely diverse. This has resulted in a large number of springs, aquifers and other natural water sources. Every spring is different, with its own balance of minerals or degree of carbonisation. The Spanish, who prize subtlety in their food and drink as well as the ability to appreciate it, will pay as close attention to the water on the table as to the wine. This is not unique to Spain. It has been common in Mediterranean societies since ancient times to give high regard to mineral springs and the waters they provide. Many springs even have religious connections.

MINERAL WATER CLASSIFICATIONS

Agua mineral natural (natural mineral water) which contains a stable composition of minerals, as well as other components that are believed to be beneficial to health. Specific legislation pronounces some of these as being also medicinal, having therapeutic qualities. They are thought to be especially useful as spa water, being efficacious in the treatment of rheumatism and stress.

Agua de manantial (spring water) is bacteriologically wholesome and good to drink, yet has no special health benefits and an unstable mineral composition. Both natural and spring waters are considered natural products that are unaltered by human processes (except for filtration).

Agua purificada (treated water) can come from any source (surface or subterranean) and has been subjected to chemical treatments to make it safe for human consumption.

There are over 100 different labels in the Spanish mineral water market. Each is unique, having its own characteristics, and its origin is clearly marked on the bottle. Vichy Catalán, from Catalunya bottles water from three separate springs, each with a distinct taste.

home cooking
& traditions

With cooking and food being such an integral part of social life in Spain, there are few secrets to be had in the Spanish kitchen. And, save for the microwave or room to build a **parrillada** (grill), there are few differences between a modern Madrid kitchen and that of a Galician village. 'Simplify' is the watchword here.

In Spain, it's difficult to say with any scientific precision where the home kitchen ends and the public domain begins. Spanish communal life is intensely social, and since dwellings are often on the cramped side, people have a need to take themselves outdoors just for some elbow room and breathing space. And they need to commune with each other, so the tapas bar, the restaurant, the cafe and the neighbourhood plaza become extensions of the home, the living room and the kitchen.

These extensions are not luxuries or places of idle entertainment. They are necessities of domestic living and Spaniards avail themselves of them regularly. For some that means every Friday night; or every morning but Sunday; or three days and four nights a week. Sometimes alone or with friends, sometimes with family. In Spain you will commonly see Mamá and Papá with two toddlers, dining with friends at a streetside restaurant at 1am.

If public life is intensely social, family life is intensely private. Family meals are sacred ceremonies, where bonds are celebrated and reaffirmed. Papá sits at the head of the table, Mamá cooks and serves, daughter helps, son misbehaves. It's a scene from a 1950s TV family.

Binibèquer, Balearic Islands

Spaniards are hospitable, but not so much in the home. Home is for family and close friends. As a guest you may never eat a home-cooked meal. It's not that the Spanish aren't accommodating, but if a Spaniard wants to entertain you, it will be in a restaurant, the extension of the home. Things are a bit different in rural areas. Country folk tend to have larger dwellings, and restaurants aren't in abundance.

D'Alt Vila, the old walled town in Ibiza, Balearic Islands

The Spanish Kitchen & Utensils

A traditional Spanish family kitchen, the sort in which the cuisine was born, is found these days chiefly in that traditional country setting. The family kitchen of Antonia Velazquez is a good case in point. She is an art teacher in Valencia. She is the first of her family to achieve a higher education, and the only one to reside in a large city. The others – mother, sisters, aunts, uncles, cousins – all live in villages and farmsteads throughout El Levante. Periodically she visits her mother and elder sister at the family farm, which is a couple of hour's drive from the city. It's a small holding, like so many. A few vines, an orange grove and a kitchen garden. The house is old, an amalgam of wood, brick and stone. The roof is tile, but Antonia says that when she was a child it was thatch. "So many things have changed in Spain in the last 25 years", she says.

Navarra

We are her guests on this visit. Her mother Lidia, and sister Alma, greet us with country charm, command us to sit in the shade on the porch and do nothing while they prepare the midday meal. They bring us water, a pitcher of rough red country wine, a small dish of olives and one of almonds. "Of course we'll have paella", Antonia says. "As soon as I told my family you would come, they said 'the foreign guests must have paella. That's what they all want and so that is what they will get as long as they are our guests!'" So we will do no labour. We are seated next to a wide, open window that looks directly into the kitchen. From here we may converse with the two women as they work, and they can refill our little dishes with ease.

The kitchen, like most in Spain, is an unfussy affair. A gas cooker with two burners, a few **ollas** (pots) for making stews or boiling water, half a dozen **cazuelas** (earthenware cooking dishes) of various sizes for the casseroles that define so much of gastronomic Spain; spoons, spatulas, knives, a small refrigerator; a **porrón** (wine bottle with a long drinking spout) sits on the bench, filled with vinegar instead of wine; two mortar & pestle sets, a small one of ceramic and a larger one of stone. There is also a baking oven, somewhat unusual in this climate, but Lidia likes to make sweets. On the ground just outside the kitchen is a fire ring with a metal grill over it, a primitive **parrillada** (grill).

Unique to the Spanish kitchen, and without which none would be complete, some blackened old **paelleras** (paella pans) hang from the wall. A true paellera is wide, round and shallow. No lid. Iron is the preferred material. It has two handles and may dip slightly in the middle where the oil can pool for easy frying. The shallow depth of the pan helps ensure that the rice cooks in a thin layer. People of El Levante say that the cooked rice should be only as thick as '**un ditet**' (the width of one finger, to a height of 1.5cm in the pan). The trick is to maximise the amount of rice touching the bottom of the pan because that's where the flavour resides. For that reason, paella pans enlarge in diameter not in height. Even those used by aspirants to the Guinness Book of World Records are shallow, though they be acres wide.

Fresh and roasted red peppers, Pamplona, Navarra

Many other dishes are named for the vessels in which they are cooked. **Calderetas** (small pots) are used for **calderetas** (stews). The **cazuela**, a low-sided earthenware dish that can be used on the stove or in the oven gives its name to many a **cazuela** (casserole). The **olla** (pot) is used for what is arguably the oldest dish in the Spanish culinary canon: **olla podrida**, the rotten pot.

Back in Valencia, Antonia's city apartment kitchen looks a lot different from Lidia's. It is less roomy than Lidia's. It's not old and blackened with age. Antonia doesn't have a baking oven but she does have a microwave and a small toaster oven, and a food processor. And in terms a chef would appreciate, a big difference between the two kitchens is that Lidia's has character, and a parrillada. As Antonia has said, so many things have changed in Spain in the last 25 years. But in this small but clean and bright place she still prepares the dishes her forbears created and nourished her on. Despite its modern conveniences and blandness, her kitchen is still a place where she imbibes the traditions of her family and country.

Woman amongst the vines, A Ponte, Arnoia, Galicia

Lidia chops and minces vegetables while Alma pounds ingredients for **sofrito** (fried tomato sauce) in a mortar. They begin to sing, softly, with the rhythm of their work. They are not even aware of it. "What song?" they ask when we ask what song they're singing. They laugh and go back to work. Alma goes outside to the woodpile, gathers an armload of orange tree prunings and deposits them next to the parrillada. Lidia continues to sing, unbeknownst to herself. We privileged characters on the porch relax and enjoy the shade.

Lidia is slicing vegetables and arranging them in a cazuela for **pisto manchego** (stewed vegetables and herbs). She crumbles some parsley in the palm of her hand, sniffs it knowingly, then sprinkles it over the top of the cazuela. In what she acknowledges is a heresy, she adds a few drops of vinegar from the porrón. Then she gives it a generous pour of olive oil. "Arbequina", she assures us. The best variety she can find. Then she places the cazuela over a very slow fire and says, "I have done my work, now the fire will do his".

Alma has been kindling her own fire in the parrillada. "We don't wait for the wood to burn down to coals", she says. "We like a little smoke. Not enough to taste like smoke, though. That would be very bad." Lidia and Antonia nod their heads. "Oh yes" we say, nodding in imitation. "Very bad." We pour more wine. As the stew simmers, Alma takes an old paellera from its hook on the kitchen wall, gathers up her ingredients and takes everything outside to her fire. "You know, paella should be cooked by men", she says, setting the pan upon the grill rack above the fire. "But since Papá died, what are we to do?"

MORTERO Y MANO (MORTAR & PESTLE)

I can't cook without the mortar & pestle. Of course I don't use it every day, but I use it often. Actually, I have three sets. The oldest one is made of vinewood from Aragón, where my family is from. My grandmother had it and it was old then. I keep it just for show now, just to decorate the kitchen. Another is ceramic, and I use it for crushing garlic and herbs. I also have a food processor, but I would have to get it down from the shelf, plug it in and select the blade. Then I would have to take it apart, clean it and put it back. Such a bother for small jobs. The mortar sits right by the sink. I pound, then a quick rinse. My third set is made of marble. This I use for grinding nuts, seeds, cinnamon, and for making **picada** (a mixture of garlic, parsley, toasted almonds and pine nuts).

The result of using the mortar is so much better than the food processor, at least for Spanish food. The food processor simply cuts things very fine, whereas the mortar & pestle mashes the ingredients, releasing the essence of the garlic or whatever. And it makes it smoother, so it coats food better, or penetrates it better, and it feels better in your mouth. And when I use the mortar & pestle, I'm always aware that this is the most ancient kitchen tool in the world. With every fall of the pestle I'm cooking a little bit of history.

Samuel de Vega

Paella

She pours Andalucían oil into the hot pan. "Picual oil, my favourite for frying." She fries rabbit, and a few small pieces of lamb's offal sausage, then removes them. In a conspiratorial tone she says, "I don't know anybody who uses sausage in paella, but Papá did, so I do too". She adds the vegetables, then the rice. She apologises that its not Bomba rice, highly prized for this dish, but sometimes it's just not available. She adds stock, a little wine, more vegetables, and after a while she returns the meat to the pan.

After about 20 minutes the fire begins to die and Alma says, "it's almost done. Now the last trick". She throws a handful of the orange tree trimmings onto the fire. They catch the flame, the heat rises, and we can hear the paella begin to sizzle. "That's how you make the socarrat", Alma says with a smile, referring to crisping the bottom layer of rice. "At the last minute. You see? This is how we cook in Spain. It's not complicated. Maybe chefs will tell you it is, but it isn't. We use the best ingredients and we cook them simply. No mistakes." And no mistakes were tasted that day in the Velazquez family kitchen.

celebrating
with food

The act of celebrating is integral to Spanish cuisine. In fact, much of the Spanish menu was borne of the need to honour a harvest, saint, or victory over an invader. Even the universally celebrated New Year will have a unique flavour here. It's often the reason for celebration that makes Spanish food so flavoursome – an Easter cheese flan without Easter is just a cheese flan.

In addition to the feasts of the calendar, there are many other reasons and excuses for Spaniards to have a party: birthdays, anniversaries, first communions, graduations, weddings, release from prison. Nowadays, sometimes, a divorce is ample reason to pour the wine, say grace and tuck in. Most often celebrations are family affairs with religious overtones. Even the Running with the Bulls is preceded by fervent prayer.

Spanish fiestas will almost always be accompanied by music. It might be a lone guitarist struggling to be heard, it might be a brass band or a rock band. Groups of women will spontaneously break into song, clapping out Gypsy rhythms. On occasion they will be answered by a chorus of the menfolk singing ballads, or folk songs or songs with suggestive lyrics. This back and forth of singing can go on and on, and you will marvel at how many songs these people know. But they love food, and music is the food of love, and they love love, too.

SAINTS' DAYS

Since every town has its patron saint, every town has its fiesta. That means at least one travelling band playing everything from flamenco tunes to Top 40 hits. It means itinerant salesfolk barking myriad methods for winning stuffed animals and kitchen appliances. It means food. While every region has its specialities, there are festival foods you can find just about anywhere. Along with the international **algodón dulce** (cotton candy), Iberian shindigs feature stands proffering pickled **berenjenas** (eggplants), **altramuces** (lupins) and different types of **jamón** (ham). One fiesta favourite is jamón served on thick, crusty bread with a hint of tomato sauce. This is all washed down with one-litre plastic cups of beer, red wine or **kalimotxo** (red wine mixed with Coca-Cola). Sweet-teeth head for the huge vat of boiling oil, with its endless production of sweets, such as **churros** (fried doughnut strips). **Tarta de Santiago** is the key dish during the Feast of St James. The gastronomically inclined will rejoice in knowing that these treats are always available – for somewhere in Spain, there's always someone celebrating something.

Brett Allan King

Día de San José	St Joseph's Day	March 19
Día de San Juan Bautista	Feast of St John the Baptist	June 24
Día de Santiago Apóstol	Feast of St James the Apostle	July 25
Día de la Virgen del Carmen	the patron saint of fisherfolk	July 16

Sailors carrying an idol in the Virgen del Carmen parade, Cadaqués, Catalunya

Processions are a common part of fiestas. If the neighbourhood or larger community is taking part, people don gaudy costumes, or make papier-mache effigies of religious or historical figures. With much ceremony, these effigies may be consigned to the flames.

Battles between Moors and Christians might be re-enacted, such as during the Fiesta de Moros y Cristianos in the Valencian town of Alcoy (April 22-24). It is astonishing to learn how many Spaniards have a suit of armour at home. Mock battles can go on for three days, the issue ever in doubt as the opposing armies sway and waver under the furious assault of a grim foe accoutred in linen and aluminium foil and armed with a broomstick. When the enemy are all slain they rise from the dead and take a meal of the symbolically named **Moros y Cristianos** (rice and black beans). And there will be much laughter. And with the singing and shouting it will be loud. It will be lusty. And it will be infectious. If you are an invited guest to a fiesta, you will be expected to be just as loud and lusty. But if you are a passer-by, a spectator, be circumspect. Remember the religious and familial nature of the fiesta. Enjoy the watching. And you might just get invited.

Nochevieja (New Year's Eve)

It's just before midnight, you are a guest in a home or restaurant, or perhaps you are on the Puerta del Sol in Madrid. Your host, or a smiling woman you've never seen before passes by laden with fresh grapes. You are given 12. When the clock tolls midnight you are to eat one grape with each sound of the bell. Get it right and swallow the last grape with the last bell and you'll have good luck in the coming year. Mess up and it's sour grapes for you.

Carnavale (Carnival)

The carnival in Cádiz marks the last festival before Lent begins. During this time the city streets are surrendered to 10 days of weird costumes, lurching processions and gluttonous feasting. Things get really raucous in the area known as Barrio de la Viña, where bands of revellers tend to congregate.

House Blessing

In rural areas during the week preceding Easter, the village priest pays a visit to all his parishioners and blesses their houses. With some blessed salt and holy water he'll ensure your house has a clean bill of spiritual health for the coming year. An honorarium is expected in the form of a couple of eggs, maybe a small cheese, placed in the basket he carries for this purpose. If his basket is too full, which can happen quickly with a very small basket, a gift of money would not be refused.

Pascua (Easter)

The most solemn time of the year. This is when people look inward, and that does not mean to their stomachs. However, there are a few special dishes associated with Holy Week. In some communities there is a Good Friday procession in which heavy floats are borne by penitents. In order to keep up their strength they breakfast on **bacalao al ajoarriero** (salt cod cooked with capsicums).

As this is the most important holiday on the Spanish calendar, there will always be food shared as families and friends come together. Dishes that appear during this time include **monas de Pascua** (figures made of chocolate), **torta pascualina** (spinach and egg pie) and **torrijas** (French toast). A popular Easter dish in Mallorca is **flan de Pascuas** (Easter cheese flan), and **cordero Pascual** (spring lamb) is common fare everywhere.

The Wine War

Taking place in the Riojan town of Haro, the wine war is yet another messy battle that takes over a community. Using **botas** (small leather wine bags) people squirt wine at each other. Later they actually drink the stuff, at least as much as they wasted.

Flag for the San Juan festival, Ciutadella, Menorca Island, Balearic Islands

CELEBRATING

NAVIDAD (CHRISTMAS)

Like the cleric stargazers of old, some tell dates by studying the heavens. The more mundane have Miss December to remind them it's Christmas. In Spain, one need only pass by a pastry shop. To everything there is a season, and for every food there is a reason.

The Spanish love celebrating with food and drink, and are also keen on marking days with saints. Nestled among the staple sweets at any **pastelería** (cake shop) are the tell-tale pastries of the saint or religious figure du jour.

You know it's All Saints' Day when the sweet, **huessos santos** (saint's bones) appear. While the first dozen Christians got wine with their bread, modern Holy Week revellers dunk their body of Christ in milk and egg to make the Easter treat, **torrijas** (French toast). On January 6, children celebrate the arrival of the gift-bearing three kings, and everyone eats **roscón de Reyes**, a spongy, family-size doughnut usually adorned with dried fruit and sugar.

Pastry shop window, Galicia

But of all the holiday seasons, Christmas is the gastronomic timepiece par excellence. With the first whiff of roasted chestnuts and sweet potatoes from streetside stands, you know that Mary had better start scouting for a manger. You know things are getting serious when the nation's supermarkets clear entire aisles to fill them with **turrón**, the quintessential Yuletide sweet. Every year, celebrities from Spain and abroad grace flashy TV advertisements for **cava**, the sparkling wine requisite for toasting 'Felices Fiestas!' nationwide.

While some households enjoy the traditional Christmas turkey, many Spaniards prefer to celebrate with **bacalao** (cod) or **besugo** (red bream). The one Spanish family with whom I had the pleasure of enjoying Christmas served the meal buffet-style, with a grand array of hams, cheeses, sliced turkey, shellfish, **tortilla española** (Spanish omelette) and other assorted dishes. A sweet, grated egg-yolk garnish seemed to go with everything. Meals will vary with region, but virtually every Spaniard can expect their Christmas to include turrón and cava.

Brett Allan King

Classic Christmas Sweets

alfajor	honey nut and cinnamon biscuit coated with syrup
almendrado	almond biscuit or cake
bienmesabe	(literally, it tastes good to me) a dessert of almonds, eggs, sugar and sponge cake
bizcochos borrachos	from the word **borracho** (drunk), cake soaked in liqueur
cabello de angel	(literally, the angel's hair) pumpkin jam
hojaldres	small flaky pastries covered in sugar
mantecado	a soft biscuit made of lard
mazapán	a marzipan of sugar and ground almonds, rendered into scores of shapes such as bite-size bells, bunnies, little trumpets, baskets, fish and even eels
membrillo	quince, often eaten with cheese
mostachones	small cakes for dipping in coffee or hot chocolate (also spelled **mostatxones**)
pestiño	honey-coated aniseed pastries
polvorón	polvo is the word for powder or dust. This biscuit gets its name because of its tendency to turn to tiny crumbs in your mouth. Made with lard, almonds and toasted flour.
roscón de Reyes	a spongy, family-size doughnut usually adorned with dried fruit and sugar
turrón	the Christmas treat par excellence: nougat made of almonds, honey and egg whites, can be plain of flavoured.
yema	small round cakes made from egg yolks and sugar
intxaursalsa	a Basque dessert of milk and walnuts

Pestiño

Almendrados
(Almond biscuits)

Ingredients
2   cups blanched almonds,
     finely chopped
2   egg whites
1   cup sifted castor sugar
1   teaspoon vanilla

Preheat the oven to 180°C. Lightly toast the almonds and set aside. Beat the egg whites until stiff but not dry. Slowly add the sugar, beating constantly. After the sugar is added, beat for another 5-8 minutes. Fold in the almonds and vanilla. Place spoonfuls of the mixture onto a greased oven tray. Bake for about 20 minutes or until biscuits just begin to colour.

Makes 3 dozen

Turrón (Nougat)

As with much of Spanish cookery, the origin of turrón is hotly disputed. The oldest written record of it dates back to the 14th century, and speaks of it being made in the Arab and Jewish quarters of Jijona in Alicante province. Who made it first the document does not reveal. According to the culinary anthropology of Claude Levi-Strauss, turrón predates Moorish, and even Christian Spain. Pagan, Jewish or Moorish, turrón is now a Christmas treat in Catholic Spain.

About thirty families scattered throughout the country produce almost all of the commercially available turrón in Spain. They use recipes that are many generations old. A few versions are dressed up with fruits or mixed nuts, but by and large the traditional turrón is plain and comes either hard or soft. The soft version is simply made from honey, almonds and sugar, cooked very slowly in a pot that is never allowed to boil. The hard version incorporates egg whites. While it is usually made in 30 sq cm sheets, it can be found in smaller packets ready to travel. Latin American countries import great quantities. And curiously, Japan was a major export market in the 16th century. Turrón has been around for a long time.

Running of the Bulls in Pamplona (July 6-14)

The festivities for this San Fermín Festival include much wine-soaked revelry. How else would you want to run with the bulls? But those in the know advise: being drunk while running away from an angry bull is a sure way to get trampled or gored. Now that's a sobering thought. But if you're not into beating the bulls, how about eating them? During the festival the streets will be rich with the smell of big bull **chuletas** (cutlets) cooking on the grill. And if bull's not to your liking, try **cabeza y corada** (lamb's head and organs), traditionally eaten here as a late breakfast.

Blessed Rice

Much has changed in the rice fields, but much remains the same. If you take a day trip out of Valencia to the village of El Palmar (and you should) you'll see modern farms with modern equipment. But you'll also see horse-drawn carts, and canal boats powered by human muscle. On Thursdays the farmers still troop to the cathedral in Valencia as they have done for a thousand years to settle the endless little disputes over water use at the Tribunal de las Aguas. No lawyers and no written record. Just a few elders putting their heads together and rendering wise decisions. And the old fiestas remain. In July, near Sueca, the people hold a mass to honour Abdon and Senen, the patron saints of rice. Their images are bedecked with sheaves of rice and carried through the town to the fields where they bless the crops and protect them against natural disasters.

Ensalada de Arroz (Rice Salad)

Ingredients

3	cups cooked rice	8	tablespoons olive oil
1	large clove garlic, minced	3	tablespoons wine vinegar
1	small onion, minced	1	teaspoon salt
2	red capsicums		green and black olives for garnish
2	tablespoons chopped parsley		salt and pepper

Make a vinaigrette sauce by combining the olive oil, vinegar, garlic, and onion. Season to taste with salt and pepper. Cut one capsicum into six narrow strips and set aside. Finely chop the other capsicum. Cool the rice slightly. Add the vinaigrette sauce, chopped capsicum and parsley. Toss gently. Spoon rice into a serving bowl. When cool, cover and chill thoroughly. Decorate the top with the reserved capsicum strips and olives.
    Makes 4-6 servings

CELEBRATING

The Tomatina

The attack of the killer tomatoes! This must be the world's largest food fight, and gloriously the messiest. In the Valencian town of Buñol, more than 120,000kg of tomatoes are heaved by townsfolk at each other on the last Wednesday of August from 11am to 1pm. At the end of the two hour sauce-making session, a bottle rocket goes off and all hands turn to cleaning up the mess. The streets are awash in tomato juice, pulp, seeds, skins. The ketchup is ankle deep and spattered all over the walls. Bring a change of clothes and a sense of the ridiculous and the sublime.

TEST YOUR TOMATINA KNOWLEDGE

The tomatina tradition is said to have been established in 1945 at an anti-Franco rally. Reportedly, the hurling of tomatoes was first directed toward El Caudillo's effigy. By chance a curvaceous young woman was caught in the line of fire and the expressed juice of the tomatoes caused the world's first ever wet T-shirt contest. A tradition was born. Creation myths are never uniform, and others say the Tomatina started during a 1945 procession for the patron saint, San Luis Bertrán. Villagers who wanted to join the effigy carrying were turned away, so they started a fight in front of a grocery store.

The tomatoes are trucked in from Extremadura because they are cheaper and said to be of lower quality. Heaven forbid you should squash the good stuff in a stranger's face. Save that for your true love.

The water for the fire hoses that clean up the stunning mess comes from a Roman aqueduct.

It's mostly a boys versus girls battle. About 20,000 participate.

The night preceding the battle over 50 contestants compete in a paella cook-off. Pans the size of medieval shields simmer over fires in a parking lot.

All Saint's Day

Falling on November 1, All Saints' Day is also known as Day of the Dead. This is by no means a solemn occasion, it is a time when families visit the graves of their kin, dust off the monuments, lay some flowers and have a dandy picnic. Pious celebrants will feast on the favourites of the departed. Look out for the biscuit or sweet bread, **huessos santos**.

regional
variations

Spain is a land of contrasts. Everything from snow-capped peaks to
sun-bleached beaches are crammed into this country, along with a
diversity of culture and, of course, cuisine. There may be culinary
elements that bind the nation, but there are just as many regional
differences that can make neighbouring areas seem like worlds away.

REGIONS

Bay of Biscay

FRANCE

La Coruña

Hondarribia

Santiago de Compostela

San Sebastián

ANDORRA

ATLANTIC
OCEAN

Barcelona

MADRID

PORTUGAL

SPAIN

Valencia

Sevilla

Mediterranean Sea

Cadiz

Strait of Gibraltar

MOROCCO

- Atlantic Spain
- The Heart of Spain
- The Pyrenees
- Mediterranean Spain

The Heart of Spain

The Heart of Spain runs from north to south. From Aragón at the foot of the Pyrenees it cuts a wide swathe through the middle of the Iberian peninsula all the way down to Gibraltar. This is the Spain of Ferdinand and Isabella, and of looming castles and medieval lanes. It is the Spain of Cervantes and Conquistadors; of Gypsies and Flamenco; hot afternoons and siestas; saffron and sangría. This is the Spain that resides in the popular imagination.

Gastronomically the Heart of Spain is – like so many other parts of the country – a land of extremes. Here you find the simplest cooking as well as the most exuberant. Perhaps 'simplest' is not the best word, as it suggests a lack of care or sophistication. Let us say instead, the most unadorned. Many people call this axis of Iberia the 'Route of Roasts', for it is roast lamb, kid and suckling pig that defines this region's culinary heart. And its imagination and verve are seen in that most Spanish of Spanish culinary inventions, **tapas** (hors d'oeuvres). In some of the cities of this region, such as Sevilla, certain trustworthy advisors would counsel you to eschew the restaurants and live solely on the tapas of the many **tascas** (tapas bars). And if your time is short, that's not bad advice. But for your sake we hope your time, and appetite, are ample.

DON'T MISS

- The morning tipple
- A world of tapas
- Dinner on Lemon Tree Lane in Cádiz
- An all-nighter in Sevilla
- Shrimp Biscuits
- **Tostada manteca colorada** (paprika-flavoured lard)
- Dinner at an asador

REGIONAL VARIATIONS

SEVILLA

Restaurant Walk
Some cosy neighbourhood joints in the middle of town.

San Jacinto and San Jorge Restaurant Walk
As festive as Betis – and cheek by jowl with it – but more working class.

Fiesta Centre
Come to this confluence of streets in the wee hours. Even in the off season, when most of the city closes by 1am, the party goes on until about 4am.

Calle del Betis
Not popular with tourists but the locals come here in their droves to patronise terrific restaurants and create a festive atmosphere. It's not cheap but not ruinously expensive either.

Puente del Cachorro
Avenida del Cristo de la Expiación
Calle Marqués de Paradas
Paseo de Nuestra Señora de
Calle de Castilla
Calle de la O
Tourist Office
Calle Reyes Católicos
C Zaragoza C Madrid
Puente de Triana (Puente de Isabel II)
Plaza de Toros (Bullring)
Paseo de Cristobal Colón
Avenida de la Constitución
Catedral
Alcázar
San Jorge
Calle San Jacinto
Plaza del Altozano
Río Guadalquivir
Calle
Alcázar Gardens
Calle San Fernando
Ay de Roma
Paseo de las Delicias
Puente de San Telmo
Plaza de Cuba

0   125   250 m
0   125   250 yd

The Heart of Spain is also where you'll find more of its Moorish history as well as Roman. In the south you'll encounter greater use of those spices that the Moors introduced. Cumin and cinnamon are good examples. It is postulated by some historians that even spinach was brought to Spain by the Moors. What is known is that **garbanzos con espinacas** (chickpeas with spinach) has been a popular dish here for centuries. It can be taken as a main dish at home, a side dish at lunch, or very often is enjoyed as a tapa served in a little saucer-size cazuela (see the recipe in the Spanish Banquet chapter).

Segovia

In cities such as Segovia you cannot ignore the roasting tradition. The rich aroma snakes its way through the winding cobblestone streets and hangs there, an olfactory siren, beckoning you to follow it to its source and find delight. The roasting is done in large woodfire ovens called **hornos asadores**. Like paella this is a dish cooked only by men. Unlike paella, it is for practical reasons. Manhandling a hundred pigs, lambs and kids over several hours requires a lot of upper body strength. Most *men* are not up to the job. Those who achieve excellence are awarded with the adoration of their fellows, and with medals and titles that would make an admiral envious. Perhaps the most titled man in Spain, after the King, was the late Cándido López. His many titles included Master Roaster of the Roasters' Guild, Head Innkeeper of Castile, and Knight of the Order of Isabella. In his eponymous restaurant he instituted the custom of demonstrating the tenderness of his **cochinillo** (roast piglet) by carving it at the table, not with a razor-sharp carving knife, but with the blunt edge of a serving platter. A life-size bronze statue of the great man stands in his city today. A plaque reads, "Honour to him who brought honour to Segovia".

Meats roasted in the asador must be true babies. Suckling pig, lamb or kid, less than 25 days old, are placed on a rack in a **cazuela** (earthenware cooking dish) with a little water in the bottom. The rising steam helps to tenderise the meat. The cazuelas are moved around constantly in the big oven with long paddles, rather like those used in a pizza oven. This ensures even roasting, a very important thing as there is very little time between the raw state and overcooked. The meat must be removed from the heat the instant it is done. It is then, sometimes, dressed with a little garlic softened in hot fat.

The end product has a skin the colour of burnished bronze. When served it is still hissing from the oven and the heat rises to your face. The aroma envelops you, and it seems that you can smell with your entire body. Table knives are superfluous. Indeed forks are unnecessary. So willingly does the meat fall apart and commend itself to you that you could literally eat it with a toothpick. It all but leaps into your mouth and chews itself.

REGIONAL VARIATIONS

Olives stuffed with peppers for tapas

Statue of Juan Bravo and Torreón de Lozoya, Segovia, Castilla y León

For a true Segovian experience, ask for the head. It's more fully cooked than the body, as the heat has to penetrate more deeply. It will come to you split lengthwise, garlanded with parsley and served with potatoes. Some people take it quite plain, lifting it and sucking the meat from the bone. Others will dress it with herbs and oil, a little vinegar or lemon. You may consider yourself much honoured if it is offered to you.

Sure, everybody in Spain eats tapas, but in the Heart of Spain they talk tapas the way mothers talk babies and brokers talk securities: with authority, with interest, with curiosity about new developments and growth. "So-and-so has much better boquerones these days. He's using that vinegar I told him about", one will say while taking the afternoon shade in the plaza. "Yes, but so-and-so is working on a new recipe for empanada. I expect great things", may come the reply. "All in all, the tortilla española made at my cousin's place has never been surpassed."

Because they are more than food, because they are a part of the way in which the community communes, tapas in the Heart of Spain loom larger than anywhere else. And as they loom, they spin out into uncountable variations, competing colours, different shapes and sizes. Some are as simple as raw clams, washed down with sherry. Others might be complex recipes cooked with sherry and much adorned such as **gambas al jerez** (prawns in sherry wine sauce). So intent are they here to make memorable tapas that Madrid, Sevilla and Cádiz **tascas** (tapas bars) will offer you a biscuit made of shrimp (see the aside Faces of Gastronomy: Jose Grimaldi in the Culture of Spanish Cuisine chapter). Wherever you go in this region, when in doubt, go for tapas.

Madrid

Two of the most loved (by locals) dishes of Madrid are **callos a la madrileña** (tripe casserole with chorizo and chillies) and **cocido a la madrileña** (stew made with meat and chickpeas). The tripe dish is flavourful and aromatic. Spaniards swear by it as a cure for a hangover and as a boost to the libido. Many of the restaurants around the Plaza Mayor in Madrid serve very decent versions.

Callos a la Madrileña
(Tripe casserole with chorizo and chillies)

Ingredients

500g	honeycomb tripe (use tripe already prepared for the pot by the butcher)
2	small onions, one coarsely chopped, one finely chopped
1	pig's foot (or veal knuckle) split in half
10	peppercorns, coarsely crushed
250g	chorizo cut into $\frac{1}{2}$cm slices
$\frac{1}{2}$	dried red chilli, crumbled
1	small tomato, chopped
250ml	dry white wine

$\frac{1}{2}$	bunch parsley	2	cloves, crushed
1	teaspoon nutmeg	2	bay leaves
$\frac{1}{2}$	teaspoon thyme	6	cloves garlic, peeled
2	tablespoons olive oil	$\frac{1}{4}$	cup cured ham, diced
1	tablespoon flour	1	tablespoon paprika
	salt to taste		

Put the tripe into a pot with 3 cups cold water and the wine, tomato, pig's foot, parsley, peppercorns, cloves, nutmeg, bay leaves, thyme, salt, coarsely chopped onion and garlic. Cover and simmer over low heat until the tripe is almost tender (4 hours). Heat the oil in a skillet and saute the finely chopped onion until it is soft. Add the chorizo and ham and cook for 5 minutes. Stir in the flour and paprika and cook 1 minute more. Add half a cup of the liquid from the tripe kettle, a little at a time, and stir until the mixture thickens. Add this and the chilli to the tripe. Cover and cook slowly for 1$\frac{1}{2}$ hours. Remove the cover and continue cooking until the tripe is very tender. Remove the pig's foot from the tripe. Remove and discard all skin, bone and fat. Cut the meat into pieces and stir into the tripe. Serve in warmed bowls with good crusty bread for sopping up the sauce.

Serves 4-6 as a main course, or 12-18 as tapas

CENTRO

NOCTURNAL MADRILEÑOS

"Nobody goes to bed in Madrid until they have killed the night."
—Ernest Hemingway.

Midnight at the Puerta del Sol, the centre of Madrid, the centre of Spain, and there's a hellish traffic jam. It's a week night, and it's perfectly normal. And while the traffic-bound **Madrileños** (people of Madrid) clog the square, their footloose countrymen crowd the sidewalks, working their way from tasca to taberna, itinerant revellers all.

No doubt most of Madrid's 3 million people turn in at a reasonable hour, as befits proud, hard-working members of the European Union. But the myth, sustained by a healthy dose of reality, persists that Madrid is a city most awake at night – all night. It's not for nothing that Madrileños are called **gatos** (cats) for their nocturnal prowling habits.

Spaniards like to say, politely yet with a whiff of superiority, that Americans live to work but Spaniards work to live. So for this American reared on Puritan values ("early to bed, early to rise..." Thanks, Ben) coming to terms with Madrid's *joie de vivre* was not easy, especially when so much of it took place well beyond my bedtime. Fortunately for me, Madrid nights begin in the afternoon, with a siesta. That's the secret to survival.

In the early evening, I met my companions, and we set off through the narrow streets of Old Madrid in search of tapas, the famous Spanish snacks. We didn't have to look far. It seemed that every second storefront housed a bar. Madrid's eating and drinking establishments are so numerous and varied that Madrileños cut a fine distinction between them. They call them tasca, taberna, meson, cervecería, cafetería, or restaurante. They even have a separate name for the outdoor cafes that spring to life during the summer, **las terrazas** (the terraces).

We ducked into the first place we chanced upon, a tasca. A long, wooden bar dominated the small room. There were no barstools and only a few tables and chairs. Patrons were packed in, wreaking convivial havoc upon the place and themselves with a blizzard of eating, drinking and loud talking. The din was truly impressive. Barely keeping up with the barrage of orders, the bartender furiously worked the beer-tap while another man slapped little plates of tapas on the bar: olives, almonds, cured ham, sauteed squid or shrimp, and **tortilla española**, a quiche-like potato omelette served in slices. It was a clean place, except for the floor just below the bar, which was covered with napkins. Trashing the floor is an old custom, one that keeps boys with brooms employed throughout Madrid.

Madrileños do the **tapeo** (tapas crawl) from about 7-10pm, or 11pm, or midnight, when it's time for dinner. Or they may just go on snacking and drinking all night. My American companions and I, in fact, chafed at

Wild strawberries for sale, Madrid

the ceaseless victualling to which our Spanish hosts subjected us. "All we ever do is eat", we complained, failing to understand that eating and drinking are secondary concerns. The main course at any Spanish meal is conversation. In fact conversation is so important that Madrileños institutionalised it a long time ago. It's called **la tertulia**, meaning social gathering. Friends or colleagues meet regularly to discuss business, politics, art, the art of living, or maybe just to gossip or talk about sports.

After conducting our own impromptu tertulia, we moved deeper into Old Madrid, pausing briefly at Plaza de Santa Ana, a small square with a large appetite for partying. The numerous bars around Plaza de Santa Ana attract loads of university students. On this night they spilled out the doors of Cervecería Alemana and onto the plaza. Cervecería Alemana is also traditionally a favourite with bullfight aficionados, so it's no surprise that it was also a haunt of Hemingway.

Fortified once more, we pushed on to Plaza Mayor, Madrid's famous landmark. The plaza is enclosed by ground-level shops set along arcades, and on the above floors are crammed 78 homes containing more than 475 small balconies. The bronze, equestrian statue of King Philip III that stands in the cobblestone plaza provides a convenient rendezvous point for young Madrileños, and an object of irreverent humour. They joke about meeting under **los huevos del caballo** (the eggs of the horse).

The area around Plaza Mayor is renowned for its rustic, subterranean taverns, called **mesones**, or **cuevas** (caves). Student minstrels dressed in traditional costumes often wander between such mesones as La Tortilla, La Guitarra, and Las Cuevas de Luis Candelas. The last is named after an 18th century rogue-about-town, whose last words before dancing on the gallows reportedly were "be happy, my beloved city". Judging from the sangría-enhanced gaiety at Luis Candelas, it appears generations of Madrileños have slavishly heeded his words.

In centuries past, royalty and other noted personages stole through the dark streets for secret trysts at dimly-lit taverns. According to legend, Goya met the business end of his lover's husband's dagger outside a meson. Madrid's movers and shakers, including the royal family, still frequent Old Madrid.

Our dinner took place uptown in the modern Madrid of sleek office towers and fashionable shops. A pricey dinner and cabaret show at the upscale Melia Castilla Hotel drew Madrid's stylishly affluent, who exited their black BMWs wearing Armani and furs. The show featured a Las Vegas-style revue with an Iberian twist, a flamenco number slipped into the American-pop line-up.

With midnight fast approaching, we schemed about how to spend the following hours. We could dance the night away – the newspaper,

El País, listed nearly a hundred clubs and discos open after 3am – or we could venture to another bar. We also had our choice of jazz, salsa, or even karaoke. But with our taste for flamenco tantalisingly whetted, we opted for Faraloe's, one of several clubs in Madrid dedicated to Andalucía's fiery music. Unfortunately, Faraloe's was virtually empty when we arrived. I thought we'd made a mistake. Perhaps we had come on the wrong night.

We were merely early.

We ordered drinks and a few more tapas, and soon the club began to fill. I was delighted to see that the audience would be almost exclusively Spanish, since I had heard that flamenco clubs in Madrid primarily cater to tourists, with shows long on slick commercialism and short on gritty, Andalucían soul. But Madrid is a city of immigrants, from other parts of Spain; they cleave to romantic reminders of home.

Prior to the performance, the audience indulged in a bit of do-it-yourself flamenco. They jammed the club's small stage to dance daring sevillanas. The official performance began at 1am. As flamenco purists will tell you, the guitar playing and the dancing, as artistic and exciting as they are, are subordinate to the singing. For it is the singing that most powerfully expresses the travails of the Gypsies, in whose culture flamenco is rooted.

The music and dancing brought shouts of appreciation from the audience, but the singing held centre stage. The singer, a wiry man with angular features and wavy black hair, strained his voice into tortured, attenuated notes, cries of pain. His passion overwhelmed the audience; his every vocal nuance twisted it into ever tighter knots of raw emotion. A stunning performance; the audience exulted when he was through.

The strains of flamenco followed us out the door. We late-night novices had acquitted ourselves respectably, but fatigue overtook us before we could achieve the traditional end to a Madrid night: eating **churros** (fried doughnut strips) dunked in hot chocolate at dawn at the classic Chocolatería de San Ginés near Plaza Mayor.

Our taxi sped along boulevards and past plazas. The lights that had shone on the sculpture of Cibeles and her lion-borne chariot in the eponymous plaza were now dark. By 5am the crowds had thinned to sparse clumps of pedestrians and freely flowing traffic.

But as the cab turned onto Plaza de las Cortes, I saw a sight that, for me, embodied the sweet joy of this wonderful, nocturnal city. A man in a tuxedo and a woman in an evening dress suddenly emerged from the Palace Hotel. Arm in arm, engaged in easy conversation, they swung down the street and headed toward Old Madrid. I could see chocolate-soaked churros in their future.

Marshall Krantz

MADRID

Convento de Corpus Cristi
Located at Plaza de Conde de Miranda 1. The nuns of this convent bake and sell delightful sweets.

Plaza Mayor Restaurant Walk
Heavily touristed but just as popular with the locals – great place to begin an evening.

Paseo del Prado
A beautiful park and promenade running down the middle of town. The best place in Madrid for a picnic of 'tapas to go'.

Sol   Calle de Alcalá   Sevilla

Mayor   Calle   Carrera de San Jerónimo

Palacio de Santa Cruz
Calle de Atocha

Tourist Office

Calle de Segovia   Calle de la Colegiada

C de Don Pedro

Latina

Plaza de Santa Ana
Outstanding precinct for a tapeo in the tascas and neighbourhood plazas.

Plaza de Santa Ana

Antón Martín

Calle del Mesón de Paredes

El Rastro Flea Market

Plaza de la Cebada
Its west side is lined with sidewalk restaurants and microbreweries. Excellent light and dark beers and fine alfresco fare await.

Restaurant Walk
Starting on Calle de Ventura de la Vega find an excellent vegetarian place. Two doors down find the eatery that boasts the 'best meat in the world'. If that isn't enough, across the street is 'Restaurante Erotico'. Continue around the corner for more good eats.

Plaza de la Cibeles
Museo Naval
Plaza de la Lealtad
Plaza de Neptuno
Museo del Prado
Real Jardín Botánico
Plaza del Emperador Carlos V

0   150   300 m
0   150   300 yd

Now to that other famous Madrid-style dish, **cocido a la madrileña**. The word 'cocido' is simply the past participial form of the verb, to cook. It is a stew of chicken, chorizo sausage, maybe some ham or other cured meat, potatoes, cabbage and chickpeas and macaroni. Eat a dinner of it and it will seem to stay with you for three days. It is typically eaten 'from front to back', starting with the broth along with the macaroni or rice, then you eat the chickpeas, then you eat the meat. You can do this at one meal, or you can do it over a span of three days. We recommend the three day approach. We have never seen anybody stagger from the table having downed an entire dinner of cocido. It is sometimes referred to as the 'miracle of the loaves and the fishes' because though there might not seem to be enough as you look at it, in the end everyone is full and there is always some left over.

But this is about the dullest dish in Spain. There are so many good things to eat that we don't know why any non Spaniard would bother with cocido except as an experiment in culinary anthropology. It's not that we think it bad. It doesn't have enough taste or smell to be bad. Its long cooking in much water seems to strip its good parts of their native goodness. And yet the Madrileños swoon for this stuff. They dream of it when away from home. They even compose songs to it. We tell no lie. To wit:

Cocido Madrileña
Don't bother telling me
about the feasts of Rome
nor the menu of the Hotel Plaza
nor of pheasants
nor pigeon froi gras
and don't talk lobster dishes.
For what keeps me awake of a night
my food of charm and delight
is the one made with woman's love
and that's cocido madrileña.

We did not make this up. This was a hit song here in the 1950s.

REGIONAL VARIATIONS

Painted tile on the wall of Los Gabrieles Cafe, Madrid

Cádiz

Cádiz is one of the most ancient cities in Europe. It was old when the Romans took it, and then held it for centuries. And throughout those centuries her soldiers stood watch upon the seaward ramparts. And in that time they imparted to the native people their language, and it is the speech

---

LOVING LARD

If you have travelled much in Mexico, and eaten the food and found it delicious, then you have enjoyed eating **manteca** (lard). Yes, the rendered fat of hogs. "Heart-stopping, cholesterol-laden pig fat?" you gasp. Oh settle down. It was tasty wasn't it? You're not dead yet, are you? A little now and then won't hurt you. And you're going to get a little now and then in Spain, especially in this region. It's what often gives Spanish biscuits and pastries their rich flavour and satisfying 'mouth feel', as professional food tasters describe it. Those delightful 'biscuit nuns' (see the aside The Unseen Hand in the Shopping chapter) have been feeding people lard for centuries, and they still do a booming business.

While all of Spain uses olive oil, it doesn't always. And it didn't always. During the inquisition the exclusive use of olive oil in cookery was thought to be strong evidence that the cooker was a secret Jew or an unreconstructed Moor. And being more expensive than lard, oil was more the prerogative of the rich. And old habits die hard.

Some areas of Spain have only recently begun to use oil as their principal cooking medium. Those famous gastronomes, the Basques, have only been using it regularly in the current generation. Before, it was too expensive. The poverty in which Spain had been mired, and made it such a cheap foreign holiday for so many years, dictated a quite different diet than what you will find today. Many older Basques still use lard when they want to taste their past. They cook with it, or spread it on toast in the morning. Truck stops and other blue collar restaurants that rarely see a foreign patron will often use it.

Lard is even more in evidence in Andalucía. In the Mercado Central of Cádiz there is a stall that sells it from great tubs. You can buy the natural white lard, or you can buy **tostada manteca colorada**, lard that has been coloured and flavoured with paprika. At El Pescador, a fine tasca, they will offer you their special worker's breakfast of a generous toasted bun spread thickly with manteca colorada, and a **doble** (long black coffee). Price, about US$1.50. So if you're up early one fine mañanita, try standing at the bar with the labourers as they fuel themselves for the day. Break bread and share the spread. It will stick to your ribs. And it might even, as is evidenced by their open collars, put hair on your chest.

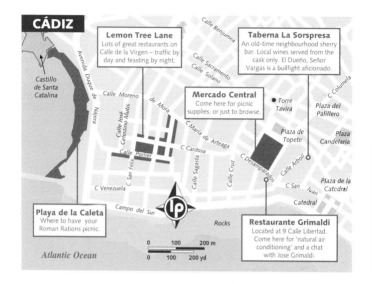

CÁDIZ

Lemon Tree Lane
Lots of great restaurants on Calle de la Virgen – traffic by day and feasting by night.

Taberna La Sorspresa
An old-time neighbourhood sherry bar. Local wines served from the cask only. El Dueño, Señor Vargas is a bullfight aficionado.

Mercado Central
Come here for picnic supplies, or just to browse.

Playa de la Caleta
Where to have your Roman Rations picnic.

Restaurante Grimaldi
Located at 9 Calle Libertad. Come here for 'natural air conditioning' and a chat with Jose Grimaldi.

Castillo de Santa Catalina

Avenida Duque de Nájera

Calle Moreno

Calle José Celestino Mutis

de Mora

Calle Portier

Calle San Feliú

C Venezuela

Campo del Sur

Atlantic Ocean

Calle Benjumea

Calle Sacramento

Calle Solano

C María de Arteaga

C Cardosa

Calle Sagasta

Calle Cruz

C Desamparador

Calle Arbolí

C San Juan

Catedral

Rocks

• Torre Tavira

Plaza del Palillero

Plaza de Topete

Plaza Candelaria

Plaza de la Catedral

C Columela

0   100   200 m
0   100   200 yd

REGIONAL VARIATIONS

of the common Roman soldier from which Spanish is descended. The Romans also gave the Iberians their gods. First the Olympic pantheon, then later, again through the medium of the soldiers, the Christian Trinity. And the Roman troops taught the people of Cádiz much about what to eat, and how.

We know much about the Roman diet. Bread was the basis, as it is today. Cheese, especially from sheep or goats, was always a treat. Fruit in abundance, grown almost year round in these southern reaches, graced much of the table. And for protein there was fish fried in olive oil. The Romans were inordinately fond of fried fish, and so too are their progeny in Cádiz. They like fried fish so much here they have fried-fish shops. They are very much like the fish & chips shops of England, minus the chips! They might offer you a bag of crisps, maybe a candy bar, but it's just a fried-fish shop, offering perhaps half a dozen varieties, wrapped in paper to take away. Very often locals will come to these shops to buy the main course for their family dinner. Or a hungry shopper will purchase a piece as a snack.

But here you may begin ro supply your Roman rations picnic. On the south side of Plaza de Topete sits such a shop. Come here and collect a few fillets of flounder. Get a hake steak. A sack of sardines. Then betake yourself around the corner to the Mercado Central for bread, cheese and fruit. Perhaps a jug of wine. From there it's just a short walk to Playa de la Caleta, or the ancient sea walls of Castillo San Sebastián, or other sites where Roman soldiers took their meal, just the same as yours, as they stood their long historical watch, and as they ate, the theatre further down the peninsula presented the latest works of Plautus and Seneca. News came of conquests and defeats. The seaside baths awaited at the end of the day's duty. The forces of history ebbed and flowed. And the Roman soldier munched his bread and cheese, savoured his fried fish, lingered over his fruit, and, on lucky days, guzzled his wine. And so shall you sit in his place and do the same. And in so doing taste the history of Spain.

Perched on a hill overlooking Granada, Andalucía

Atlantic Spain

This region is sometimes known as 'Green Spain'. Nothing you have ever seen from Hollywood, or read of in Hemingway, or heard of in song or legend will prepare you for this. As you walk down the streets of a city like La Coruña you could be persuaded that you are in Ireland. You will hear not Gypsy castanets, but bagpipes. There are bartenders here that don't know that **un fino** means a glass of dry sherry, but they know the difference between Jameson's and Bushmill's Irish whiskey. They even know the political difference! This is Celtic Spain. The same ancient tribes that found their way to Ireland and Scotland and Wales found their way here. They brought their pipes and drinks. They brought their **trasgos** (goblins) and leprechauns. It causes one to wonder if there is any significance to the fact that both Francisco Franco and Fidel Castro are **Gallego** (Galician).

LA CORUÑA

Restaurante Bania
7 Calle Cordelería.
Outstanding vegetarian restaurant.

Plaza María Pita
The smarter restaurants are located around here.

Ciudad Vieja
Moseying around the beautiful old town will stimulate your appetite as well as your soul.

Playa del Orzán

Ría de la Coruña

Paseo Marítimo

Calle de la Maestranza

Ayuntamiento

Calle de San Andreas

Calle Nueva

Calle Estrella

Calle del Real

Avenida de la Marina

Tourist Office

Dársena de La Marina

Museo Aqueológico

Paseo del Parote

Jardín de San Carlos

Jardines de Méndez Núñez

Paseo Marítimo

Calle Estrella Olmos
Lots of small seafood places oozing with character. You'll also find **tigres rabiosos** (mussels in a spicy sauce) if you crave spicy food.

Avenida de la Marina
Large restaurants with terraces facing the sea. Check out Sidrería Trasgo at number 3. It's a great place to have your cider poured from a great height and take bets on how much will end up on the floor. Also a great place to try **percebes** (goose barnacles).

0   100   200 m
0   100   200 yd

Like their counterparts across the Irish Sea their cookery is simple, but they have learned from their near neighbours how to expand upon that simplicity and extract the most from any piece of provender that might come their way.

Octopus is normally rather unremarkable, a blank canvas upon which to paint, and most people don't know how. But the Gallegos make of it

Pulpo Gallego (Spicy boiled Octopus)

something to remember long after you have left them. **Pulpo gallego** (spicy boiled octopus) is tender and flavourful and you can eat lots of it without feeling too full. It is simply boiled whole, then cut up and dressed with a sauce of oil, paprika and garlic. The trick is in the boiling. Dipping the octopus into the water, drawing it out. Dipping again, so that it cooks at just the right rate. It is a simple dish, but unforgiving of mistakes.

In Galicia

breakfast	al-mor-thoh	*almorzo*
lunch	shan-tahr	*xantar*
supper	say-ah	*cea*
Cheers!	Sah-oo-day!	*Saúde!*

Asturias and Cantabria, along with Galicia, provide Spain with some of the best dishes. Perhaps the most famous, at least it's famous if you are from Asturias, is **fabada asturiana** (stew made with pork, blood sausage and white beans). In historical terms, fabada is the saviour of Spain. To look at it you would say it was nothing more than franks and beans, and such it is. But it is franks and beans raised to the nth degree. In the 8th century the Moors had conquered all of Spain except for the little outpost of Asturias. Unwilling to countenance this, the Moors dispatched an army to subdue the insolent infidel, and so bring the whole of the peninsula under the arm of Al-Islam. The army stopped at the border for lunch. It was their misfortune to have a porkless fabada. One characteristic of fabada is that it is so satisfying that it brings on sleep. We can attest to this. The story goes that the Moors gorged, fell asleep, and were attacked by the Christian knights of Asturias. After that the long reconquista began. Asturias was never under Moorish control. To this day the Asturians say to each other "Have a care. Asturias is Spain. The rest is Araby."

REGIONAL VARIATIONS

Fabada Asturiana
(Stew made with pork, blood sausage and white beans)

Ingredients
2 cups Asturian white beans soaked overnight
1 smoked black pudding
1 chorizo
4oz salt pork
4oz lean pork, smoked if you like
1 pinch saffron
Salt and pepper to taste

Rinse and drain the beans, place them in a pot with enough water to cover and bring to the boil. Add the pork, reduce the heat and simmer for one hour. Add the chorizo, black pudding and the saffron. Cook for half an hour. Add the salt and pepper. Serve immediately.
Serves 4

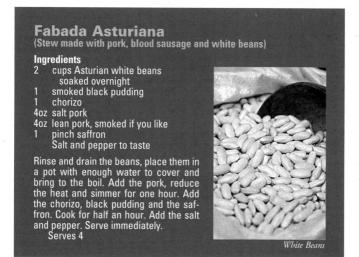
White Beans

Octopus with paprika

REGIONAL VARIATIONS

Like their neighbours, the Basques, the Atlantic Spanish live largely from the sea. Their bread may be the best in Spain, their cheeses superb, they may make good cider and decent wine, but the sea is where their soul is, and they harvest it with religious fervour. They bring in its bounty and celebrate its abundance. **Merluza** (hake) a kind of cod, is the most popular fish. You will find it on the menu in nearly every restaurant along the coast. Most recipes for it, as with most recipes for anything in the Atlantic, are simple as far as ingredients. The trick is always in the process. Just the right kind of heat for just the right length of time for just the right kind of fish, yielding the most genuine taste of the sea. When flavourings are used they tend to be those locally available. And in the Atlantic region those are apples, onions and white wine, the most popular being from the **Albariño** grape.

DON'T MISS

- The morning tipple
- Heavenly Bread
- Mussels in La Coruña
- A Galician cheese tasting
- Irish whiskey in a Celtic pub
- **Percebes** (goose barnacles)
- **Pulpo gallego** (spicy boiled octopus)

Green chillies at the market, Santiago de Compostela, Galicia

Merluza Encebollada (Hake with onion sauce)

Ingredients

6	hake fillets
6	shallots
3	tablespoons olive oil
4	tablespoons bread crumbs
1/4	bunch parsley, finely chopped
2	onions sliced very thin or grated coarsely
250ml	cider
	Salt and pepper to taste

Wash the hake fillets and dry them with a paper towel. Heat the oil in an ovenproof pan. Fry the onion and shallots for 2 minutes, then cover the pan, reduce heat and simmer for 10 minutes. Add the cider, bring to the boil and reduce to a third of its original amount. Remove from the heat and set aside. Season the fish with salt and pepper. Add it to the pan, spooning over some of the onion mixture. Sprinkle with the parsley and crumbs, and drizzle with a bit more oil. Bake at 200°C for 15 minutes.

Serves 6

Spices are used so sparingly and so rarely that we feel compelled to tell you of the one great spicy dish to be had along the Atlantic coast: **tigres rabiosos**. These are **mejillones** (mussels) braised and served in a very spicy red capsicum sauce. You won't see them often, but they can be found in the town of La Coruña. And they are hot. And delicious. We are not sure why the Atlanticos bother to eat them, given as they are to the unadorned. But we are glad they do.

Onions and garlic at the market, Santiago de Compostela, Galicia

The soup known as **caldo gallego** is known all over Spain. Of course it will be common here. It can be flavourful and thick, or watery. Neither way is considered right or wrong. Indeed the concept of caldo gallego is so freestyle that we could give you a cogent argument that there is no such thing as a correct definition. It normally contains greens, meat, potatoes and beans. What kind of meat depends on what's available. Same for the greens. White beans are favoured, but no duel has ever been fought over the use of something else. In Cantabria we saw it made with fish, and no one made comment. Caldo gallego is largely what the chef says it is.

Grapes, beans and tomatoes at the market, Santiago de Compostela, Galicia

Among the exotica of the Atlantic region are **percebes**, goose barnacles, as in Barnacle Bill the Sailor! Trash from the sea, scourge of seagoing vessels since the bronze age. Barnacles, by Saint Elmo's Fire! No good, labour making, destructive, damned, and delicious, barnacles. Lovely barnacles. Big tasty barnacles. It is hard to describe them. They are black, and as wide and as long as your little finger. At one end is what appears to be a three-toed claw. They taste like clams. And they are among the most pleasant things to eat in all the world. They are pricey, but it takes a long time to eat them, and so you may spend time lingering over them, conversing, laughing with each other over your inability to eat them without squirting their juice all over you. Yes, they are pricey. But they are worth every peseta.

Santiago de Compostela

In Santiago de Compostela lies the object of one of the most important pilgrimages in all of Christendom: the tomb of Saint James the Apostle. For nearly a thousand years the faithful have made the long walk from southern France, across the Pyrenees to the extreme end of Celtic Spain to venerate the saint. When they arrive it is not only a time for exaltation and prayer. It is a time for joy, for singing and dancing, and a time to feast. A time to feast both humbly and grandly. And there could be no grander humble feast than a simple picnic under the trees by the Catedral del Apóstol, which houses the Apostle's bones.

The old Mercado is worth a visit, and you can supply much of your picnic here. Excellent Gallego breads are available at Panadaria Elena

SANTIAGO DE COMPOSTELA

Rúa das Rodas   Centro Galega de Arte Contemporánea

Vía Sacra
Come here for one-stop shopping for your Pilgrim's Progress picnic.

Rúa das Carretas

R de San Francisco

Panadaria Elena Suarez
Sensational Gallego breads.

Rúa das Hortas

Praza do Obradoiro

Catedral del Apóstol

Praza do Quintana

Agostiño

Rúa da Virxe da Cerca

Arca de Vela Restaurant
Come here for a break from the hordes of tourists.

R de Gelmirez

Rúa do Pombal

Viliar

Rúa Nova

R de Santo

Carballeira de Santa Susana

Rúa do Franco

Rúa do

Rúa

ℹ️ Tourist Office

Mercado Central
A good morning walkabout rewarded with great coffee at a local restaurant.

Rúa de Senra

Fonte do Santo Antonio

Rúa do Castro de Ouro

0   100   200 m
0   100   200 yd

Old Town Restaurant Walk
A beautiful cluster of tasty restaurants. Start in the middle and go in any direction.

Rúa de Montero Ríos

Cabbages at the market, Santiago de Compostela, Galicia

Suarez across the street at number 6. And at number 7, Meson el Hispano sells water and wine. For one-stop shopping there are several **tiendas** (stores) along Rua Da Acibechería between the cathedral and Praza de Cervantes. From any of these it is just a brief walk to the tree-lined Praza da Inmaculada. When the church bells toll midday, come here and find some friendly shade. A few sparrows or humming birds may visit you as you break your bread. It is written that man does not live by bread alone, but it was this very bread that fuelled the pilgrims' progress and brought them the hundreds of miles to this very spot where now you sup. Here, in your bread and wine, you take not only nourishment, but you imbibe that which fuelled the untold thousands of pious travellers gone before.

In Madrid there's a Museum of Gallego Breads. It isn't really a museum, it's a bakery, but it illustrates the high esteem in which Gallego breads are held. And deservedly so. While the rest of Spain seems to be doing its best to 'modernise' its bread production and bring it to market with the least amount of taste and nutrition possible, here in Green Spain the bread is still largely an artisan product. Whether you buy it at a family grocery or bakery, you will find it the best bread in Spain.

It is truly a bread culture here. Rice is not grown, and while it is eaten it is not common. **Maíz** (corn) is more common, and it is often used in bread making. The loaves are often monuments to baking, huge constructions, thick crusted beasts, meant to last for days. They are substantial in weight and texture, rich in flavour, abundant with nutrition. Look out for **hogaza**, a dense, thick-crusted bread.

That natural next step beyond bread, the **empanada** (savoury pie) is best here as well. It can be made with wheat, rye, barley or corn flour. Or mixes thereof. It can be filled with anything. In most of Spain there seems to be an unwritten law that empanandas are filled with tuna. Celtic Spain seems not to have been read the culinary riot act. Here the empanada is limited only by the cook's imagination. You will find it made of rabbit, thrush, quail, cod with dried fruit, eels, scallops, sardines, cockles and mussels alive alive oh. And tuna.

Alongside your empanada you may be served a plate of the regional speciality, **pimientos de padron**, pungent little green capsicums fried in oil and sprinkled with coarse salt. Most of them are flavourful but sweet, not hot. Most of them. You play a game of gastronomic Russian roulette with pimientos de padron and now and then you get a fire in your mouth. If you don't care for it, you can douse it with floods of the local **sidra** (cider). This, along with a few thin white wines such as Albariño, is the preferred tipple on the fogbound coast of Atlantic Spain. And cider is widely considered the only drink with which to enjoy the famous cheeses of this region.

Atlantic region cheeses are for the most part like bread, artisan products. The moist, cool climate produces rich grasses that make for fat, contented cows who produce flavourful milk. The breeds have gorgeous sounding names like Rubia Gallega, Parda Asturiana, and Carreña. The cheeses tend to be mild and creamy rather than assertive or hard. And they are usually small. While the mellifluously named cows eat much grass and give tasty milk, they do not give a lot of it. They simply aren't bred for quantity. It is interesting to note that the individual cheese maker of the Atlantic is almost always a woman. While the men are in the fields, or out to sea or working a job elsewhere, the women of the farm are tending the kitchen gardens, preserving family traditions, and making all the cheese. Think about that when you eat it.

San Simón is a Gallego mountain cheese and until recently was hard to find in restaurants and shops. This slightly smoked cheese is beautiful to look at, with the appearance of a polished brass knob. It looks like an artefact. Slice it horizontally, so it won't dry out, and you find an interior that is dense and yellow with a creamy texture.

Cabrales is named for the Asturian town where it is produced. It is a blue cheese, cured in the cool, damp caves found in the nearby Picos de Europa mountains. It is wrapped in maple leaves, giving its rind a slight ochre tint, which contrasts beautifully with the blue penicillium mould. Cabrales is very creamy, salty and assertive. It coats the mouth when you eat it, giving you plenty of reason to drink more cider to prepare your palate for the next bite, and more cider. It is widely available in better restaurants all over the country.

Afuega'l Pitu is from the Asturian town of Oviedo. This is a valley cheese, and is salted. Sometimes the makers add a bit of paprika to it for variety. Before you buy you should ask first if it had paprika. At the very least, ask for a taste because it will be gladly given. For an Atlantic cheese it's a bit on the dry side, with a granular quality, and it sticks to the roof of your mouth. It has a nutty flavour and a long finish. This is a cheese you can really linger over.

Tetilla (literally, nipple) from Galicia is so named because of its distinctive shape. One wonders if the original was in any way a representation of that of its maker. It is a quickly ripening cheese, full fat, and with a mild and sweet, not a salty, taste. Tetilla has a very creamy texture. It melts easily, which makes it good for cooking, if the Spanish were given to cooking with cheese. Perhaps they will be some day.

Ahumado de Aliva is from the area around Liebana in Cantabria, and was originally made by shepherds during their stays in the highland pastures. This cheese is smoked over juniper wood, giving it a unique aroma. It reminds us of gin. Its taste is like butter, rather mild except for the smoke. A very good cheese with beer or white wine.

A GALICIAN CHEESE TASTING

Manuel Angel Lopez, of Trasgo Sidrería in La Coruña, is in his element: cheese. Before him sits a platter of some of the most beguiling cheeses in Spain. "I think we eat more cheese here than anywhere in Spain" he says. "Sometimes we even make a meal of it. You can taste why." Manuel has laid out his selections thoughtfully. We start with **Tetilla**, a mild and creamy Galician cow's milk cheese, as a waiter pours cider from his highest reach. **Ahumado de Aliva** follows. It is also mild, and buttery tasting, but a little more assertive due to being gently smoked. With this Manuel offers some dried fruits and breaks a loaf of bread. More cider. "Now let's go next door, to Asturias" he says. **La Peral** is soft-ripened cheese, with a taste reminiscent of brie. We spread it on the bread. The cheese is bolder in the mouth, and we take it with sliced radishes. Manuel serves it with a glass of crisp white Albariño wine. "And now that you are truly ready" he says, "the **cabrales**!" This is a strong tasting, salty blue cheese that is made in caves. And we enjoy it with salad and red wine. Galicia offers the best salads in Spain, and bites of the fresh crispy greens scour the palate between bites of rich cabrales. And with what shall we end this, Manuel? "Brandy, of course." Of course.

Mediterranean Spain

The most emblematic dish of the Mediterranean region is **zarzuela de mariscos** (spicy shellfish stew). This dish is testament to the region's harvest of the sea, and by the sea, the importation of new foods and new ideas. Mediterranean Spain is also a stalwart supporter of the Mediterranean diet: low in cholesterol and fat, high in fibre and vitamins. In addition to rice, fish and tangy sauces, you will find that you have arrived at the garden of Spain.

In Catalunya		
breakfast	**es-mor-sar**	esmorzar
lunch	**dee-nahr**	dinar
supper	**soo-pahr**	sopar
Cheers!	**Bon proh-feet!**	Bon profit!

REGIONAL VARIATIONS

More vegetables are grown, and consumed here, than any other region. In El Levante and Catalunya, restaurants offer whole dishes of vegetables! Yes, it's true. Nothing but vegetables. There are even dedicated vegetarian restaurants here, 40 in Barcelona alone. But don't be fooled, they also like their animal foods and will polish off a plate of ham and chorizo like the most carnivorous Extremaduran.

This is also a land of legumes, which are highly prized as winter fare and provide more dietary fibre to the Spanish diner than almost anything else. Chickpeas are also here, and have been since Phoenician times. Lentils are popular, cooked with onions and mushrooms, or cooked plain and dressed with vinaigrette. Beans here are combined with almost anything that is not a bean. Not just the predictable like sausage and ham. Even clams, fish steaks, and all kinds of vegetables are cooked with beans. Rice is mixed with beans to make **Moros y Cristianos** (Moors & Christians). And sometimes, yes, even beans are mixed with beans. Ever heard of a three bean salad?

La Boquería Market, Barcelona, Catalunya

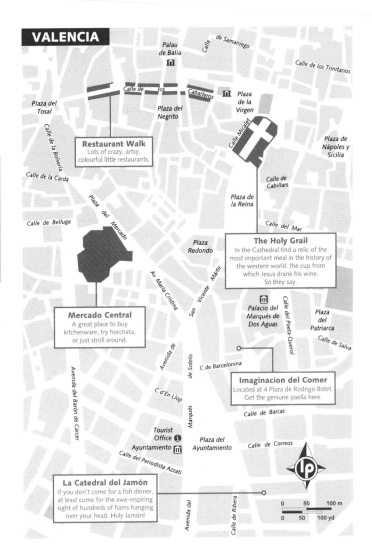

VALENCIA

Palau de Balia

Calle de Samaniego

Calle de los Trinitarios

Plaza del Tosal

Calle de los Caballeros

Plaza del Negrito

Plaza de la Virgen

Calle Micalet

Plaza de Nápoles y Sicilia

Calle de la Bolsería

Calle de la Carda

Restaurant Walk
Lots of crazy, artsy, colourful little restaurants.

Calle de Cabillars

Plaza de la Reina

Plaza del Mercado

Calle de Belluga

Calle del Mar

Plaza Redondo

The Holy Grail
In the Cathedral find a relic of the most important meal in the history of the western world: the cup from which Jesus drank his wine.
So they say.

San Vicente Mártir

Av María Cristina

Mercado Central
A great place to buy kitchenware, try horchata, or just stroll around.

Palacio del Marqués de Dos Aguas

Calle del Poeta Querol

Plaza del Patriarca

Calle de Salva

Avenida de Sotelo

C de Barcelonina

Avenida del Barón de Cárcer

C d'En Llop

Imaginacion del Comer
Located at 4 Plaza de Rodrigo Botet. Get the geniune paella here.

Marqués

Calle de Barcas

Tourist Office

Ayuntamiento

Plaza del Ayuntamiento

Calle de Correos

Calle del Periodista Azzati

La Catedral del Jamón
If you don't come for a fish dinner, at least come for the awe-inspiring sight of hundreds of hams hanging over your head. Holy Jamón!

Avenida del

Calle de Ribera

0   50   100 m
0   50   100 yd

But to return to the emblematic zarzuela. This is the most sophisticated and worldly, most sybaritic region of Spain. Its people are the most demonstrative. And so is its art. Just look at the works of Gaudí. Had Gaudí been a cook he would have specialised in the almost Baroque and dreamy zarzuela de mariscos.

Zarzuela De Mariscos (Spicy shellfish stew)

This most Mediterranean of recipes is also one of the most laborious and time-consuming.

Ingredients

1/4	cup olive oil
3	cloves garlic, finely chopped
1	onion, finely chopped
1	green capsicum, seeded and finely chopped
1/4	cup serrano ham, chopped
1	cup tomatoes, chopped
1	bay leaf
1/4	cup sweet red capsicums, finely chopped
1/4	teaspoon oregano
500g	swordfish or other white fish, skinned and cut into chunks
1/4	cup dry sherry
1/4	cup dry white wine
2	cups fish stock or water
2	teaspoons salt
1/4	teaspoon saffron (or 3 to 4 saffron threads, crushed)
12	mussels, de-bearded and scrubbed under cold running water
12	clams scrubbed under cold running water
3	tablespoons parsley, finely chopped
	lime or lemon wedges for garnish

In a large heavy pot, heat the oil over low heat, then add the garlic, onion, green capsicum and ham, and cook, stirring, until the onion is tender. Add the tomatoes, bay leaf, capsicums and oregano. Cook until the mixture has reduced (10-15 minutes). Add the swordfish, sherry, wine, stock, salt, and saffron, stir and bring to a boil, uncovered over high heat. Add the mussels and clams, reduce the heat to medium, cover, and cook for 6-8 minutes. Remove and discard any mussels or clams that do not open, add salt if needed, transfer the stew to a serving bowl and serve hot, garnished with parsley and lime wedges. Best accompanied by rice.

Serves 6 to 8

DON'T MISS

- The morning tipple
- A feast of Gaudí architecture
- Picnic fare from La Boquería
- Restaurante Gorduña
- The hunt for mushrooms
- A vegetarian blowout
- Eating a bikini

Looking out upon the Mediterranean as it does, this region has always been Spain's window on the world. Though Columbus sailed from the southern port of Cádiz, it is through the Mediterranean that new world crops were suffused into Spain. The mighty statue of 'Colon', as he is known in Spanish, standing on a tall pedestal and pointing westward, is not in Cádiz, but Barcelona. Another important historical fact is that for some two centuries Sicily and Naples were ruled by Spain. The culinary exchange between Spain and 'the Boot' was intense. As a result, while most Spaniards don't eat pasta except in soup, Catalunya has a long tradition of pasta cookery, specialising in **canalones** (cannelloni). As the people here will tell you, "most of Spain looks inward, we look outward".

Garroxta

The region of Catalunya is famous for **garrotxa**, a goat's milk cheese which, like blue cheese, is inoculated with penicillium mould. However, this is not a blue cheese. The penicillium grows only on the outside. The interior is white. This is strictly an artisan cheese, made by former professional people who began a 'back to the land' movement about twenty years ago. Their product is meltingly soft on the tongue, and a bit tangy, as goat cheeses often are. You will recognise it by its steely blue-grey coat.

Mahón cheese comes from the island of Menorca and is produced year round except in August, when everyone go on vacation. It has a well-oiled rind that is coloured by paprika. Mahón comes in both full and medium fat versions, both very aromatic. It has a salt-sour taste and is semi hard, making it useful for grating over vegetables or meat, which is what people of Menorca do with it.

Mussels from Los Carocoles Restaurante, Barcelona, Catalunya

Most of Spain's **azafrán** (saffron) is grown in La Mancha, in the Heart of Spain region. But Mediterranean cookery makes more and more varied use of it. Its subtle yet piquant flavour, its vibrant yet subdued colour, its enigmatic aroma all speak to the Mediterranean character. It is believed that the Romans introduced it to Spain, but after the Visigoth invasions following the fall of Rome its cultivation went into decline. Enter the Moors. Along with rice, almonds and numerous other crops they brought the crocus flower into Spain. Each blossom yields three little stamens, no more. They must be picked with dextrous fingers, for no machine has been invented that could do the job. Harvesting often at night or in the early hours, it is usually families who work the saffron. Hired hands are often paid in saffron. With retail prices at US$2800 per kilogram that's not bad wages, if you can pick enough. Tens of thousands of flowers will yield a few grams. Once gathered, the little threads of magic are slightly roasted to conserve their flavour. This process reduces their weight by as much as two thirds.

Barcelona, the capital of Catalunya, a fiercely independent region with its own language and smouldering history, was the perfect venue for the iconoclastic works of Antoni Gaudí (1852-1926). A solitary artist, Gaudí found his inspiration in the medieval forms of the past and the Art Nouveau movement sweeping Europe in the late 19th century. His expression of those concepts produced works of unparalleled exuberance and imagination never seen before or since. The apartment buildings, fountains, parks and his signature work, La Sagrada Família, were all a synthesis of tradition and radical experimentation.

Gaudí's buildings are sea swells caught in stone. Onion-domed copulas line brightly-tiled roofs while blasts of colour speckle buildings with intense blues, greens and yellows, fading to pale pastels. Straight lines did not exist for Gaudí, all were curved, twisted, arched or looped. Everywhere there are shimmering mosaics of fantastic patterns and designs, climbing in a riot of colour to mysterious towers crowned with fruit basket pinnacles.

Since much of Gaudí's work is outside, it can be quietly contemplated from a distance; time to savour the subtle changes that the play of light brings to his buildings. Such contemplation can be intense work, and intense work needs sustenance. Only a picnic that reflects the master will do, however, and a Gorgeous Gaudí Picnic can be easily gathered at the city's market, La Boquería on La Rambla. Brightly glazed fruit reminiscent of the pinnacles of La Sagrada Família can be bought at the kiosks near the front door. If you prefer the fresh variety, you can create a lovely basket of fresh fruit. Pineapple, peaches and oranges would be apropos, topped with a scattering of cherries and apricots. The numerous fish stalls will provide

The tiled mixtures of Gaudí's chimney pots, Parc Güel, Barcelona, Catalunya

BARCELONA

Plaza del Sol
Excellent place to wander and follow your nose. A lovely warren of food and drink without the tourist hordes.

Carrer de Balmes
Upmarket joints frequented by young business types. Food here goes beyond the Spanish.

La Rambla
This whole promenade is lined with bars and restaurants. It's the perfect place for a tapeo and the street people are the best entertainment in town.

Restaurant Biocenter
Located at 25 Pinto Fortuny. One of 40 vegetarian restaurants in Barcelona. This one specialises in legumes and things faintly Moorish.

La Boquería and Restaurante Garduña
Excellent place to wander and follow your nose. A lovely warren of food and drink with not many tourists.

Travessera de Dalt · El Putxet · Lesseps · Gràcia · Hospital de Sant Pau · Plaça de les Glòries Catalanes · Glòries · Monumental · Via Augusta · Muntaner · Plaça de Joan Carlos I · Avinguda Diagonal · Plaça de Francesc Macià · Avinguda de Sarrià · Carrer de Muntaner · Carrer del Numància · Carrer de València · Carrer d'Aragó · L'Eixample · Passeig de Gràcia · Carrer de Balmes · La Ribera · Parc de la Ciutadella · Via Laietana · Ciutat Vella · Gran Via de les Corts Catalanes · Estació de França · La Barceloneta · Sants · Hostafrancs · El Raval · La Rambla · Plaça de Sants · Carrer de la Creu Coberta · Mercat Nou · Avinguda del Paral.lel · Poble Sec · Ronda Litoral

0   400   800 m
0   400   800 yd

you with small pre-cooked blue crabs, like so many pieces of mosaic. Tetilla cheese, for its sensuous shape and rich taste is a must. Here at one of the restaurant stalls such as Clemen's you might also get a few **bikinis**. This is the Catalan sybarite's term for ay sandwich cut diagonally into halves. The triangular pieces call to mind bikini bottoms. At least in Catalunya.

Just outside the market is Escribá, the legendary pastry shop located at the corner of La Rambla and Petxina. You'll need **cava** (sparkling wine) to wash down this feast and it can be purchased here, as well as water. Gaudíesque in design, the shop contains a fine selection of lovely sweets and biscuits as well as artisan bread in knots, bows and rounds. Right down the street is L'Arc (stall 77) where a variety of especially fancy tapas can be found and tucked away with your provisions.

Your picnic can take place at a Gaudí work of your choice. The lovely park across from La Sagrada Família on the Nativity Facade side is a delightful place to enjoy your feast and contemplate this extraordinary building. Parc Güell, Gaudí's miniature garden city, was never completed but it's still the premier location for a Gorgeous Gaudí Picnic. The park sits high on tree-covered hills providing beautiful vistas of city and sea. You can spread out your goodies on swirling, snake-like benches covered in mosaics, or climb the rustic stairways that thread though the hills. Pick a shady spot for your repast and enjoy views of the few imaginative homes that Gaudí was able to build. It's an enchanting place to savour the art of Antoni Gaudí and your picnic in his honour.

Fresh cherries in a basket, Caceres, Extremadura

The Pyrenees

The Pyrenees stretch across the top of Spain from the Mediterranean Sea to the Atlantic Ocean, and were formed when what is now Iberia collided with the European continent. They make Spain Europe's most mountainous country outside Switzerland. They also represent a cultural and historical unity. One not created by tectonic movement but by pilgrimage, politics and war. Through them lay the path of the Camino de Santiago, the long road to the tomb of Saint James the Apostle. Through them lies the Roman road linking Gaul to Zaragosa, the path of Moorish armies and later their pursuers under Charlemagne. And along these mountain roads and their debouchments onto the two seas can be found the foods of the region, and those of its many and sundry travellers.

The Pyrenees have always teemed with game, and trout. The mountain valleys have long held fine pastures for goats and sheep, and the seas at either end have always provided plenty. As long as people have dwelt along this great mountainous spine there have been these gastronomic constants. With the passage of time new crops have come along: cherries, pears, almonds, varieties of wine and table grapes. New ways of doing things. The Romans brought the recipe for cured ham. The Moors for almond sweets. They tell tales of Hemingway teaching people his favourite ways with trout. Today, French and German families on ski holidays bring the latest culinary inspirations from their homelands. And the people of the mountain chain take what they like and leave the rest, as they have done for millennia.

Of course the most famous part of this region is the Basque Country (also known as País Vasco), a small jewel on the westernmost extreme of this long sinuous body. Among the people of Spain the Basques think about food, and talk about it, and feel about it more than any other community. Many people will tell you with passionate conviction that the best restaurant in Spain is Arzak in San Sebastián. And we find the argument persuasive. But even if it did not exist it would hardly matter. This would still be the most dedicated gastronomic community in Spain. This is where the famous

DON'T MISS

- The morning tipple
- Getting invited to a gastronomic society
- An evening in a sidrería
- **Bacalao** (cod)
- Restaurant walks in Hondarribia
- Casa de Irene, in Artíes

REGIONAL VARIATIONS

Inside the Luis Irízar Cooking School, San Sebastián, Basque Country

SAN SEBASTIÁN (DONOSTIA)

Mar Cantábrico
(Kantauri Itsasoa)

31 de Agosto
Puerto Iñigo
Alameda del Boulevard
Av Zurriola

Av de la Libertad

Calle de San Martin
Mercado de
San Martín
RENFE

ET/FV
Station

Paseo de Vizcaya
Río Urumea

Av Ategorrieta

Paseo Ulia
Jose Elosegi
Mendiola

Paseo Zaratagi

A8 Bilbao - Behobia

**Bar Txepetxa,
Percaderia #5**
Here find Jose Marañón, the
undisputed 'King of Anchovies'.
More pintxos (tapas) made
from anchovies than you'll
find anywhere else.
And all very tasty. A
favourite of local food writers.

Restaurant Arzak
What many will say
is the best restaurant
in Spain.

**Fermin Calbetón
Restaurant Walk**
Where Basque
conviviality is at
its most intense.

0   250   500 m
0   250   500 yd

STRANGER IN A STRANGE LAND

I had resigned myself to a long walk on the lovely half-crescent bay of La Concha, while Richard was to visit the men-only cooking society of San Sebastián. Much to my delight, our host Louis Irízar, world-famous chef and founder of the Irízar Cooking School, invited me along on the tour. This would be very special; even General Franco's wife wasn't able to arrange such a visit.

As we wandered through the narrow streets of the old town, Louis explained the club's purpose: a place for men to come, relax and make themselves or their friends a meal in the modern kitchens.

On arrival I was surprised to see that the club opened directly onto the street. The only thing distinguishing it from other restaurants around was a discreet sign marked **privada** (private). As we entered, I hung back a bit, allowing Louis and Richard to walk a few steps ahead. I felt shy at my invasion of such a male dominion, and hoped Louis would introduce us quickly as journalists so that the members wouldn't gasp in horror at my appearance and begin throwing bread, or something harder. Not to worry. The moustached gentlemen seated at the long

tables rose as one, pushed back their benches and with gracious smiles and bows invited me to sit, and please, to have lunch. Succulent ruby-red tuna cooked to perfection sat next to a platter of crisp lettuce and ripe tomatoes drenched in olive oil and vinegar. There was also a **tortilla** (omelette) fresh from the pan, made of fluffy eggs and buttery potatoes. A plate was quickly filled for me, presented with aplomb, and my opinions on the feast eagerly awaited. Cider was poured from an arm's length into my glass and the group delighted in my exclamations at such a feat. I felt I should be wearing long, full skirts and some kind of Elizabethan ruff, being the object of such gallantry! Richard had lunch, too, but he had to stand.

Later that day we passed the club, now packed with members singing at the tops of their lungs. Women married to the members passed by, and one said to me, "we tell them, 'please, get out of the house, go to your club! But do come back'".

Gina Comaich

MUSHROOM MANIA

Most Spaniards don't eat mushrooms. Andalucíans think of them as deadly toadstools. Gallegos have for centuries connected them with witchcraft. These attitudes are slowly, very slowly, turning around, but in the Mediterranean, especially in Catalunya (and the Pyrenees) there is no turning around needed. People here love mushrooms of all kinds. Not only will they buy them at the market and order them by the platter in restaurants, they will make a social event of a mushroom hunt. There are clubs and societies that exist for this purpose alone. On a spring or autumn weekend in the Pyrenees it is no unusual thing to see a group of Catalans wandering the woods, baskets and knives in hand and eyes focused studiously on the ground. The hunt is on. Tally Ho, the fungus!

This mushroom mania is rarely mentioned in Spanish cookery books or tourist brochures. Foreigners simply don't think of mushrooms when they think of Spain. For that matter, most Spaniards don't think of mushrooms when they think of Spain! But now you will know better. Now you will know that there are even restaurants that, during mushroom season, specialise in dishes using the tasty little nubbins. They might be something as simple as a tapa of **setas**, a popular wild variety, fried quickly in oil and garlic. It could be an omelette with several varieties cooked into it. It might be mushrooms stuffed with sausage, or simmered in red Rioja wine, or flamed with Sherry brandy.

Setas at market

Tapas bar, San Sebastián, Basque Country

THE JOKE'S ON ME

The Basques love to eat, drink and laugh. For them food is not food without drink. And drink is not drink without laughter. You will hear it pealing out onto the street whenever the bars and restaurants are open. But they are circumspect in their laughter and never let it conflict with their good manners. If you are not a practised Spanish speaker you will certainly make a few linguistic gaffes. One of the easiest mistakes to make in a bar is when ordering a glass of beer. You should ask for **una caña**. But you might slip and say **una canon** (a cannon). No one will laugh at you. They might look perplexed, or even embarrassed. But they won't laugh, unless you, realising your error, laugh first. Then they will roar with laughter! Gales of guffaws will burst forth. They'll repeat the request, and they'll say things like, "hey, the señor wants to drink from a cannon! He must be real thirsty! Har har har!" Then when others enter the bar they will be let in on the big joke and the laughter will go round again. And if you are a good sport about it, and laugh along with them, someone is likely to say to you, "hey, Señor Cannon, that drink is on me". Oh yes. We've made this mistake many times.

all-male gastronomic societies are (see the aside Stranger in a Strange Land). This is where pilgrims of another kind come to pay their respects. The Basque influence is felt all through the Pyrenees. The vineyards and bodegas are either owned largely by Basques or heavily influenced by them, just as the English own or influence many of the sherry bodegas.

When you are near the sea you must of course look for seafood. Among the most famous dishes of this region is **bacalao al pil-pil** (salted cod in garlic and oil). Also popular is **pimientos rellenos** (stuffed red capsicums). Perhaps your mother fed you stuffed capsicums at home. Unless she was Basque you don't know how good stuffed capsicums can be. Here they're usually stuffed with fish, but we prefer them stuffed with pork. No matter how good the fish is, we can have a surfeit of it.

HONDARRIBIA

San Pedro Kalea Restaurant Walk
The main drag is the best place to dine while watching the world go by. You'll also find shops where you can fill your Basket of Basque picnic.

Santiago Kalea Restaurant Walk
Set back from the main drag, quieter and more contemplative.

Rio Bidasoa Ibaia

Picnic Spot
A lovely view from a hillside underneath the old palace.

The cheese here is called **Idiazábal**. This is sheep's milk cheese, and one of the most popular in Spain. You can eat it when it's fresh and mild, and the rind is soft, but true cheese lovers like it aged and hardened. Basque shepherds make it in their mountain huts while grazing the sheep. They smoke it slightly, and they swear that the direction of the wind during smoking will affect the quality of the cheese. Annually the shepherds come

---

In Basque country

breakfast	go-sah-ree	*gosari*
'lunch' at 10am	am-ahr-reh-tak-oh	*amarretaco*
'lunch' at 11am	am-ay-cah-tak-oh	*amaicataco*
lunch	baz-kah-ree	*bazkari*
early dinner	a-pal-owr-ree-ow-dee-ak	*apalaurreaudiak*
supper	a-fah-ree	*afari*
Cheers!	To-pah!	*Topa!*

REGIONAL VARIATIONS

down to the village of Idiazábal for the cheese making contest. They lean on their crooks as the judges judge, perhaps wondering if such city dwellers really know how to judge such a thing. When the winner is announced his cheese is auctioned off, usually to a local restaurant who advertises the product on its menu for as long as it lasts.

It won't take you long to discover the ruling precept of this cuisine: take the best ingredients you can find, interfere with them as little as possible, then enjoy the result in the most pleasant company you can find. The Spanish in general are a convivial people. But the Basques are most convivial of all. We wonder sometimes if there is a Basque eating alone somewhere, if so, is it an occasion for sadness? To ensure that the ingredients are up to

The Guggenheim Museum, Bilbao, Basque Country

Pimientos Rellenos (Stuffed red capsicums)

The Filling
100ml olive oil
1   onion, peeled and chopped
1   garlic clove, peeled and chopped
1   tablespoon parsley, chopped
150g serrano ham, minced
200g ground pork
1   tablespoon flour
     Salt and pepper to taste

The Capsicums
12   sweet red capsicums, roasted, peeled and seeded
300ml oil
200g flour
2   eggs, beaten

For the stuffing heat the oil to medium low in a skillet and fry the onion, garlic and parsley for about 10 minutes. Increase the heat to medium and add the ham and pork and cook for another 10 minutes. Stir in the flour, salt and pepper. Set aside to cool. When cool enough to handle, stuff the capsicums with the mixture and secure their mouths with toothpicks. Heat the remaining oil in a deep vessel. Dredge the capsicums in the flour then dip in the beaten eggs. Using a slotted spoon, lower the peppers into the hot oil and cook until they begin to brown (10-15 minutes). Serve with **alioli** (garlic mayonnaise) and toasted bread.
    Serves 6

Roasted red peppers

A BASKET OF BASQUE

A picnic in the Basque Country is the easiest thing in the world. Ask any Basque how they would do it. "Easy" they will say. "Just tell the concierge! Or the chef!" Hotel concierges and restaurant chefs are used to taking orders for a picnic basket. From the simple fare of shepherds to the grand goods of a grandee, the able servant knows just where to get the best of what, when to get it and what the price ought to be. Just give him 24 hours notice. He'll even map out the route to his favourite picnic site if you haven't picked it already.

To keep it authentic, be sure to ask for **sidra** (cider), or for **txakolí** (sharp white wine). It's the only wine produced in this region. Any Basque with a sense of Basqueness is going to insist on including fish in your basket. A **bacalao** (cod) salad would be very fitting, or fried **bonito** (tuna) cheeks which can easily be eaten by hand. Crab is available and a few legs would make good cracking. With France so near, froi gras is everywhere. And, as everywhere in Spain, there is ham aplenty. Now just find yourself a lasting hillside, this little corner of Spain is blessed with many. It might overlook the sea, or it might be host to a little flock of sheep, and it might be cloaked in the perfume of freshly-pressed apples from a nearby sidrer´a. Buen provecho.

snuff, many restaurants here use small dedicated gardens or farms to supply their fruits and vegetables. This way the chef has complete control over what produce is used in the kitchen. Take a walk through the less populated parts of the towns and you will see these gardens. Some of them are simply the back yards of private homes.

Moving inland you'll see less seafood and more trout, lamb and game. Still, the ruling principle applies. Roasts are treated with little more than the heat of a fire. Sometimes they are rubbed with garlic or basted with fat. A sprig of rosemary might enter the oven to perfume its air. Here lamb is known as **ternasco**, rather than **cordero**. Game or rabbit might be cooked with wild mushrooms, for as in Catalunya, the mushroom fear does not reside here. In the town of Jaca, an ancient pilgrimage stopover, you will find an unusually good land of cakes, and pastries. One emblematic pastry from Aragón is **adoquines**, caramel-filled, rectangular pastries wrapped up with paper bearing an image of the Virgen de Pilar.

As you make your progress through this region be on the lookout for one of its most rewarding features. Here and there in small villages in the high valleys and in the passes, you'll find some of the finest restaurants in existence. Superb cooks who have trained at the best schools and restaurants

High Mountain Trucha (Trout)

Ingredients

4	trout, cleaned and patted dry
100g	breadcrumbs
4	red capsicums, roasted, peeled, seeded and chopped
4	bacon strips
100ml	olive oil
2	tablespoons minced parsley
1	garlic clove
	Salt to taste

Combine the breadcrumbs and capsicums and stuff the trout with the resulting mixture. Wrap the trout in the bacon strips and secure them with toothpicks. Place the trout in a roasting pan and baste with oil. Bake at 180°C until the trout flakes easily (30 minutes). Transfer the trout to a serving dish. Saute the garlic and parsley in the pan juices. Deglaze with a little water, wine or lemon if necessary. Pour the juice over the trout.

Serves 4-6

of Spain and France find themselves longing for their old mountain homes. They return, convert the family residence to a small restaurant, and find contentment. When you arrive, so will you. You'll be served family recipes and other dishes of the village. You might get civet of wild boar, or lambs offal sausage. Pig's trotters with turnips is fine mountain fare. If you go fishing for trout, and they bite, bring your catch and they'll cook it for you. Perhaps the best example of the small Pyrenean restaurant is Casa Irene, operated by Irene España, in the village of Artíes at the border between Aragón and Catalunya.

shopping
& markets

Spain is as modern as any other western European country, with a strong allegiance to supermarkets. But explore a little and you'll find shopping for food, especially in a busy Spanish market, with its colourful produce and displays of fresh flesh, can be just as much a unique Spanish experience as the Cádiz carnavale.

La Boquería Market, Barcelona, Catalunya

Shopping in Spain is most often just like shopping at home. In the newer parts of the cities you will even find shopping malls just the same as you would at home. They are so like home that were it not for the language being used you might think you were in Walnut Creek, California or Milton Keynes. They even have restaurants that serve bad food. This may be the land of Don Quixote, Gypsies and shepherds leaning on their crooks as they watch their flocks, but it is also a fully integrated member of NATO and the EU. It's a modern country. Welcome to 21st Century Spain!

But there are pockets of old Spain, if you know where to look. There are a few places remaining where the nation's exuberance, and traditions, and character are still on display.

Mercado (Market)

As you visit the various cities of Spain, look to the map. Near the centre of the old town you may see a **mercado** (market). In Santiago de Compostela the mercado is near the cathedral, and it looks like a cathedral, as it's built from ancient and reclaimed stones. Valencia has a mercado, also near the cathedral, that's as artful and colourful as the city itself. And San Sebastián has one underground. But the grandest of the grand and the bestest of the best is in Barcelona.

Mercat La Boquería (101 La Rambla, open Monday-Saturday 7:30am-9pm) looks like it was originally a railway station, with its vast wrought-iron roof covering an area as big as a football field. There has been a market in this area since medieval times, the earliest record dating to 1301. In those days the merchants were spread out over a wider area and in the open or under temporary shelter. The name Boquería comes from the word **boq** (sheep's stomach) and so may refer to the butchers who set up shop here. In 1836 the market was finally consolidated, government health regulations being the principal driving force. Many of the stalls and the market's main ornamentation were designed by local artists. The floor plan might have been conceived by an English gardener for its maze-like layout. It follows a numbered grid pattern, like city blocks, but with just enough irregularities to keep it from being predictable.

The main entry is in the eastern wall on La Rambla. At the centre is a **glorieta** (traffic circle). This is the heart of the market, and is where the fishwives sell seafood. Everything that was ever pulled from the depths of the Mediterranean is here: finfish, shellfish, kelp and seaweed, spread out on beds of shaved ice or swimming live in tanks; fresh fish, canned fish, cooked fish, whole, filleted to order, or salted and dried; octopus and squid (with or without their ink), giant tuna and tiny anchovies, buckets of clams, mountains of mussels and shoals of shrimp. And everywhere the flashing of cutlery as pinafore-clad women work the catch with huge and deadly knives. They shout to each other, and they whisper of bargains to be had. Their arms never cease as they hone their blades and attack a new fish every minute. The lorries arrive from the docks and 150kg of albacore and tuna are surrendered to their hands. With meat-hooks and gaffs they haul the weighty beasts in and, pausing to adjust their skirts, take up their weapons again, divide and conquer. Blood-spattered and wise in the ways of fish anatomy and cookery, they'll pause to advise you on the best way of preparing this cut of that fish. They'll tell you at what stall to buy the best vegetables to go with it. Who has the right wine, the finest rice. They know everything. These mighty women with their merciless blades, girlish dress, salty language and flirtatious winks. These bloody coquettes are the soul of the market.

SHOPPING

178

If you want to buy some **bacalao** (cod) this is the place. At stall 737 Señora Goma will sell it to you dry or revived. You can choose your cod from one of the marble basins in which they are soaking. Señora Goma will remove the bones for you, but at a slightly higher cost. The most expensive cut is the **morro** (middle fillet). Use the small strip cuts called **esqueixat** for **esqueixada** (cod salad). She also has wonderful delicacies such as **mojama** (dried tuna) to drench with oil and serve as a tapa. But her rarest offering is **callos de bacalao** (salt cod tripe). This stuff is as rare as truffles and if she has any on hand you should try it.

Seafood at La Bouquería Market, Barcelona, Catalunya

SHOPPING

You can find a world of olives at stall 742. Nice for a snack as you walk about. Also find a nibble at stall 318 where Carmen Naudi sells all manner of pulses, including the popular snack, pre-cooked **garbanzos** (chickpeas). If you're in the mood for ready-to-eat meat, head to Mantequería Casa Guinart at 95 La Rambla, at the front of the market. Here you'll find all kinds of cheeses, pâtés, excellent wines, and that very Spanish treat, **cecina de caballo** (cured horseflesh).

La Boquería Market, Barcelona, Catalunya

Among the 500 market stalls of La Boquería you'll find all the makings of Spanish cuisine. The market is so full of goods, buyers and sellers that it spills out onto side streets and alleys where lively trade continues. As many tourists as locals come here to ogle and gawk and see and smell – to hear the shouts and feel the press of bodies and business. A busy time at La Boquería is an intense time. You may feel the need to seek shelter. Never fear. There is plenty of respite to be found in the bars and kiosks that dot this interior landscape. A cold beer to combat the heat, or a leisurely glass of sherry, or a full meal, or a sandwich and a Coke are always within reach. Some have stall numbers and some don't, but we'll tell you how to find them.

Bar Clemen's (stall 114) is so small that one of the three family members who operate it has to work on the outside of the bar. They serve breakfast, lunch, sandwiches and tapas. Alberto, the tall one, speaks English and is most helpful. Look for Bar Clemen's on the south wall.

Bar Boquería (stall 285) is tucked into the corner at the far western end. It's good for coffee, pastries and a few tapas.

Bar Pinotxo (not far from Bar Boquería) is probably the best known of the Boquería eateries. It has been run by the Asim family for 60 years, and Juanito Asim is quite possibly the most photographed waiter in Barcelona. It's a good stop for tapas and pastries.

Sandvitxeria Central (stall 497) is a Spanish sports bar where there is always a game on the big screen. They specialise in **mariscos** (seafood) and they have more elbow room than most.

Bar Kisoco (stall 66) is just to your right as you enter through the La Rambla gate. It looks a little like a truck-stop, a bit scruffy. And they serve hearty truck-stop fare such as stew. Ironically, they also specialise in **cava** (sparkling wine) and Champagne.

Kiosco Universal (next to stall 699) is the biggest place under the roof. It has a horseshoe-shaped bar, a grill, several employees scurrying about and full bar service. It has an extensive menu. If it weren't for the lack of tables this would be a proper sit-down restaurant.

Petit Bar is in the alley just outside the south wall (go out the exit near Clemen's). It's a tiny little place with only one table outside. Not a sidewalk restaurant really, as it's deep in an alley. But it's got charm.

Kiosco Moderno is right in the heart of the market, on the **glorieta** (traffic circle). You can't miss it. It has a fully stocked bar so is good for an afternoon gin & tonic, or for a morning tipple.

Bar Sant Josep is just inside the main gate of the market. It's a small, bright place set amongst the aromas of the fruit stalls.

La Boquería Market, Barcelona, Catalunya

ANTONIO MAGAÑA – Faces of Gastronomy

Restaurante Garduña is connected, as though by an umbilical cord, to La Boquería at the southwest corner. And La Boquería feeds it both its raw materials and many customers. This is where you go when you want the market to distil itself into a single splendid dinner. It is owned by Antonio Magaña. We met him quite by accident while having a drink in the downstairs bar. The place was crowded with shoppers and tourists so he invited us upstairs to a cosy dining room. "Here you can look out over the market", he said as he opened a window and let in some evening air, slightly cooled by a Summer rain.

We had heard that his was the oldest restaurant in Barcelona, so we asked him.

"Oh no. Not at all. My restaurant is only 170 years old. There are some that are 200 years old. I've been in my restaurant for 28 years. For the first 20 I was a waiter. And all through those 20 years I saved. Then eight years ago I was able to buy it. I suppose I could have retired, but I love my restaurant. Why should I retire?"

"Do all of your ingredients come from La Boquería?"

"Yes. The market is my kitchen. I have my usual suppliers, but I'll switch if another has a better selection or higher quality. It changes from time to time you know."

"What makes Mediterranean, especially Catalan, cooking different from the rest of Spain?"

"Well that's hard to say sometimes. We use the same ingredients. I can take the same things offered in La Boquería and make the same food that they eat in Andalucía. The chief difference is in the preparation. We have a lot of French and Italian influence, so we think about other ways to do things. We like to make it a little more colourful. We make more use of sauces. We eat pasta as a dish, not just as an ingredient. I serve cannelloni here for example. And of course I serve **zarzuela** (spicy fish stew), which in the Spanish opinion is rather spicy.

When we asked if he ever uses Tabasco, he blushed. "Well, I do have a bottle on hand" he said with a shy smile. And it was brought to the table with the zarzuela we had for dinner.

Dried fish, La Boquería Market, Barcelona, Catalunya

Speciality Shops

Tienda (family grocery) These stores are still common, especially in smaller cities and in Galicia. If you can't find a bakery, these are good places to buy good bread. They are sometimes known as **tienda de alimentación**, or **tienda de comestibles**, or as **almacén**.

Carnicería (butcher's shop/stall) Look for these in the older grand markets and mercados centrales. In the supermarkets the meat section is just like in any country.

Charcutería (delicatessen) A good place to find packaged cured meats and other delectables, for picnics or for taking home.

Confitería/Pastelería (cake shop, also selling confectionery) These are most common in Barcelona and Madrid.

Frutería (fruit shop/stall) These are found almost everywhere. They are most often family-run operations, also selling beverages and snacks such as bread, sweets, and cheese.

Panadería (bakery) For the best bread, look for **panadería artesana**. Except in Galicia where the 'artesana' goes without saying.

Unbaked bread waiting for the ovens, Barcelona, Catalunya

Pescadería (fish shop/stall)

Pollería (stall or shop specialising in chicken)

Verdulería (greengrocer) You'll find these mainly in the grand markets.

Bodega (wine producer/cellar/shop) A bodega could be any commercial operation having to do with wine. A **tienda de vinos** (wine shop) is a small sales point for wine. These aren't as common as you might think, as people tend to buy their wines where they buy their groceries.

Produce available from J. Murria Fine Foods, Barcelona, Catalunya

Supermercado (Supermarket)

There are supermarkets everywhere, and most Spaniards shop at them regularly. Some supermarkets are independent operations but most are members of commercial chains. They can be found in the basements of huge department stores, such as the Corte Ingles. Every city in Spain has at least one Corte Ingles. The larger ones have several. They have the virtues of being open six, or even seven days a week and during **mediodia**

THE UNSEEN HAND

I moved quickly through the cool of Plaza Mayor's porticoes, trying to avoid the piercing Spanish sun and Madrid's citizens hurrying home to lunch and a siesta. A homeless person I often passed, always in a state of perpetual siesta, was burrowed even deeper in his piles of blankets.

Only a sudden desire to buy **galletas** (biscuits) could have sent me out into that summer heat – galletas made by the nuns of Convento de Corpus Cristi. I'd often heard of these cloistered women who supported themselves by making all sorts of delicious pastries from ancient and contemporary recipes. Being a sweet tooth, I needed to find them.

Many feel that the secular world depends on the prayers of these nuns to get it through its various gyrations and tribulations. Prayers are constantly streaming out from the walls of this convent seeking to give spiritual sustenance to an unconsciously ravenous world, but pastries too? Wonderful!

The convent was buried deep in the old city on Plaza de Conde de Miranda and even with my map, I kept blundering around finding all sorts of charming plazas but not the Conde de Miranda or its cloistered bakery. Soon the crowds began to thin and the banging of shops' steel shutters grew quiet. A single bell began to toll, and following its sound I rounded a corner and came, at last, into the sun-baked silence of Plaza de Conde de Miranda.

The convent's tall, impressive walls glowed warmly in the sun and I followed them to a high, brass studded door. A small door within it had a note tacked on inviting me in if I wished to make a purchase. Feeling somewhat like Alice, I gently turned the handle and pushed the ancient door open. There was no one about and the only promising thing I could see was an another door further on. I walked toward it very aware of my heels clacking on the paving stones, breaking the restful quiet. I found myself in a minuscule courtyard, but still not a person in sight.

I moved on and entered a small room with a large wooden turntable taking up much of the left wall. This was it, the entrance to my sought

(midday). Supermercados carry virtually anything you should wish to buy. In addition to food and drink, on the upper floors you may buy cookware, tableware, dishwashers, furniture. This is true one-stop shopping. They even have information booths staffed with friendly and helpful multi-lingual personnel. As wine shops are not as common as you might think, people tend to by wine at the grocery or the supermarket. This is the same for beer, soda and water.

---

after bakery. The ancient turntable spun around, making me jump with surprise. Then a cheerful voice from behind it asked what I'd like to purchase. It was then I noticed the list of pastries on the wall. Feeling somewhat self-conscious speaking to the turntable, I shyly asked for half a kilo of tea galletas, placing the requisite amount of pesetas on the turntable. It promptly rotated and in a minute reversed once more, with my galletas packaged and ready to go. I mumbled a gracias, got one back with a smile which I could hear. I took my galletas and made my way back to the entrance.

Stepping out into the sunshine, I felt slightly disoriented. I had just completed a purchase without seeing anybody. The delicious lemony smell of the galletas set me right, though, and I hurried off for a strong espresso and a taste.

They were perfect: a rich, sweet shortbread with just a hint of lemon to tang your tongue and involve your nose. I quickly ate three looking about the cafe somewhat guiltily. Packing up my remaining galletas, I headed back to the hotel wondering just what I was going to do with the rest of them. They were wonderful but to keep them all to myself seemed selfish. My travelling companions were not sweet lovers and these were heavy-duty galletas to be savoured by chronic sweet devotees.

As I turned the corner, I noticed that the homeless person I'd passed earlier had wandered away, leaving his small bundles in a heap. He might enjoy these if he comes back, I thought, and placed the package beside his things.

The next morning on my way to breakfast I passed him again. This time he was awake and sitting crossed-legged drinking a large cup of coffee from the nearby cafe and delicately biting into one of the galletas. I thought the nuns would be very pleased; their labours working, as always, unseen but effective.

Gina Comaich

Buy your blessings from Convento de Corpus Cristi,
Plaza de Conde de Miranda 1, Madrid.

Things to Take Home

Azafrán (saffron) is one of the best deals in Spain. Because of its extremely high market value it has always tempted fraud. Something so small and highly prized has in the past created something like an illicit drug trade. There was a time in parts of Europe when adulterating saffron was a capital offence. More than a few people have been burned at the stake or hanged for it. You won't have such recourse if you're defrauded with turmeric or other saffron simulators. For this reason, do not buy ground saffron. Ever. Look to see that all the threads are of uniform length and a deep, burnt orange colour. Get to know the aroma of the genuine article. You'll never forget it and never be fooled. The nose will know.

Other edible souvenirs include **cecina** (cured meat). You can also buy ham and all kinds of sausages vacuum packed, ready to go. In Galicia you can even buy vacuum-packed **fabada asturiana**, the uncooked beans and the smoked meats sealed side by side. They need no refrigeration and will keep indefinitely. There are also many tinned or bottled foods that carry the taste of Spain and are unavailable or hard to find elsewhere. And take home some short-grain **Bomba** rice, grown in Spain. It's expensive but worth it. Like saffron, all of these are available in charcuterías and supermercados, as well as in La Boquería. Spanish wines are nowadays easy to find at home, but **sidra** (cider) is not. If it is to your liking, take some with you.

Spain exports relatively little of its olive oil, and less still of its better stuff. However, when you are in Spain you might want to buy some. It makes a very fine souvenir if you buy the local oil from areas you visit, and it makes for popular gifts. And when you've returned home and want to taste your favourite little corner of Spain, you'll have it bottled and on the shelf, ready for a feast of memory. When shopping for olive oil or any other foodstuffs, check labels for Denominations of Origin and Specificity, a guarantee that you're getting what you paid for. (See the boxed text Denominations of Origin and Specificity in the Culture of Spanish Cuisine chapter.)

Two items of cookware are essential for your Spanish kitchen. The **paellera** for making so many of your rice dishes, including paella. Cast iron is the traditional material, but stainless steel also works. They are available in non-stick versions these days. The non-stickers are roundly condemned by all and sundry, and used by many, especially by those who must clean them when they are encrusted with rice. Look for the design with the extra heavy bottom. It has a better heat distribution and so needs less movement over the flame. The other vessel is the **cazuela** (earthenware cooking dish) with a flat bottom and straight sides about 5cm high. These are the best things for cooking stews, and for roasting meats and fowl. They come in several sizes, from tapa to family.

SHOPPING

Display of glassware at the Alambique Cooking School, Madrid

A proper **queimada** bowl, and its matching cups, is the only proper vessel with which to prepare, serve and enjoy **queimada**, the flaming aguardiente of Galicia. They are for sale in gift shops all over Santiago de Compostela. Most of them are made of ceramic and are painted in complex designs. Other drinking vessels include **chupitos** for drinking cordials and liqueurs. These are small and usually made of clear glass, but sometimes coloured. **Jarras** (pitchers) are good for beer as well as sangría.

Spanish linens for your table are beautiful. They are no longer cheap, but they are nevertheless still beautiful. And to complete your table setting, Toledo cutlery. The swordsmiths of Toledo were famous for centuries as makers of superior weapons. The state of sword fighting being what it is today, they don't do as much business now, so they have taken to making dinner and kitchen knives. Lucky for us.

eat & drink

Feel like hogging into a suckling pig? Or how about just a beer and
a plate of olives? No matter what your budget or belly size, you'll
find an establishment to suit. Nowhere else in the world is eating
and drinking out such an institution. And what greater Spanish
experience is there than the tasca (tapas bar), where eating and
drinking come together in a balance worth raising your caña to.

If you can't find a place to eat, and eat well, in Spain it's because you're holed up in your hotel room wondering where to go. Restaurants have been a part of Spanish culture for centuries. Indeed Spain is home to the oldest restaurant in the world. According to the Guinness Book of Records that would be Sobrino de Botín (established 1725) just off Plaza Mayor in Madrid. Botín is merely the oldest and you'll find many other eateries that are well over 100 years old.

Outdoor cafe at the Guggenheim Museum, Bilbao, Basque Country

Most of these restaurants began as coach houses, places where travellers stopped for the night. Or they were like Botín, what today we might call a working-class tavern or pub. Botín is located on Calle Cuchilleros (Cutlers Street). It was then a lane full of workshops, smithies, potters and the like. At mealtimes the workmen would come to Botín for bread and wine, a bit of ham or chorizo, and some respite from the afternoon sun.

Cafe life, Madrid

Where to Eat
Horno Asador (Roasting Oven)

At some time Botín developed into that quintessentially Spanish restaurant, the **horno asador** (literally, roasting oven). The actual oven is round, with portals and a cooking floor about half way up. It's made of roofing tiles or adobe. One made of firebrick is said to provide a too intense heat. Beneath the cooking floor burns a fire of wood, preferably pine boughs, ash or broom. Baby lambs or kids, suckling pigs, sometimes fowl are placed in **cazuelas** (earthenware cooking dishes) and slid into the oven. In Summer, if the horno asador has no air-conditioning, dining can be challenging. But in the bitter Spanish winter there can be no better place to be. The air is thick with conversation and conviviality. The aromas are maddeningly delicious. Many of them, including Botín, have several floors including a basement where the most romantic setting is. To dine in a horno asador is to slip away from this century into another. Unless you are seated next to a party of cigar smokers. Then it's best to quietly ask for a table on a floor above. Horno asadors are very popular with tourists and locals alike. During high season it's good to get reservations. Dinner costs anywhere between US$10-$30. More if you drink a fine wine.

Terraza (Terrace)

The Spanish love to eat outdoors, so you will find streetside restaurants, known as **terrazas** (terraces) in every city. All you have to do is walk down the street, and you will eventually encounter several. This assumes you are walking in the centre of the city, its 'old town'. All major cities in Spain these days have modern metropolises growing like tumours at the edges. Many of them look as though they were designed by Soviet rationalist architects. We make no guarantees about what you will find there. But as a tourist you probably will be staying in the old town. So take a walk when you get hungry. When you find a terraza there will be awnings, umbrellas, even trees to fend off the sun. Most of them also have an interior dining room, if you prefer to get out of the weather. Whole blocks will be given over to these establishments. And when you find them thus clustered, you'll discover that they all tend to have very similar menus. So make your choice of restaurant based less on the menu and more on its ambience, service or view of the world passing by. Reservations are generally not taken, but if there is a crowd they will start a waiting list. If you absolutely must dine at that terraza, then do put your name on the list. But there are always others.

Outside Los Caracoles Restaurante, Barcelona, Catalunya

WHERE TO EAT & DRINK

Parador Restaurante, Santiago de Compostela, Galicia

Restaurante (Restaurant)

A proper sit-down restaurant in Spain is like any other in the western world. The customs and protocols are pretty much the same. No real pitfalls. One style difference is that they tend to be small and intimate. If they want to increase floor space they increase the number of floors, not the space. Real estate is expensive, and besides, the Spanish like intimacy. Reservations are accepted, and often required during high season. If it is one of the famous temples to gastronomy like Arzak in the Basque Country or Bulli in Catalunya, reservations are required year round and often far in advance.

Tipping is problematic in Spain. It is not really the custom among Spaniards, and there's always a service charge in restaurants, so the staff are being paid a living wage, in theory at least. In observing Spanish diners we have rarely seen them leave a tip, and then little more than loose change. If you pay by credit card there isn't even a space on your charge form for a tip amount. And if you do leave a tip it all goes into a common pot, so your waiter will not really be rewarded for good service. And since he isn't expecting to be rewarded, you just might not get very good service. Usually restaurant service is matter-of-fact and workman-like. Nothing to condemn, but nothing much to reward either. Our advice? Leave your small change. It accumulates in your pocket very quickly.

Casa de Comidas (Working-Class Restaurant)

There is one type of restaurant that is never mentioned in guide books. And we are reluctant to do so here. But we trust you not to spread this around. Want a cheap meal of wholesome fare with good service? Unless you are staying at an expensive hotel, you could ask the receptionist "where do you go for lunch?" or ask them "where can I find a working-class restaurant?" They will probably direct you to a place across the street or otherwise very near. Working-class restaurants are, penny for penny, the best deal in Spain. You can get a lunch at the Costa del Sol (7 Tres Cruces, Madrid) consisting of two fried trout, potatoes, bread, a tall can of beer, salad and a platter of vegetables for about US$8. And on the subject of vegetables, since they are cheaper than meat, these fibre-friendly restaurants will have them on the menu.

CLOSED FOR LUNCH

Many business enterprises, including restaurants, tascas and bars, close for **mediodia** (midday) – which actually means somewhere between 4-8pm. In some areas, especially rural or small town areas, this is the norm. To let you know where you may still come for a tipple or a bite or both, those that remain open during the long, hot afternoon will display a sign proclaiming: **no cierramos por la mediodia** (we don't close at midday).

Cerveza, agua, good food and company, Santiago, Galicia

Tapas bar in San Sebastián, Basque Country

Tasca (Tapas Bar)

Then there is the tasca. This is the most common type of eatery in the Heart of Spain region, and very common everywhere else. They are sometimes large, they are often small, and they are sometimes the bar of a proper sit-down restaurant. Tascas can be grand or grotty. They can have marble floors or floors covered with sawdust, spit, cigarette butts and substances you'd rather not contemplate. But these tascas are sometimes the best! At least the most fun.

Consider a tasca in the Lavapies district of Madrid, at about 10pm. Patrons pressed against the bar, shouting their orders to the barman. It's smoky, a bit gritty, reflecting the working-class and student neighbourhood. A guitarist is trying to make himself heard. Soon the crowd swells, and spills out onto the streets. Per custom, the patrons carry their drinks and tapas with them and the party continues outside, spreading into a nearby plaza or parking lot. In this tasca there is an open window near the bar where the people outside can pass in empty glasses and receive them recharged, a tapa resting on top. You avoid puns like 'sitting on tapa the world'. You gingerly shoulder your way in through the bustle and surrender yourself to the aromas of garlic, vinegar, boiled shrimp, ham, cheese, saffron, all emanating from a bar groaning with bowls and platters heaped high with tapas. Perhaps the last bar you were in (for you surely have been at another already) had a **lista de precios** (price list) on the wall, and the barman kept track by writing down your selections in chalk on the wooden bar. But here you just take what you like as the evening progresses, keeping track yourself. The honour system is in play. In some bars, tapas are served on toothpicks and the barman will count them to add up your tariff. Let's see, three toothpicks and a **vino de la casa** (house wine) comes to about US$4. Plenty left in your pocket for the next tasca.

Fish for tapas, San Sebastián, Basque Country

WHERE TO EAT & DRINK

Tapas, San Sebastián, Basque Country

One of the great things about tascas is that they'll sell you any of their goods **para llevar** (take away). Need a bottle of water or a can of beer as you trudge down the heated highway? Step into the nearest tasca. No problema. Do you like that wine you just had a glass of? Get a bottle. They'll even open it for you. Carry it with you when you go. And the same goes for tapas when it's time for an impromptu picnic.

Jamónería (Ham House)

The Spanish don't merely enjoy, or even love, their **jamón** (ham). Truth be known they worship the Holy Ham. You will see shrines to it everywhere. Jamónerías, all hung heavily with hams, are among the most common type of restaurant. Inside, hams hang thickly from the ceilings and walls. They grace the bar. Their hammy scent fills the air. And the establishments have names that sing the importance of ham. You will see names like The Palace of Ham; The Jewel of Ham; The Museum of Ham; The Salon of Ham. But the ultimate ham sight in all of Spain, the hammiest, the jamónissimo, is La Catedral del Jamón (The Cathedral of Ham), Palacio de la Bellota, Mosen Fernandes 7, Valencia. 'Donde jamón es jamón!' is their proud motto. 'Where ham is ham!' Within this hammy cloister the hams are so numerous that they obscure the ceiling from which they hang. They are a forest of hams! A stalactite cavern of cured hindquarters! To take a table in this place is almost intimidating, as though you are sitting beneath some terrible Sword of Jamónocles. If you are an observant Muslim or Jew it could give you the creeps, or fill you with a strange desire to convert among this hammy host of hundreds. Ironically, this is a seafood restaurant. And the fried fish is especially good. Nevertheless, the hams are not just here for show. They are the popular appetiser, and the restaurant goes through a lot of them. For fish may be fish, but here ham is ham!

A delivery of ham, Santiago de Compostela, Galicia

Vegetarians & Vegans

To our friends who are vegetarian or vegan, we offer some advice. So you've come to Spain for the artworks, the architecture, the history. Ahh, España! Now all you have to do is keep from starving. Well, if you are vegetarian, you'll survive. You may get tired of living on salad and bread and the odd vegetarian paella. But you'll get by. You'll probably become a familiar face at the local **frutería** (fruit stall), and they'll be glad to see you. At the tasca you'll find more plant kingdom comestibles than at a proper sit-down restaurant. Many tapas are vegetables or fruits. **Garbanzos con espinacas** (chickpeas and spinach) are a favourite in the Heart of Spain region, as are salads of beetroot and onion, and potato dishes such as **patatas bravas** (potatoes in a spicy tomato sauce). Dishes of pulses, such as **lentejas** (lentils) are here and there, and cheese is plentiful. Artichokes are popular and olives are always good. The occasional pastry will be rewarding. However most vegetable dishes are had in the home. Be aware. People go to restaurants to eat flesh.

The one place in Spain where you could dine for 40 days and 40 nights on vegetarian fare without fear or loathing would be in Barcelona. That is because Barcelona currently has 40 vegetarian restaurants. By our estimate, that is equal to all the other vegetarian restaurants in Spain combined. Madrid has a few, Sevilla one, Cádiz none, Galicia two. The Basques haven't heard of vegetarianism, except as a survival response to famine and war, or as a foreign cult designed to make men less manly and women more so. Try to pry them from their cod and you risk life and limb. A vegetarian restaurateur, owner of Restaurant Banía in La Coruña, advises that you search for vegetarian restaurants on the internet before coming to Spain. We think this is sound advice. If you don't do this before your arrival, at least consult the restaurant listings in the telephone book afterward. You may find something. You can also ask your hotel reception. It is unlikely they will know of a vegetarian eatery, but they might be able to help you find one.

I'LL HAVE THE VEGETARIAN VERSION, PLEASE

One thing to remember in Spain is that the concept of vegetarian isn't always readily understood. I was sitting at a cafe in León with friends. The menu listed a 'vegetarian sandwich' and a 'special vegetarian sandwich'. One of my friends asked the waiter what the difference was. He explained that the 'special vegetarian' had everything on it that the 'vegetarian' had, but also included ham and cheese.

John Buczynski-Carlson

Toros de Osborne, Andalucía

GRAZING HELL – Tips For The Transient Herbivore

Dead pig is a vegetable. Many Spanish cooks will attest to this. You specifically ordered your dish 'without meat' and incredulously watch the straight-faced waiter defend those surprise bits of mystery flesh with "that's not meat, it's ham".

The visiting vegetarian must pack a small stash of vitamins and a big sense of humour. It's not to say you can't enjoy a wide variety of Spanish delicacies, but if you find devouring any of God's creatures repulsive, you'll need to be diligent. A strategy for the transient herbivore might be to map out all the vegetarian restaurants and stick to that route. This would be about as typically Spanish as pursuing a route of Hare Krishna temples. You can do it, but where's the Spain in it?

Upon moving to Madrid many years ago, I was a non-smoking, non-drinking, coffee-eschewing, militant vegetarian. In tribute to that virtuous but deprived youth, I still embrace the herbivorous realm. With time, though, I make further concessions to this meat-and-potatoes culture and slip into what I call 'fuzzy logic' vegetarianism (it's kind of, sort of, not meat). Basically, I'm a whore. But if you're Snow White – and want to leave without having devoured any of the seven dwarves – there are ways to swim with the omnivores.

All 'normal' restaurants offer a three-course **menú del día** (the day's set menu). Courses offered are often filling and vegetarian friendly. These fixed-price daily specials are clearly advertised outside the restaurant, thus saving you problems within. Politely tell the waiter your preference; but remember, in Spain the customer – particularly the vegetarian one – is never right.

Children

Are you travelling with children? Good. The Spanish adore children, and take them everywhere, even to bars and to all but the smartest restaurants. They dress them up like living dolls, parade them on the paseo, fuss over them and buy them far too many sweets. Even newborn babies are proudly conveyed in gorgeously expensive prams and parked next to an outdoor cafe table. You are most welcome to make goo-goo noises to them and ask their parents how old they are, and they will be delighted. Ah, the blessed sound of little feet. And voices. You will often hear them squealing with delight, shrieking in protest, and hollering to each other as they play a spirited game of tag or hide-and-seek around, or under, your table. And as long as they don't break anything or eat from your plate their parents will look upon them with adoration, or just ignore them.

We are fortunate to count beer and wine as offspring of the plant kingdom. When it comes to tapas, and you make no exceptions for fish, your experience will be dominated by various incarnations of potato, egg and cheese. If you eschew both eggs and dairy products, brace yourself for the Spanish Potato Famine.

In a country where vegan means pagan, you might as well pack a lunch and listen to the culinary accounts of others. Unless you've been invited to some esoteric vegan-crudivore convention, it's time to get in the picnic frame of mind. Whether it's tomatoes, lettuce and avocado, or canned white asparagus and artichoke hearts, the markets always offer something fresh and delicious to stick in a baguette.

We all occasionally need to be loved, to be doted on by one of our own. This is where vegetarian restaurants come in. Spanish vegetarian food is topographically ambiguous fare – what in polite circles is called 'international'. Dishes tend to lean toward the ovo-lacto, but you can be assured there were no squealing animal deaths during preparation. These meat-free zones also offer a menú del día, usually including a choice of soup or salad followed by a mixed plate of assorted entrees. It is also easy to find vegetarian paella, **croquetas** (croquettes) and other meatless, whole-grain versions of Spanish classics. While some establishments are relatively upmarket, others have a sectarian 70s health food feel to them. By the time the sandal-clad waiter brings your herbal tea, you will have perused all the flyers offering to teach you yoga, cleanse your chakra, and open your third eye.

Once back in the real world of Spanish gastronomy, don't drop your guard. March onward in your quest for meatless dishes, armed always with the culinary caveat, "without meat – and without ham".

Brett Allan King

A quiet Sunday lunch can suddenly turn into a cacophony if someone brings enough offspring. It is rewarding to watch tray-laden waiters weave through them, never dropping a thing. But the diversion is poor payment for your whispered conversation being forced to a sustained shout. The kids might eventually settle down. Or they might not. You could try scolding the children. But it's unlikely they will listen. You could complain to the waiter. But he will only shrug and wonder why you don't just stay home if you hate children so much. You could complain to the parents; this can be effective for as much as one full minute. You could get up and walk out in a huff, stating you'll never come back to this place again! But you'll still have to pay the bill. So why not just do as the Spanish do: order another drink. Or two.

After all, if the kids are having fun, shouldn't you?

Where to Drink

Firstly, a few practical matters. In Spain eating and drinking are things done together. The notion of going to a bar where only alcohol is served is foreign to the Spaniard. But the Anglo-American world (and we include the Aussies, Canadians and Kiwis among the guilty) is making inroads. Slowly, very slowly, but measurably. If you really must have a properly made dry Martini, and we must now and then, betake yourself to the Palace Hotel in Madrid. The bar staff know exactly what they are doing. And they don't buy the notion of the dry, dry, dry, desiccated dry Martini. They actually put a splash of vermouth in it, and they shake it into submission with plenty of ice. Other luxury hotels are similarly staffed and equipped. If it has four or more stars, it has good drinks.

La Fontana de Oro, wine shop and bar, Madrid

The only other alternative we can offer at this time is Bar Antillano Coctelería (5 Calle Coloreros, Madrid). Here they make a scholarly study of mixology. In a faintly Cuban atmosphere with lovely old-time jazz played discreetly in the background, you can order classic cocktails and play stump the barman. Outside these and no doubt a very few other venues, the only properly mixed cocktail you can count on is gin & tonic. And that's a fine drink. But neither man, nor woman, lives on gin & tonic alone.

Tio Pepe sign, Puerta del Sol, Madrid

Pubs, saloons, cocktail lounges, **tabernas** (bars), **mesones** (subterranean taverns) and **cervecerías** (beer bars), all those watering holes that you take for granted as part of a civilised life, are rare things in Spain. Many places are called 'bar' though they are really tascas. You may stumble onto a small, dark hole in the wall that serves little more than beer or sherry. Its patrons are almost all elderly men, and the ambience is rather subdued. They aren't sleazy dives, though they are less expensive than tascas. The old pensioners might spend a lazy afternoon in them, but don't come here for a party at night. Andalucía is the best region to find such places. But you should always keep in mind that Spain is an intoxicating, not an intoxicated, culture.

Night life in Habanilla Cafe, Sevilla, Andalucía

Eating and drinking in a bodega in the Santa Cruz district, Sevilla, Andalucía

Sidrería (Cider Bar)

The best way to enjoy cider is in a **sidrería**, an establishment where cider is made, served, or both. Sidrerías are common in the Atlantic region and in the Basque Country. They are usually rustic places, with plain wooden benches and long tables. Huge wooden vats line the walls, and each vat is named, for a patron saint, a sports hero, a movie star. There is one in Asturias said to be named for a man's mistress.

Cider must be poured with ceremony and enjoyed in prescribed fashion. If poured from the vat, a tube about the size of a cigarette is pounded into the vessel's side at about shoulder height to act as a tap. You, the drinker, stand at the ready with a wide glass in hand. When the tap is opened it shoots a thin stream of golden cider out to a distance of about five feet. The sight of this cannot but help recall the image of a gentleman passing – shall we say – cider. Holding your glass out you catch about half a glass and no more. This is because you must drink it rather quickly. Once exposed to air the cider goes off in minutes. There should be a bucket or a keg nearby, or there will be a porcelain-lined trough along the bottom of the bar. Pour your dregs into this.

This kind of 'draught' cider also comes in 1 litre green bottles. In order to achieve the same aeration that the vat method provides, the cider server takes the bottle and holds it up as high as possible while holding the glass in the other hand as low as possible. Much cider ends up on the floor. If you order cider in a Galician or Asturian restaurant, it will be served in a bottle with a cap that opens automatically when the bottle is tipped.

Non-Alcoholic Drinkeries

If a tipple isn't on your mind, you can find establishments dedicated to the drinking of non-alcoholic beverages. **Horchaterías** serve **horchata** (tiger nut milk) and little else. The grander ones also offer horchata ice cream, as well as coffee and soft drinks. Look for them most often in Valencia. The **chocolatería** is an institution in Spain, though at first glance it looks hardly any different from a bar or tasca. It will have a long, stand-up bar as well as tables or booths. You might think it's something like a coffee shop, but the sign over the door says chocolatería. They usually stop serving chocolate by lunch time, but you can always get a soda or a snack. Except in Barcelona and parts of Madrid, you won't see much in the way of dedicated coffee or tea houses. Virtually every eating and drinking establishment in the nation serves coffee, and few people drink proper tea. In the dining cars of trains you will often see 'bitters' offered as an aperitif. In the Anglophone world, bitters are often mixed with gin or whisky. In Spain they drink their bitters plain, or 'without'. In Spanish the word for 'without' is **sin**. So no matter how virtuous you are, you can always enjoy a 'bitter sin'.

understanding
the menu

The food may be new, the waiters slick, but don't be intimidated by the ordering process. Spanish menus are straightforward, and even if you order dessert first (by mistake or by choice) no one will scold you. Just take a moment to familiarise yourself with a few words and you'll be ordering your primer plato with the best of them.

Let the Spanish menu hold no dread for you. Among other European examples it is one of the more user friendly. There is only one landmine to be mindful of, and we'll reach that shortly. There are actually two genres of menu: the sitting and the standing. The standing menu is always posted on the wall of the **tasca** (tapas bar). It may be a simple printed poster, it might be a chalkboard with entries in colourful florid script (the Spanish love florid script). In Madrid it's common to see a crafted wooden board, polished and fixed with slots into which smaller boards can be inserted or removed as selections change. And in the Basque country the whole thing is greatly simplified. A small notice on the wall announces that tapas – or **pintxos** as they are known here – are priced at X pesetas and **raciones** (full portions) are priced at something more, usually double. The pintxos are all laid out upon the bar in a beautiful display of culinary abundance and all you need to do is begin eating. When you are satisfied, tell the barman how many you ate and you'll be charged accordingly. It's the honour system in much of the Basque country. So much for the menu. Elsewhere, just look up at the wall or at the display, see what you like, and tell your tapster. He'll serve you and keep track of your bill. All you have to do is eat, drink and pay. Then, even in the humblest little, darkest little, most out of the way little tasca, the Spanish niceties will be observed: your change will be presented in a little dish, never given from hand to hand or hand to bar. Printed menus that are brought to your table are of two sorts: the **menú del día** (the day's set menu) and the **menú la carta** (a la carte menu).

Gazpacho y vino tinto (sounds better than soup and a glass of red), Sevilla, Andalucía

Menú del Día (Day's Set Menu)

By law all restaurants in Spain (as opposed to tascas) are required to offer a luncheon known as the menú del día. It must consist of three courses plus bread, and water or wine. The third course is always dessert. The price of the menú del día is always less than if you were to order the same items a la carte. Typical prices for the menú del día run between US$8-$12. It's one of the best deals in Spain. When you are presented with the menú del día you will see that it is divided into three course groups followed by the bread, water or wine notice. There may be only two or three offerings per course; there may be as many as 20. Choose one from column A, one from column B, and one from column C. Some restaurants will offer two versions of the menú del día: one of meat, the other of seafood. The seafood will always be more expensive.

Updating the menu at Parador Restaurante, Santiago de Compostela, Galicia

The **primer plato** (first course) will include the lighter dishes such as soups and salads. A common primer plato soup is **caldo gallego**, a concept more than a recipe but usually a clear broth with greens and a bit of meat. **Gazpacho** (cold tomato soup) is also a standard and quite variable. And there is often some kind of seafood soup, anything from a simple bisque

to a hearty **zarzuela** (spicy fish stew) bursting with shellfish. There will be a simple **ensalada** (salad) available, consisting of lettuce, onion and tomato. Also common is **ensalada mixta** (mixed salad) with extras such as asparagus or even fresh tuna. You will see **asparragos con dos salsas** (asparagus with mayonnaise) and **salsa rosa** (mayonnaise with paprika).

And here on the menú del día we depart from all that we have been taught about gastronomic order and continuity, digestive common sense and moderation. Under the wise influence of the French, the Greeks and the Italians we have come to agree that dishes early on in the course of a satisfying meal should be low in calories, or light upon the tongue, or cleansing to the palate, or high in acidity, or some combination thereof, all in order to stimulate the gastric juices and prepare the stomach and the mind for the great gastronomic work ahead. Surely there are exceptions such as froi gras, a traditional appetiser not so light, cleansing or acidic, but taken in traditionally small portions, stimulating the appetite. But the bulk of Spanish primeros platos are exactly that: bulk!

Seafood platter at Los Caracoles Restaurante, Barcelona, Catalunya

Paella, full of rice, oil and meat or fish, served in great portions, is a common first course. A big platter of fried sardines or anchovies, freshly caught that morning, are another. They are delicious, and usually enough to feed two! **Empanadas** (savoury pies); fish puddings; 'salads' consisting of heaps of cod plus a few bits of lettuce; casseroles of beans, sausage and bacon;

An orderly fashion of chairs, Barcelona, Catalunya

trenchers of ham with cheese and the odd slice of tomato masquerading under the name of something like 'ensalada catalana' make up some of the dishes you will be confronted with in the primer plato selection. And you haven't even looked at the second course yet. Beware!

Now your choice of **segundo plato** (second course) will be simplified in comparison with the first. This is basically the meat, fish and potatoes section of the menu. Almost everything here is fried: steaks, chops, fish, and chips. If it isn't fried it's prepared in a brick or adobe **horno** (oven), or baked in a **cazuela** (earthenware cooking dish). And if you think that the primero plato was huge, wait until you're called upon to assail the mighty fortress of the segundo plato! Unless you're used to the Spanish regimen, you will run up the white flag of surrender long before you have made serious inroads into the segundo plato. And, of course, you will have bread and your choice of mineral water or wine. And then will come the **postre** (dessert). Mercifully, this will be a small dish, such as a flan, **crema catalana** (creme brulee), or a small dish of fresh fruit, the most popular Spanish dessert.

Now here is the good news and the bad news about the menú del día. The good news is that if you are not dining alone it is perfectly acceptable to **compartir** (share). Simply order one lunch and tell the waiter that it is '**para compartir**' (to be shared). There will be no questions asked, no disapproving glances, just two sets of plates for one order of the menú del día. You will probably want to order another beverage, but that will cost little. With this plan, two of you can have a cheap hearty lunch and not send wasteful portions back to the kitchen. Win win situation.

Now for the bad news. There are no substitutions. There are no changes permitted. There is no allowance for customer preferences. You'd rather have two primeros platos and no segundo? Or vice versa? Diablos! Never! What? What? You want something not clearly spelled out on the menu? Are you trying to cause trouble? You want to deviate from the plan? We accommodate no deviants here, Senor! The chef is *un artiste*! Well, maybe he's not exactly *un artiste*, but he *is* an unyielding sod who *thinks* he is *un artiste*. And you are not going to get even the slightest deviation from the hallowed precepts of the lawfully defined menú del día! Harumph!

The only way around these ramparts of cultural implacability is through subterfuge. You can, if you are willing to be looked upon as somewhat odd, tell the waiter that you are a vegetarian. He will assume that you are a person not to be reasoned with and, rather than take the time to correct you, accommodate you. Of course you have now limited yourself to salad and gazpacho or, if you are lucky, an onion tart, but we have found this not a bad thing.

Menú la Carta (A la Carte Menu)

The menú la carta is also available at lunch, and it is the only one for your evening meal. It is simplicity itself, divided into food types: meat, fish, fowl, dessert and so on. In the smarter restaurants the menu may lead with a selection of **entreméses** (starters) but you are free to have anything you wish and in whatever order. There is no overweening sense of culinary punctilio. In grander restaurants, especially in the Basque country, you may see two sections of dessert items: those that must be ordered **al principio de la comida** (at the start of the meal) and those that can be ordered **al momento** (at any time). And in the grandest restaurants there is the excellent custom of the **menu degustación** (tasting menu), which comprises selected small portions of many dishes. It usually requires a minimum number of diners. Only one note of caution on the menú la carta: don't try to get anything not specifically listed, or cooked in some slightly different way. Spanish cooks don't like to improvise and waiters don't like to confront them.

NOTHING ON THE SIDE

A conversation overheard in a restaurant.

Diner: And please bring me a side order of fried potatoes.

Waiter: Sir?

D: French fries. You know, chips.

W: Side order, sir? I don't understand.

D: You know, on the side. Just a dish of fried potatoes.

W: Nothing else, sir?

D: Right.

W: Sir I can't give you that. It's not on the menu.

D: But that man over there is having them with his lamb chops.

W: That's because they come with the lamb chops. The cook won't give them to me separately.

D: You mean I have to order the chops to get the chips?

W: Yes sir.

D: Why don't you just bring me lamb chops and chips but hold the lamb chops.

W: I'll have to charge you for the lamb chops, Sir. I wouldn't know what to charge for the chips alone. They're not on the menu.

Carta de Vinos (Wine List)

Like the menú la carta, the carta de vinos is straightforward, listing reds, whites, the odd rosé or **cava** (sparkling wine). Sherry is so common it is taken for granted. You will seldom see imported wines on the list. If you are not familiar with the wines listed don't bother asking the waiter for advice.

Food and wine outside Bodega de Sarria, Navarra

He probably hasn't tasted them all, and at any rate he will only tell you what he likes. And that is the Spanish way with wine. They put up with no Frenchified horse feathers about serving only the correct crisp Loire Valley white (second growth of course) with your shrimps, crayfish and other minor crustacea. Down, down to hell with such ways, say the Spanish. Drink what you like. The Spanish will even mix their wine with water, or put ice in it on a hot day. While they will generally drink red wine with meat and white wine with fish, if you do the opposite you will not be punished. So if you can't decide on your wine, order the **vino de la casa** (house wine). You won't be disappointed. Considering the rigidity of the menú del día, the wine list seems almost schizophrenic.

In the grandest restaurants, and this only in the last decade or so, **sommeliers** (wine stewards) have started to appear. These people are certified caretakers of and advisors on the wines offered by the house. They know the characteristics of each and every wine on the list, and each year they taste many of them again as they age. Their advice is impeccable, and disposable. You may still have absolutely anything you like. Salud!

a spanish
banquet

The simplicity of Spanish cuisine means a banquet need not be a tiresome chore for the host, and Spanish food tastes better when shared with friends anyway. Indeed no matter if you're risking a paella creation or just throwing together olives and other easy morsels, if friends are to be had, the banquet will be a success.

Paella de la Huerta
(Paella with Rabbit and Vegetables)
In cooking paella, you should use a heat source as big as the pan. Traditionally, and in the best places today, the source is an open fire of vine cuttings or citrus trimmings. If you're using an ordinary gas stove (cooker) you'll want to straddle the pan over two burners or set it on your largest burner. And you'll still want to move and rotate the pan to distribute the heat. Or you could just set the pan on the barbecue. One other detail: paella should be cooked by men. After working in the fields and orchards, the menfolk gathered, kindled a fire and cooked and ate together. This tradition lives on.

3	cups chicken stock, simmering
8-10	saffron threads, toasted, ground and added to the stock
	salt to taste
1/4	cup pure olive oil
4	pieces of rabbit (or chicken) seasoned with salt and pepper
1	red capsicum, cored, seeded, and cut into thin strips
1	small whole bulb of garlic
6	medium-size garlic cloves, peeled
250g	asparagus, washed and cut into 2cm pieces
100g	green beans, trimmed
1/2	medium onion, finely minced
1	ripe tomato, peeled and chopped
1 1/2	cups short grain rice
1/2	cup cooked (or canned) white beans
1	lemon, quartered

In a 36cm paella pan or skillet heat the oil over medium-high heat. Saute the rabbit pieces until thoroughly browned (10-15 minutes). Transfer to a platter and set aside.

So now you've been to Spain and can't wait for the taste of more. Or maybe you haven't been but would like to experience what you can at home. By now you know well what a Spanish meal is composed of: the Holy Trinity (bread, oil, wine) and two touchstones (garlic, conviviality). Serve these and no Spaniard will fault you. Even if it doesn't quite taste like Spain, it will savour of a good attempt. Aviento!

Your Spanish banquet will be thick with conviviality. It will not be stodgy or ponderous or fussy. It will be as lively as **cava** (sparkling wine), as colourful as saffron, and as rich as fine olive oil. Set your table simply,

Reduce the heat to medium low and saute the red capsicum, bulb of garlic and garlic cloves until the capsicum is translucent (5-10 minutes).

Set aside the capsicums and garlic cloves. Saute the asparagus and green beans until al dente (3-5 minutes). Set aside.

Pour off excess oil from the pan, increase the heat to medium and saute the onion until soft (about 5 minutes). Add the tomato and the reserved garlic and cook until the mixture is reduced to a thick puree (10-15 minutes). If you're not cooking the rice immediately, remove the paella pan from the heat. The mixture in the pan is called the **sofrito**, and it is the flavour base for the paella. This is what you want the rice to stay in close contact with during cooking. You can set this aside for several hours before finishing the dish.

Add the rice, stirring until translucent (1-2 minutes). Stir the pan to evenly distribute the rice. Manoeuvre the bulb of garlic to the centre and add the stock. When the stock comes to a boil lay the vegetables in the pan in a pinwheel pattern. Add the rabbit pieces and the white beans. Do not stir the rice once the stock is boiling. Increase the heat to medium high and cook, rotating and swirling the pan to distribute the heat evenly. When the rice absorbs enough liquid to rise to the surface (8-10 minutes), reduce the heat to medium low.

Continue to simmer until the liquid has been absorbed (10 minutes). Taste a grain just below the top layer of rice; it should be tender but not mushy. If the rice is not done but all the liquid has been absorbed, add more hot stock and cook a few minutes longer.

At this point you can cover the pan or put it in the oven at 180°C for a few minutes until the top surface is fully cooked. Then, on the burner, raise the heat to medium high for about 2 minutes until the bottom of the rice begins to toast, creating the socarrat.

Remove it from the heat and let it rest about 5 minutes. Set the pan on the table and give each diner a wedge of lemon. Eat from the pan.

Serves 4

with a minimum of dishes, utensils and display. A white cloth, glasses for water and wine, knife, fork and spoon for each diner. If you would like a centrepiece, a colourful bowl of fruit is better than flowers. Or a pitcher of sangría looks festive, even if you don't drink it (see the recipe in the Drinks chapter). Make sure every diner is served bread on a small plate. Also provide a cruet of olive oil rather than butter.

So what's on your menu? You could take two basic approaches. You could serve regional fare, or you could make it pan-Spanish, taking a bit from each region for a national **menu degustación** (tasting menu). A

Garbanzos con Espinacas
(Chickpeas with Spinach)

Ingredients

300g	spinach, chopped
2	cloves garlic
1	slice of white bread
1	pinch of salt
1	pinch paprika
1	pinch cinnamon
1	pinch cumin
1	pinch cayenne
½	teaspoon sherry vinegar
¾	cup chickpeas, soaked and cooked
2	tablespoons olive oil

Wash the spinach and cook it in ½cm of water, in an uncovered pan until tender and dry. Heat half the oil in a skillet and fry the bread and garlic until both are brown. Transfer them to a mortar, add salt and vinegar and pound to a paste. Heat the remaining oil and fry all the ingredients together for 5 minutes. Thin with a little water if it gets too dry. It should have a consistency that holds together in a spoon. Let the mixture rest about half an hour so the flavours marry. Serve hot or at room temperature in small bowls.

Serves 4 as a tapa

Compota de Peras (Pear Compote)

Ingredients
1kg   pears
250g   sugar
2   cups water
2   cinnamon sticks
grated zest of half a lemon

Peel and core the pears. Place in a pot with the remaining ingredients and bring to a boil. Cook for 10-15 minutes, or until the pears are very soft but still hold their shape. Serve at room temperature along with some of the cooking syrup.

Makes 5 servings

Pears, Santiago de Compostela, Galicia

Mediterranean dinner might be the easiest to pull together outside Spain. To keep a true Barcelona feeling, your music should not be flamenco. Bright and cheery string quartets would be more in keeping with Spain's most European city. Greet your guests with glasses of cava. If you can't find the genuine article, California sparkling wine would be a closer substitute than French Champagne. Let your guests sit and relax with their wine, and give them some olives or almonds to nibble. Or, for a real hands-on Spanish experience, serve **pá amb tomáquet** (tomato bread). Serve a platter of toasted, rough textured bread. Give each guest a peeled clove of cut garlic and half a small tomato. Show them how to first rub the bread with the garlic, then the tomato. Sprinkle it with salt then drizzle it with a fruity Catalunyan olive oil. If they complain about their hands smelling of garlic, scold them, and make them lick their fingers.

Meanwhile, you will have made your paella up to the point of the **sofrito** (see the recipe). Serve a fresh **ensalada mixta** (mixed salad) on chilled plates, before beckoning the guests to table. Finish your paella, adding the rice and stock. This will take you about 20 minutes, during which time you can see

that the cava keeps flowing and the guests are convivial and redolent of the garlic, also known as 'stinking rose'. When the paella is done, cover it with foil and place it in a warm oven. Dinner is served. Sangría will go well enough with your salad, as will **agua mineral** (mineral water), or even more cava. To go with your paella, serve a lighter Rioja, red or white. And don't forget a scoop of mayo.

And for dessert, eat your fruity centrepiece with chocolates and cream sherry. Or prepare a **compota de peras** (pear compote).

But why not make your Spanish banquet a night of tapas. As you have discovered, anything can be turned into a tapa, from olives on toothpicks to the hearty vegetable stew, **pisto manchego**. But how to make them with the real tastes of Spain? Firstly, take everything outside, and bring the kids. The Spanish would. And what about the tapas? Obviously you can't take your guests out on a genuine **tapeo**, a tapas crawl. But you can bring at least some of the spirit of the **tasca** (tapas bar) to them. Outside in the fine weather, play a little flamenco music and tell your friends that they are now in the plaza or on the street outside the first of many tascas. See that Spanish wine, sherry and beer (local if need be) are poured freely. Start up the engines of conversation, open the vessels of mirth, swirl the air with conviviality. Then bring on the tapas. Bring them one selection at a time, not en masse. With each new selection served, announce your arrival at the next tasca. Change the music. Change the wine. Change your clothes if you must. But keep changing and keep serving until they cry for mercy. Then inform them that no one goes to bed here in Madrid until they have killed the night.

Other possibilities for a tapas spread include tuna and green capsicum; preserved olives, whole or pitted, stuffed with almonds or anchovies; clams in their juices; anchovies, sardines and tuna fillet in olive oil; marinated mussels or tuna. You could prepare more expensive items such as **anguilas a la vasca** (eels with chillies and garlic) or **pulpo** (octopus) in olive oil. These tapas can be made a little more substantial by spearing them to a piece of bread with a toothpick, perhaps drizzling them with olive oil.

Tapas from **latas** (cans) are common in Spain and easy to buy in shops to take home. If you live in a large city you might find them at speciality importers. **Calamares en su tinta** (squid cooked in its ink) is a popular choice, as is a canned version of pisto manchego.

What with Spanish cheeses being exported in greater variety you can serve a **tabla de quesos** (cheese board). A rich addition you can make easily is **Manchego** (hard sheep's milk cheese) preserved in olive oil. Cut the cheese into square slices, then diagonally to form triangles. Pierce the triangles several times with a toothpick so the oil soaks in well. It will keep

Eating in Los Caracoles Restaurante, Barcelona, Catalunya

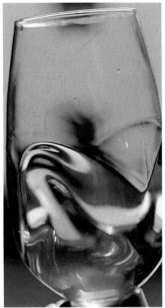

Extra virgin olive oil

like this for up to a year, with the flavour constantly maturing, but you can enjoy it after a month in the soak.

Whole Spanish hams, as well as **cecina** (cured meats) and **salchichón** (cured white sausage) are slowly becoming available outside Spain. They are easily had in the UK. Remember to slice along the grain into wafer-thin, translucent pieces in order to bring out the full taste and aroma. Or buy it pre-sliced and vacuum packed.

If all else fails, remember the *sine qua non*: olive oil. If you have Spanish olive oil you can pour it on anything and call it Spanish. "Yes" you will say. "These are Spanish bangers. Aren't they delicious? And do try one of these pie floaters, or some of this Spam. The olive oil is from Andalucía." Be a fearless cook and never apologise. The Spanish wouldn't. Buen Provecho!

fit & healthy

There's no hiding the amount of oil used in Spanish fare, and sometimes oil seems to be the main ingredient of a meal. But there is enough fresh and healthy produce here to make for a balanced diet. Also, Spain has the perfect climate for aimless wandering and summer swimming, plenty of opportunity to shed what you may gain round the gullet.

So you want to eat your way through Spain and not get sick or gain weight? You want to broaden your mind without loosening your bowels? The short answer, then, is to watch your intake and get plenty of exercise. Easily said and not so easily done. The food in Spain is often very rich, mainly due to the heavy use of olive oil. And as restaurants in most areas serve little vegetation, you might want to do the following:

- Carry a vitamin supplement.

- Carry a calorie counter and use it. Balance your intake with your activity.

- Avail yourself of local fresh fruit as often as possible. It will help to keep you fit, balanced and regular.

- Most Spanish cities are eminently walkable. So walk. Walk everywhere you can as often as you can. Get out of the car and walk. It's the most convenient and cheap way to exercise anywhere. Walk!

- If it's too far to walk, rent a bicycle.

- Go swimming, in the hotel pool, in the nearby river if it's clean, in the ocean, at the ol' swimmin' hole.

- Go dancing. Often. Spain has many discos if you like dancing in a disco. Couples dancing is not really a tradition for most Spaniards, but Barcelona has an active swing-dancing scene.

- Take along your running shoes. The best place to use them in the cities is in parks. And on the beaches, use the beaches.

- Carry your skipping rope, flexigrips or other portable exercise equipment.

- Make time for some kind of regular exercise, even if it's only twenty minutes in the morning before sallying forth to feast.

- If you belong to any kind of athletic club or social/business club with athletic facilities, find out if clubs along your route have reciprocal privileges.

Crowded beaches on Ibiza Island

OIL OVERLOAD

A word of warning: if you are travelling to Spain you are going to eat olive oil whether you like it or not. You are going to eat it every day, and possibly at every meal. This was written in your fate the moment you booked your airfare. You cannot escape. Few people actually dislike olive oil, but even those who love it can have a surfeit of it (unless we are Spanish). This can result in a slightly bloated feeling, even when the stomach is empty. Even if you haven't eaten for half a day you can still feel rather full, as though extra virgin olive oil is pumping through your veins. To combat this, try to get as much exercise as you possibly can. Burn that stuff off! Also eat fresh fruit or raw vegetables every day. Regular trips to the market or to the local **frutería** (fruit shop) should provide you well.

But while you're planning on getting lots of good healthy exercise, don't plan on hitting the ground running, especially if you're on a long trip. It's worth allowing yourself time to adjust physically and mentally to your new environment and lifestyle, especially in the first week. Factor in some time to take a breather, recover from jet lag and catch up on sleep. Don't overdo the booze or the mayo; work up to your usual party vigour slowly. Try the Spanish schedule of an afternoon siesta. It will make a lot of difference to your stamina.

Hygiene & Water
Basically, sanitation is not a problem. The water is clean. Health codes are of the western European standard. The tap water in Madrid is better than that in London. So go. Have a good time. Don't worry.

Fluid Balance
It is hot in Spain for most of the time. Plain water, lots of it, is the best preventative and remedy for dehydration. Always carry drinking water with you and remind yourself to sip from it regularly while you're out, or stop at lots of places to drink.

Use how much urine you're passing as a rough guide to whether you're getting dehydrated. Small amounts of dark urine suggest you need to increase your fluid intake. Passing reasonable quantities of light yellow urine indicates that you've got the balance about right. As a rule of thumb, drink enough so you produce a reasonable quantity of light-coloured urine every three to four hours while you're awake.

Eating the Right Stuff

Eating well should be fun, but it's also about making sure you get enough of the right nutrients to enable you to function at your best, mentally and physically. While on the road, your diet will be different from normal; in addition, a different lifestyle, stress and new activities may mean your nutritional requirements are increased.

With the help of this book you'll be able to identify available foods for a diverse and nutritious diet. But when you eat can be as important as what you eat. If you're on the move, be careful not to miss meals as this will make you more easily fatigued and vulnerable to illness.

Everybody needs six basics for life (seven if you count beer): water, carbohydrates, protein, fat, vitamins and minerals. Foods aren't a pure source of just one nutrient, they contain various elements in different quantities, so the best way to make sure you get enough of the right things is to eat a varied diet.

You shouldn't find it difficult to maintain a balanced diet here, where the national diet consists of a carbohydrate staple (rice, bread, potatoes) which you eat with a protein source (meat, fish, beans) and vegetables. Fresh fruit is widely available.

As a guide, you need to eat a variety of foods from each of five core groups:

- **bread, other cereals** (rice, potatoes) – eat lots of these, they provide carbohydrate, fibre, some calcium and iron, and B vitamins, though be aware that potatoes will normally be cooked in or dressed with a lot of fat.

- **fruit & vegetables** – eat lots of these, they give you vitamin C, carotenes (vitamin A), folate, fibre and some carbohydrate

- **milk and dairy products** – eat moderate amounts for calcium, zinc, protein, vitamin B12, vitamin B2, vitamin A and vitamin D

- **meat, fish, nuts, beans** – these provide iron, protein, B vitamins (especially B12; meat only), zinc and magnesium; eat in moderation

- **fat and sugary foods** (butter, oil, margarine, cakes, biscuits, sweets, etc) – eat sparingly from this group, which mainly provides fat, including essential fatty acids, some vitamins and salt

Bear in mind that if you're already sick, your requirements change and you may need to increase the amounts of some food groups to increase your intake of protein, vitamins and minerals, for example.

Fading Away?

Losing weight when you're travelling is pretty common. There are lots of reasons for this, including getting sick, having a change in diet and perhaps being more active. You may have a bit of padding to spare, but keep a close eye on how much weight you are losing and don't allow yourself to shed too much, as this may put you at risk of illness, as well as draining you of energy.

If you find you're losing weight, remember that with a vegetarian diet you generally have to eat larger quantities of plant foods to get the same amount of energy. Increase your quota of energy-giving foods, including fats. If you've just turned vegetarian be aware that your body takes a bit of time to adjust to getting some nutrients from plant sources, so it's worth taking a bit of care with your diet. Getting enough protein isn't generally a problem, especially if you eat dairy products or eggs. Note that proteins from plant sources often lack one or more amino acids (the building blocks of protein). Vegetarian diets have traditionally dealt with this by basing meals around a combination of protein sources so that deficiencies are complemented. Examples of combinations include: pulses and rice, pulses and cereal, and nuts and cereal.

Because iron from plant sources isn't absorbed as well as iron from meat, iron-deficiency anaemia is a risk if you aren't careful, especially in menstruating women. Another vitamin you might not get enough of is vitamin B12 as it's only derived from animal sources. If you cut out all animal foods from your diet, you'll need to take a supplement to make up for this. Yeast extracts and fermented soybean substances like tempeh and miso contain a substance similar to B12 but it doesn't have the same effect in the body, so you will still need B12 supplements. Good sources of nutrients include:

protein	pulses, bread, grains, seeds, potatoes, soybeans
calcium	seeds, green leafy vegetables, nuts, bread, dried fruit, tofu
iron	pulses, green vegetables, dried fruits, nuts; absorption of iron is increased by consuming a source of vitamin C at the same time (fruit & vegetables, fruit juice). Tea, coffee, and phytate and oxalates from plants will reduce the absorption of iron

Diarrhoea

Diarrhoea should not be a problem. Although the mere change in the water's mineral balance could bring on a short bout of it. Don't let yourself get run down. Your immune system is suppressed when you're tired, so pace yourself and get sufficient rest. Practice the art of doing nothing now and then. If, despite taking precautions you still get a bout of travellers diarrhoea, don't panic. A few rushed toilet trips with no other symptoms is not indicative of a serious problem. Diarrhoea caused by contaminated food or water is more serious. Dehydration is the main danger with any diarrhoea, particularly for children where dehydration can occur quickly.

If diarrhoea strikes, you should rest – this gives your body the best chance to fight whatever is making you ill. Drink plenty of fluids and check you're not getting dehydrated – weak black tea with a little sugar, carbonated drinks allowed to go flat and diluted 50% with water, are all good. Be aware of how often you're passing urine and what colour it is (see Fluid Balance earlier in this chapter).

Note any other symptoms as diarrhoea can occur in other illnesses, including malaria and hepatitis. Remember that diarrhoea is contagious so be scrupulous about washing your hands after you use the toilet.

What to Eat

It's easy to get hung up about what, if anything, to eat when you have diarrhoea. But relax, use your common sense and try to tune in to what your body is telling you – if you feel like eating, go ahead, especially starchy foods which are known to promote salt and water absorption (such as rice and crackers). If you don't feel like eating, don't force yourself to. Unless you're roughing it, you're going to be basically well nourished and able to withstand a couple of days with little or no food. It may make you feel a bit wobbly, so make sure you add a bit of sugar or honey to your drinks so as to keep your energy levels up.

Your overworked guts will appreciate small amounts of food at regular intervals rather than great big meals, and this may also make you feel less nauseated. You may find that eating brings on cramps and you have to dash to the toilet. We all have a natural reflex whereby eating increases the activity of the gut, but this can get exaggerated in a diarrhoeal illness. It doesn't make you a great dinner companion, but you'll probably find that once you've answered the call of nature you can return to finish your meal (but remember to wash your hands very thoroughly).

Food on the Runs

When you have diarrhoea, it's good to eat:
- plain rice and potatoes
- plain bread
- dry biscuits, salty or not too sweet
- bananas

If possible, it's best to avoid:
- fruit & vegetables, except bananas
- dairy products, including yoghurt
- spicy foods
- oily, greasy foods

Contrary to the spirit of this book, you should stick to a more limited diet while you have diarrhoea and as you recover. You should also go easy on fibre providers like fruit, vegetables and nuts. Bananas are good as they tend to stop you up, and are a source of potassium and glucose. As the diarrhoea clears up and you start to get your appetite back, gradually add in more foods until you are feeling back to normal, and can resume your culinary adventures.

Indigestion
A change in diet, stress, anxiety and fatty foods can all make indigestion (burning pains in your upper abdomen) and heartburn (burning in your gullet, often with an acid taste in your mouth) more likely when you're travelling. The discomfort is often worse when you're hungry or just after meals. Smoking and alcohol exacerbate it.

Simple measures you could try are to eat small, regular meals – don't eat a huge meal just before you go to bed. Milk and yoghurt can be soothing, as can eating plain, starchy foods like bread. You could consider trying antacids (there are many products available without prescription) although stomach acid has a protective effect against infective agents, so this taking antacids may make you more vulnerable to gut infections.

Children's Health
Like many places in the Mediterranean, travelling with children in Spain can be a lot of fun, as long as you come with the right attitudes, equipment and the usual parental patience. All the usual health tips regarding food, heat and diarrhoea mentioned earlier should be followed with extra care, as kids tend to jump into everything with both feet, and can be especially susceptible to the heat.

Parents needn't worry too much about health concerns though it pays to lay down a few ground rules – such as regular hand-washing – to head off potential medical problems. Kids are welcomed everywhere by Spanish people except in the smartest restaurants. If they get sick or sunburned, you'll be able to find ordinary medicines at a corner pharmacy. Children (and adults) should be warned to be careful of traffic.

Heat
Spain's hot weather can get to you, so take it slowly until you have fully acclimatised. Drink plenty of liquids to replace all the water lost through perspiration. Always use sunscreen, even when overcast.

Contrary to popular belief, salt tablets interfere with the absorption of water by the body. 'Dehydrating' or 'electrolyte' solutions have a similar effect if consumed too often.

When the weather is hot, avoid the sun between midday and 4pm. Stick to the shade. Literally. When walking at this time of day, go from shade to shade. And wear a hat! With a wide brim.

Allergies

Anyone with an allergy to shellfish should be aware that the Spanish love it. But you should be able to tell when a dish includes it. The dish's name will normally include the word **mariscos**. If in doubt, ask '**Hay mariscos?**' (Are there any shellfish?).

Diabetes

If you are diabetic, bring everything you need, then pack some more. If you're travelling with a companion it's a good idea to split your supplies between you in the event your luggage is lost. And leave some with a hotel or a friend. Carry your prescription or other documentation so the local police won't think you're dealing in drugs.

Last Word

Above all, observe balance, contrast, moderation and variety. Food is a very important aspect of your journey, but it isn't the only one. Taken out of context it's mere gorging. Balance your dining with visits to farms, wineries, museums and theatres. Contrast the local cuisine with local sports or arts. Moderate your intake, vary your gastronomic experience, journey well, eat well, and return home well.

Recommended Reading

Delicioso: The Regional Cooking of Spain (Knopf, 1996) by **Penelope Casas** is an excellent reference and supply of recipes.

Life and Food in the Basque Country (New Amsterdam, 1989) by **Maria Jose Sevilla** is an intimate look at the table and life in the Basque Country.

A Taste of Spain (Flammerion, 1992) is a magnificent work of Spanish gastronomy by one of her pre-eminent novelists, **Xavier Domingo**.

To the Heart of Spain (Berkeley Hills Books, 1997) by **Ann and Larry Walker** is the record of one of their gastronomic and cultural journeys through Spain.

Websites

www.trasgo-es.com
Well laid out website for Sidrería Trasgo in La Coruña, Galicia.

www.tourspain.es
Website of the Spanish Tourist Office

www.donlorenzo.com
Very informative and personal website of an English expat hotelier living in Spain.

FIT & HEALTHY

Photo Credits

Oliver Strewe Front & back cover p1, p5, p8, p9, p10, p11, p13, p14, p16, p17, p20, p21, p23, p24, p26, p30, p32, p34, p36, p40, p45, p48, p49, p50, p52, p53, p54, p55, p56, p59, p62, p64, p65, p67, p68, p70, p71, p72, p74, p77, p80, p81, p82, p83, p85, p86, p87, p88, p90, p92, p94, p95, p98, p100, p101, p102, p103, p104, p106, p107, p109 top right, bottom left, p112, p113, p114, pp122, p123, p124, p129, p130, p134, p139, p142, p144, p145, p146, p147, p148, p149, p150, p153, p155, p158, p159, p163, p164, p165, p166, p167, p168, p169, p171, p172, p175, p176, p178, p179, p180, p181, p182, p183, p186, p189, p190, p191, p192, p194, p195, p196, p197, p198, p199, p200, p205, p206, p207, p209, p210, p211, p212, p213, p216, p217, p220, p221, p222, p224, p225 top, bottom left.

Damien Simonis p12, p109 top left, bottom right, p111, p117 top, bottom right, p120, p127 top right, bottom left, p132, p160, p204, p226.

Mason Florence p127 top left, bottom right.

Guy Moberly p19, p42.

Bethune Carmichael p117 bottom left.

Gerry Reilly p60, p116.

Jon Davidson p29, p110.

John Noble p119.

Greg Elms p27.

Veronica Garbutt p225 bottom right.

Dashan Cooray p200.

eat your words
language guide

- **Pronunciation Guide** 236
- **Useful Phrases** 237
- **English - Spanish Glossary** 245
- **Spanish Culinary Dictionary** 259

Pronunciation

As transliterations give only an approximate guide to pronunciation, we've included this guide for those who want to try their hand at pronouncing Spanish more like a native speaker.

Vowels

a	as the 'u' in 'nut'
e	as the 'e' in 'met'
i	like the 'i' in 'machine', but shorter
o	like the 'o' in 'hot'
u	as the 'oo' in 'fool'

Consonants & Semiconsonants

b	as the 'b' in 'book' at the start of a word or after 'm', 'n' or 'ng'; elsewhere a sound between English 'b' and 'v'
c	as the 'c' in 'cat' before 'a', 'o' or 'u'; as the 'th' in 'thin' before 'e' or 'i'
ch	as the 'ch' in 'cheese'
d	as the 'd' in 'dog' at the start of word; elsewhere as the 'th' in 'this'
g	as the 'g' in 'gone' at the start of a word if followed by 'a', 'o' or 'u'. When followed by 'ue' or 'ui', the 'u' is silent unless it has diaeresis (ü). Before 'e' or 'i', similar to the 'h' in 'hello'.
h	always silent
j	similar to the 'ch' in Scottish 'loch' or German 'ich'
ll	between the 'ly' sound in 'million' and the 'y' in 'yes'
ñ	like the 'ny' sound in 'canyon'
q	as the 'k' in 'king'. As in English, 'q' is always followed by a silent 'u'.
r	a rolled sound which is stronger when at the start of a word or when a word has a double 'r'
s	as the 's' in 'sin'
v	the same as Spanish b
x	as the 'x' in 'taxi' when between two vowels; as the 's' in 'sin' when before a consonant
y	as the 'ee' in 'meet' at the end of a word or when it stands alone; elsewhere as the 'y' in 'yes'
z	as the 'th' in 'thin'

Stress

When a word ends in 'n', 's' or a vowel, stress falls on the second last syllable. When a word ends in a consonant other than 'n' or 's', the final syllable is stressed. Any deviation from these rules is indicated by an accent, as in **atún**

Useful Phrases
Eating Out

Do you speak English?
  say ab-lah in-glays?

¿Se habla inglés?

Do you know a good restaurant (that's cheap)?
  kon-oh-thes al-guhn res-tor-an-tay
  (kay no say-ah moy ka-roh)?

¿Conoces algún restaurante
  (que no sea muy caro)?

Table for ..., please.
  uhn-ah mes-ah pa-rah ..., por fah-vohr

Una mesa para ..., por favor.

Do you accept credit cards?
  a-sep-tan tar-khe-tas de kre-di-to?

¿Aceptan tarjetas de crédito?

Would you like to go for a drink/meal?
It's on me.
  kee-ehr-es kay by-am-os a
  to-mahr al-goh/a sen-ahr?
  tay in-vee-toh

¿Quieres que vayamos a
  tomar algo/a cenar?
  Te invito.

Just Try It!

What are they eating?
  kay es-tan koh-mee-en-doh el-yos?

¿Qué están comiendo ellos?

I'll try what she/he's having.
  pro-ba-ray loh kay el-yah/el es-tah
  koh-mee-en-doh

Probaré lo que ella/él
  está comiendo.

What are the specialities of this region?
  kwal-es son las es-pes-ee-al-ee-dah-des
  loh-kal-es?

¿Cúales son las especialidades
  locales?

What's the speciality here?
  kwal es la es-pes-ee-al-ee-dad
  de es-tay res-tor-an-tay?

¿Cuál es la especialidad
  de este restaurante?

What is today's special?
  kwal es el plat-oh del dee-ah?

¿Cúal es es plato del día?

What do you recommend?
  kay may rek-om-ee-en-dah?

¿Qué me recomienda?

What's that?
  kay e eso?

¿Qué es eso?

What's in this dish?
  kay in-gred-ee-en-tays tee-en-ay
  es-tay pla-toh?

¿Qué ingredientes tiene
  este plato?

The Menu

Can I see the menu please?
pwe-doh ver el men-oo, por fah-vohr?

¿Puedo ver el menú, por favor?

What's the soup of the day?
kwal es la so-pah del dee-ah?

¿Cuál es la sopa del día?

What desserts are available?
kay ay de pos-tray?

¿Qué hay de postre?

I'd like the set lunch, please.
kee-see-ehr-ah el men-oo del dee-ah,
por fah-vohr

Quisiera el menú del día,
por favor.

What does it include?
kay in-kloo-yay?

¿Qué incluye?

Does it come with salad?
bee-en-ay con en-sah-lah-dah?

¿Viene con ensalada?

Is service included in the bill?
el ser-vith-ee-oh es-tah in-cloo-ee-doh
en lah kwen-tah?

¿El servicio está incluido
en la cuenta?

I'd like ...
kee-see-ehr-ah ...

Quisiera ...

Not too spicy, please.
po-koh pee-kahn-te, por fahv-ohr

Poco picante, por favor.

Bon appétit!
bwen pro-vech-oh!

¡Buen provecho!

I'd like something to drink.
kee-ehr-oh al-goh pa-rah beb-ehr

Quiero algo para beber.

Can I have a (beer) please?
uhn-ah (ser-veh-sah), por fah-vohr

Una (cerveza), por favor.

A glass/bottle of red/white wine, please.
(uhn bah-soh /uhn-ah bo-tel-yah) de
vee-noh tin-toh/blan-koh, por fav-or

(Un vaso/Una botella) de vino
tinto/blanco, por favor.

Can you please bring me ...?	may pwe-day try-ehr ... por fah-vohr?	¿Me puede traer ... por favor?
an ashtray	uhn se-ni-seh-roh	un cenicero
more bread	mas pan	más pan
a cup	uhn-ah ta-thah	una taza
a glass	uhn bah-soh	un vaso
a knife/fork	uhn koo-chil-yoh/ten-eh-dor	un cuchillo/tenedor
a napkin	uhn-ah ser-vil-yet-ah	una servilleta
some salt/pepper	lah sal/pi-mee-en-tah	la sal/pimienta
a spoon	uhn-ah koo-chah-rah	una cuchara
a toothpick	uhn pal-il-yoh	un palillo
more water/wine	mas ag-wah/vee-noh	más agua/vino

The food is ...   lah koh-mee-dah es-tah ...   *La comida está ...*
- burnt   kay-mah-dah   *quemada*
- cold   free-ah   *fría*
- stale   ran-see-ah/pa-sa-dah   *rancia/pasada*
- undercooked   po-koh koh-cee-doh   *poco cocida*

Thank you, that was delicious.
moo-chas gra-si-as,
es-tah-bah bwe-nee-si-mo
Muchas gracias, estaba buenísimo.

Our compliments to the chef.
fay-leece-ee-tas-ee-ohn-es
al koh-see-ne-roh
Felicitaciones al cocinero.

The bill, please.
lah kwen-tah, por fah-vohr
La cuenta, por favor.

I didn't order this.
no ped-ee es-toh
No pedí esto.

You May Hear
kee-ehr-eh al-goh pa-rah beb-her?
Do you want anything to drink?
¿Quiere algo para beber?

Family Meals
Can I bring anything?
pwe-doh try-er al-guhn-ah koh-sah?
¿Puedo traer alguna cosa?

Let me help you.
tay ay-oo-doh
Te ayudo.

No thank you, I'm full.
no pwe-doh mas
No puedo más.

Special Needs
I am a vegetarian.
soy veg-et-ar-ee-an-ah/oh
Soy vegetariana/o.

I don't eat meat.
no koh-moh kar-nay
No como carne.

I don't eat chicken, fish, or ham.
no koh-moh pohl-yoh, nee pes-kah-doh,
nee ha-mon
No como pollo, ni pescado, ni jamón.

I'm a vegan. I don't eat meat, fish or dairy products.
soy veg-et-ar-ee-an-ah/oh es-trik-tah/oh.
no koh-moh kar-nay, nee pes-kah-doh, nee
prod-uk-tos lak-tay-os
Soy vegetariana/o estricta/o. No como carne, ni pescado, ni productos lácteos.

Do you have any vegetarian dishes?
tee-en-en al-guhn plat-oh
veg-et-ar-ee-an-oh?
¿Tienen algún plato vegetariano?

Does this dish have meat?
yeh-vah kar-nay oh ha-mon
es-tay plat-oh?

¿Lleva carne o jamón
este plato?

Can I get this without the meat?
may pwe-day prep-ar-ahr es-tay
plat-oh sin kar-nay?

¿Me puede preparar este
plato sin carne?

Does this dish have gelatin?
es-tay plat-oh yeh-vah gel-at-ee-nah?

¿Este plato lleva gelatina?

Can you recommend a vegetarian dish?
may rek-om-ee-en-dah uhn plat-oh
veg-et-ar-ee-an-oh?

¿Me recomienda un plato
vegetariano?

I'm allergic to (peanuts).
soy al-er-hee-kah/koh a
(los ka-kah-weh-tes)

Soy alérgica/o a
(los cacahuetes).

I don't eat ...
no koh-moh ...

No como ...

Does it contain eggs/dairy products?
yeh-vah hway-vos/prod-uk-tos
lak-tay-os?

¿Lleva huevos/productos
lácteos?

I am diabetic.
soy dee-ah-bet-ee-kah/koh

Soy diabética/o.

Is this kosher?
es ap-toh pa-rah los hoo-dee-os?

¿Es apto para los judíos?

Is this organic?
es or-gan-ik-oh?

¿Es orgánico?

I follow a ... diet.	es-toy a dee-et-ah ...	Estoy a dieta ...
gluten-free	sin gloo-ten	sin gluten
lactose-free	sin lak-toh-sa	sin lactosa
sugar-free	sin as-oo-kah	sin azúcar
wheat-free	sin tree-goh	sin trigo
carbohydrate	ee-drah-toh de kahr-bon-oh	hidrato de carbono
fat	gra-sah	grasa
high fibre	ri-kah en fee-brah	rica en fibra
low-fat	de bak-oh kon-ten-ee-doh gra-soh	de bajo contenido graso
nutritional analysis	in-for-mas-ee-on noo-tris-ee-on-al	información nutricional
organically-grown produce	prod-uk-tos bee-oh-lo-gee-kos	productos biológicos
protein	pro-tay-ee-nah	proteina
sodium	soh-dee-oh	sodio

Children

Are children allowed?
  say ad-mit-en nee-nyos?   *¿Se admiten niños?*

Is there a children's menu?
  tee-en-en men-oo in-fan-til?   *¿Tienen menú infantil?*

Do you have a highchair for the baby?
  tee-en-en uhn-ah sil-yee-tah   *¿Tienen una sillita ara el bebé?*
  pa-rah el beh-bay?

Self-Catering

Where is the nearest (market)?
  don-day es-tah (el mer-kah-doh)   *¿Dónde está (el mercado)*
  mas ser-kah-noh?   *más cercano?*

I'd like to buy ...
  kee-see-ehr-ah kom-prar ...   *Quisiera comprar ...*

Where can I buy ...?
  don-day pwe-doh comprar ...   *¿Dónde puedo comprar ...?*

Who's next?
  kee-en es lah ul-ti-ma?   *¿Quién es la última/el último?*
  (lit: Who's last? – When you join a queue at a food counter, it's normal to
  ask 'who's last', so that you'll know when it's your turn to be served)

price   pres-ee-oh   *precio; PVP*

How much is (a kilo of cheese)?
  kwan-toh vah-lay (uhn ki-loh   *¿Cuánto vale (un kilo*
  de ke-soh)   *de queso)?*

Do you have anything cheaper?
  tee-en-ay al-goh mas bah-rah-toh?   *¿Tiene algo más barato?*

Can I taste it?
  pwe-doh pro-bahr-lah/loh?   *¿Puedo probarla/lo?*

Do you have anything better?
  tee-en-ay al-goh mas mek-ohr?   *¿Tiene algo mejor?*

Can I have ...?
  kee-see-ehr-ah ...   *Quisiera ...*

I'd like (six slices of ham), please.
  pon-gah-may (say-is lon-chas de   *Póngame (seis lonchas de*
  ha-mon), por fah-vohr   *jamón), por favor.*

Give me (half) a kilo, please.
  pon-gah-may (med-ee-oh) ki-loh   *Póngame (medio) kilo,*
  por fah-vohr   *por favor.*

How long will this keep for in the fridge?
  kwan-toh say kon-serv-ah   *¿Cúanto se conserva*
  en el free-goh?   *en el frigo?*

Where can I find the (sugar)?
don-day pwe-doh en-con-trahr (el as-oo-kah)?

¿Dónde puedo encontrar (el azúcar)?

I'd like some ...
kee-see-ehr-ah (un po-koh de) ...

Quisiera (un poco de) ...

best before ...
kon-soo-mir an-tes de ...

consumir antes de ...

At the Bar

Shall we go for a drink?
va-mos ah to-mahr uhn-ah koh-pah?

¿Vamos a tomar una copa?

I'll buy you a drink.
tay in-vee-toh ah uhn-ah koh-pah

Te invito a una copa.

Okay.
day ak-wer-doh

De acuerdo.

What would you like?
kay kee-ehr-es to-mahr?

¿Qué quieres tomar?

I'll have ...
may a-peh-teh-say ...
pa-rah may, ...

Me apetece ...
Para mí, ...

It's on me.
pag-oh yoh

Pago yo.

You can get the next one.
lah prox-ee-mah lah pag-es too

La próxima la pagas tú.

No ice.
sin ee-el-oh

Sin hielo.

Can I have ice, please?
con ee-el-oh, por fa-vohr

Con hielo, por favor.

Same again, please.
oh-trah de loh mis-moh

Otra de lo mismo.

Thanks, but I don't feel like it.
loh see-en-toh, pehr-ro noh may a-peh-teh-say

Lo siento, pero no me apetece.

I don't drink alcohol.
no beb-oh

No bebo.

Good health!/Cheers!	**sa-lood!**	¡Salud!
	ah too/soo sa-lood!	¡A tu/su salud!
	chin chin!	¡Chin chin!
	to-dah lah swer-tay!	¡Toda la suerte!
	to-pah!	Topa! (Basque)
	bon proh-feet!	Bon profit! (Catalan)
	sah-oo-day!	Saúde! (Galician)

This is hitting the spot.
may loh es-toy pah-san-doh moy bee-en/bom-bah

Me lo estoy pasando muy bien/bomba.

I'm a bit tired, I'd better get home.
es-toy can-sah-dah/doh, kee-ehr-oh ear-may ah ka-sah

Estoy cansada/o, quiero irme a casa.

Where's the toilet?
don-day es-tah el lah-vah-boh?

¿Dónde está el lavabo?

Is food available here?
sir-ven koh-mee-dah ah-kee?

¿Sirven comida aquí?

I'm feeling drunk.
es-toh may es-tah soo-bee-en-doh moo-cho

Esto me está subiendo mucho.

I think I've had one too many.
kray-oh kay ay tom-ah-doh dem-as-ee-ahd-as koh-pas

Creo que he tomado demasiadas copas.

Excuse me! (to get attention)
por fa-vohr!/oy-gah!

¡Por favor!/¡Oiga!

I was here before him/her!
yoh es-toy an-tes kay es-tay sen-yaw/ es-ta sen-yaw-rah!

Yo estoy antes que este señor/esta señora!

| I feel ill. | **may see-en-toh mal** | *Me siento mal.* |
| I'm hung over. | **ten-goh res-ak-ah** | *Tengo resaca.* |

Wine

May I see the wine list please?
lah kar-tah de vee-nos por fah-vohr

La carta de vinos, por favor.

Can you recommend a good local wine?
may rek-om-ee-en-dah uhn bwen vee-noh del pay-ihs?

¿Me recomienda un buen vino del país?

May I taste it?
pwe-doh pro-bahr-lah/loh?

¿Puedo probarla/lo?

Which wine would you recommend with this dish?
kwal may rek-om-ee-en-dah pa-rah ak-um-pan-yar es-tay plat-oh?

¿Cúal me recomienda para acompañar este plato?

This is brilliant!
es-toh es-tah ree-kis-ee-moh!

¡Esto está riquísimo!

Please bring me another bottle.
try-ga-may o-trah bo-tel-yah, por fah-vohr

Tráigame otra botella, por favor.

This wine has a nice/bad taste.
es-tay vee-noh may sa-bay bee-en/mal

Este vino me sabe bien/mal.

This wine has a nice/bad colour.
  es-tay vee-noh tee-en-ay bwen/mal kol-ohr   *Este vino tiene buen/mal color.*

This wine is corked.
  es-tay vee-noh sa-bay a kor-cho   *Este vino sabe a corcho.*

Celebrating with Food
Christmas

Christmas Day	nav-ee-dad	*Navidad*
Christmas Eve (evening)	not-chay-bwen-ah	*Nochebuena*
New Year's Eve	fin de an-yoh	*fin de año*
New Year's Day	an-yoh noo-eh-voh	*año nuevo*
Epiphany, 6th January	dee-ah de los ray-es ma-gos	*día de los reyes magos*

Happy Easter/Christmas!
  fay-leece pas-kwas!   *¡Felices pascuas!*

Happy Christmas!
  fay-leece nav-ee-dad!   *¡Feliz navidad!*

Happy New Year!
  fay-leece/pros-pay-roh an-yoh noo-eh-voh   *¡Feliz/Próspero año nuevo!*

Birthdays & Saint's Days

birthday cake	pas-tel de kum-ple-an-yos	*pastel de cumpleaños*
candles	vel-as	*velas*

Congratulations!
  fay-leece-ee-dad-es!   *¡Felicidades!*

Happy birthday!
  fay-leece kum-ple-an-yos!   *¡Feliz cumpleaños!*

Happy saint's day!
  fay-leece san-toh!   *¡Feliz santo!*

Many happy returns!
  kay kum-plas moo-chas mas!   *¡Que cumplas muchos más!*

Christenings & Weddings

Baptism	bow-tis-moh	*bautizo*
engagement	kom-prom-ee-soh	*compromiso*
honeymoon	loo-nah de mee-el	*luna de miel*
wedding	bo-dah	*boda*
wedding anniversary	ah-nee-ver-sah-ri-oh de bo-das	*aniversario de bodas*

To the bride and groom!
  bee-ban los nov-ee-os!   *¡Vivan los novios!*

In Spanish, nouns always have a feminine or masculine form. With some exceptions, there are some ways to tell which form a word should take. Generally speaking, feminine forms end in -a and are preceded by the definite article la (the), or the indefinite article una (a). Masculine forms generally end in -o and are preceded by the definite article el (the) or the indefinite article un (a).

A

afternoon tea	me-ree-en-dah	merienda
aged (of cheese, etc)	vee-e-khoh	viejo
ale	ser-veh-sah	cerveza
almond	al-men-drah	almendra
anchovy	ahn-cho-ah	anchoa
anise	ah-nees	anís
appetiser	a-bray-boh-kas	abrebocas
apple	man-tha-nah	manzana
apricot	al-bari-ko-ke	albaricoque
artichoke	al-ka-choh-fa/al-kah-oo-sil	alcachofa/alcaucil
ashtray	se-ni-seh-roh	cenicero
asparagus	es-parr-ah-gos	espárragos
aubergine	be-ren-ken-ah	berenjena
avocado	ag-wah-ka-te	aguacate

B

baby food	koh-mee-dah de beb-ay	comida de bebé
bacon	ba-kon	bacón
bag	bol-see-tah	bolsita
baked	al orr-noh	al horno
bakery	pan-ah-der-ee-ah	panadería
(baking) tray	ban-dek-ah	bandeja
banana	plat-an-oh	plátano
bar	bahr/tab-er-nah/tas-ka	bar/taberna/tasca
barbecue	bahr-bak-ow-a	barbacoa
barrel	ton-el	tonel
basil	al-ba-aka	albahaca
basket	ses-tah	cesta
bay leaf	oh-kah de lor-el	hoja de laurel
beef	ba-ka; va-koo-noh	vaca; vacuno
beer	ser-veh-sah	cerveza
best before ...	kon-soo-mir an-tes de ...	consumir antes de ...
bib	bab-ehr-oh	babero
bill (check)	kwen-tah	cuenta
birthday	kum-ple-an-yos	cumpleaños
birthday cake	pas-tel/tahr-tah de kum-ple-an-yos	pastel/tarta de cumpleaños

biscuit	gal-yet-ah	galleta
bitter	ah-mahr-goh	amargo
blackberry	zar-zam-or-ah	zarzamora
blackcurrant	grow-sel-yah neg-rah	grosella negra
black olive	a-say-too-nah neg-rah	aceituna negra
black pepper	pi-mee-en-tah neg-rah	pimienta negra
black pudding	boo-tee-far-rah neg-rah	butifarra negra
blender	bat-ee-dor-ah	batidora
blueberry	a-rahn-ah-doh	arándano
blue cheese	ke-soh a-thul	queso azul
boiled ham	ha-mon dul-say/york	jamón dulce/York
bone	weh-soh	hueso
bottle	bo-tel-yah	botella
–opener	a-bray-boh-tel-yas	abrebotellas
bowl	bol	bol
box	ka-kah	caja
bran	a-fray-cho	afrecho; salvado
brandy	kon-yak	coñac
bran flakes	kop-os de sal-va-doh	copos de salvado
bread	pan	pan
breakfast	des-ai-yoo-noh	desayuno
(Basque)	go-sah-ree	gosari
(Catalan)	es-mor-sar	esmorzar
(Galician)	al-mor-thoh	almorzo
breakfast cereal	ser-ee-al-es	cereales
bream	bra-mah/sahr-goh	brama/sargo
broad bean	ab-ah	haba
broccoli	brok-o-leh	brócoli
brown rice	ah-rroth in-teg-ral	arroz integral
brown sugar	as-oo-kah mor-en-oh	azúcar moreno
Brussels sprouts	kol-es de broo-sel-as	coles de bruselas
buckwheat	tree-goh sar-rah-sen-oh	trigo sarraceno
butcher's shop/stall	kahr-nee-seh-ree-ah	carnicería
butter	man-tek-il-yah	mantequilla

C

cabbage	ber-sah/kol	berza/col
cafe	ka-fay-teh-ree-yah	cafetería
cake	pas-tel/tahr-tah	pastel/tarta
cake shop	pas-tel-er-ee-ah	pastelería
can	lat-ah	lata
–opener	a-bray-lah-tas	abrelatas
candle	vel-ah	vela
cantaloupe	kan-tal-oo-poh	cantalupo
caper	al-kah-pah-rrah	alcaparra
capsicum	pi-mee-en-toh	pimiento

English	Pronunciation	Spanish
carp	*kahr-pah*	carpa
carrot	*zan-a-or-ee-ah*	zanahoria
carving knife	*trin-chan-tay*	trinchante
cashew nut	*ah-nah-karh-doh*	anacardo
casserole	*kath-way-lah*	cazuela
cauliflower	*kol-i-flor*	coliflor
caviar	*kav-ee-ah*	caviar
cayenne	*kay-en-ah*	Cayena
celery	*a-pee-oh*	apio
chamomile tea	*man-thah-nil-yah*	manzanilla
champagne	*sham-pan-yah*	champaña
check (bill)	*kwen-tah*	cuenta
Cheers!	*sa-lud!*	¡Salud!
cheese	*ke-soh*	queso
cheesecake	*tahr-tah de ke-soh*	tarta de queso
chef	*chef*	chef
cherry	*se-ray-sah*	cereza
chestnut	*kas-tan-yah*	castaña
(chewing) gum	*chic-leh*	chicle
chicken	*pohl-yoh*	pollo
–soup	*so-pah de gal-yee-nah*	sopa de gallina
chickpea	*gar-bahn-thoh*	garbanzo
children's menu	*men-oo in-fan-til*	menú infantil
chocolate	*chok-oh-lah-tay*	chocolate
–cake	*pas-tel de chok-oh-lah-tay*	pastel de chocolate
chop	*choo-let-ah*	chuleta
chopping board	*tak-oh*	tajo
chopsticks	*pal-il-yos*	palillos
cider	*see-drah*	sidra
cinnamon	*kan-el-ah*	canela
clam	*al-meh-kah*	almeja
clove (of garlic)	*dee-en-tay*	diente
clove (spice)	*kla-voh*	clavo
cocktail	*kok-tel/com-bin-ah-doh*	cóctel/combinado
cocoa	*ka-kow*	cacao
coconut	*koh-koh*	coco
cod	*bak-al-ow*	bacalao
coffee	*ka-fay*	café
black	*ka-fay soh-loh*	café solo
decaffeinated	*ka-fay des-kaf-ay-in-ah-doh*	café descafeinado
grinder	*mol-in-il-yo de ka-fay*	molinillo de café
ground	*ka-fay mol-ee-doh*	café molido
instant	*ka-fay in-stan-tah-nay-oh*	café instantáneo
–pot/maker	*ka-fay-teh-rah*	cafetera
–with milk	*ka-fay kon le-chay*	café con leche
with whipped cream	*vee-en-es*	café vienés

colander	es-koo-rree-dor	escurridor
cold	free-oh	frío
–drink	beb-ee-dah fres-kah	bebida fresca
–meats	fee-am-brays	fiambres
confectionery	re-pos-teh-ree-ah	repostería
conserves	kon-fit-oo-ras	confituras
cookbook	re-set-ahr-ee-oh	recetario
cookie	gal-yet-ah	galleta
coriander	koo-lan-troh	culantro
corkscrew	sa-ka-kor-chos	sacacorchos
corn flakes	korn-flek-ays	cornflakes
cornmeal	ah-ree-nah de may-iz	harina de maíz
corn oil	a-say-tay de may-iz	aceite de maíz
courgette	ka-lab-ah-sihn	calabacín
crab	kan-gre-koh	cangrejo
cranberry	a-rahn-ah-doh	arándano
cream	kre-mah/nat-ah	crema/nata
–cake	pas-tel de nat-ah	pastel de nata
–cheese	ke-soh kre-mah	queso crema
croissant	kra-sont	croissant
cucumber	pep-ee-noh	pepino
cumin	koh-mee-noh	comino
cup	ta-thah	taza
currant	oo-bah de kor-in-toh	uva de corinto
curry;	ku-rri	curry
curry powder		
cutlery	koo-bee-ehr-tos	cubiertos
cutlet	choo-let-ah	chuleta
cuttlefish	sep-ee-ah	sepia

D

dairy products	prod-uk-tos lak-tay-os	productos lácteos
date (fruit)	dat-il	dátil
delicatessen	char-koo-teh-ree-ah	charcutería
dessert	pos-tray	postre
–spoon	koo-chah-rah de pos-tray	cuchara de postre
dining room	kom-e-dohr	comedor
dinner/dinner party	se-nah	cena
dish of the day	plat-oh del dee-ah	plato del día
double (shot of spirits)	doh-blay	doble
draught beer	ser-veh-sah de bar-ril	cerveza de barril
drinking water	ag-wah pot-ab-lay	agua potable
drinks	beb-ee-das	bebidas
dry	se-koh	seco
duck	pa-toh	pato

E

eel	*ahn-gwee-lah*	anguila
egg	*hway-voh*	huevo
boiled	*hway-vos koh-cee-doh*	huevos cocidos
fried	*hway-vos free-tos*	huevos fritos
eggplant	*be-ren-ken-ah*	berenjena
endive	*en-dib-ee-ah*	endibia
entree (starter)	*en-trah-dah; en-tran-tay*	entrada; entrante
espresso	*ka-fay ex-pres*	café exprés
extra virgin olive oil	*a-say-tay de ol-ee-vah vir-khen ex-trah*	aceite de oliva virgen extra

F

fat	*gra-sah*	grasa
fennel	*in-ok-oh*	hinojo
fig	*ee-goh*	higo
fillet	*sol-oh-mil-yoh*	solomillo
first course	*pree-mer plat-oh*	primer plato
fish	*pes-kah-doh*	pescado
–shop/stall	*pes-kah-der-ee-yah*	pescadería
–soup	*so-pah de pes-kah-doh*	sopa de pescado
fixed price menu	*men-oo de lah ka-sah*	menú de la casa
flavour	*sa-bor*	sabor
flour	*ah-ree-nah*	harina
flower shop/stall	*flor-is-teh-ree-ah*	floristería
food processor	*roh-bot de koh-see-nah*	robot de cocina
fork	*ten-e-dor*	tenedor
free-range chicken	*pohl-yoh de kor-ral*	pollo de corral
free-range eggs	*hway-vos de gran-kah*	huevos de granja
fresh	*fres-koh*	fresco
fried	*free-toh*	frito
frozen	*kon-gel-ah-doh*	congelado
fruit	*froo-tah*	fruta
–salad	*en-sah-lah-dah de froo-tas*	ensalada de frutas
–shop/stall	*froo-teh-ree-ah*	frutería
frying pan	*sahr-ten*	sartén
fungi	*on-gos*	hongos

G

game	*ka-sah*	caza
garlic	*ah-khoh*	ajo
–mayonnaise	*al-ee-ol-ee*	alioli
–mushrooms	*sham-pin-yon-es al a-kil-yoh*	champiñones al ajillo
garlic press	*try-too-rah-dohr de ah-khos*	triturador de ajos

English	Pronunciation	Spanish
gelatin	*gel-at-ee-nah*	gelatina
general store	*al-mah-sen*	almacén
gherkin	*pep-in-il-yoh*	pepinillo
gin	*hin-eb-rah*	ginebra
gin & tonic	*ton-ee-kah kon hin-eb-rah*	tónica con ginebra; gin tonic
ginger	*hen-ee-bray*	jengibre
glass	*bah-soh*	vaso
glass of beer (250 ml)	*kan-yah; too-boh*	caña; tubo
goat	*ka-bra*	cabra
goat's cheese	*ke-soh de ka-bra*	queso de cabra
gourmet	*trip-as-ai*	tripasai
grain	*gra-noh*	grano
grams	*gram-os*	gramos
grape	*oo-bah*	uva
grapefruit	*pom-el-oh*	pomelo
grater	*ral-yah-dor*	rallador
green bean	*hoo-dee-ah ver-day*	judía verde
greengrocer	*ver-dul-ehr-ee-ah*	verdulería
grilled	*ah lah par-ril-yah/ plahn-chah*	a la parrilla/plancha
grocery store	*al-mah-sen*	almacén

H

English	Pronunciation	Spanish
hake	*mer-loo-thah*	merluza
half	*med-ee-oh*	medio
half a litre	*med-ee-oh li-troh*	medio litro
ham	*ha-mon*	jamón
a handful	*man-ok-oh*	manojo
hard	*doo-roh*	duro
hazelnut	*av-el-yah-nah*	avellana
herbal tea	*in-foo-see-on*	infusión
herbs	*ee-er-bas*	hierbas
highchair	*sil-yah al-tah; sil-yee-tah*	silla alta; sillita
high-fibre	*ri-kah en fee-brah*	rica en fibra
home-made	*ka-seh-roh*	casero
honey	*mee-el*	miel
hot dog	*per-ree-toh kal-ee-en-tay*	perrito caliente
hot drink	*beb-ee-dah kal-ee-en-tay*	bebida caliente
hot (temperature)	*kal-ee-en-tay*	caliente
house specialities	*es-pes-ee-al-ee-dah-des de lah ka-sah*	especialidades de la casa
house wine	*vee-noh korr-ee-en-te vee-noh de lah ka-sah*	vino corriente; vino de la casa

I
ice	*ee-el-oh*	hielo
ice cream	*el-ah-doh*	helado
ice cube	*koo-be-toh de ee-el-oh*	cubito de hielo

J
jam	*mer-mel-ah-dah*	mermelada
jar	*tar-roh*	tarro
jug (of wine)	*har-rah*	jarra
juice	*hoo-goh/soo-moh*	jugo/zumo

K
kettle	*pa-vah*	pava
kidney bean	*hoo-dee-on*	judión
kilogram	*ki-loh-gram-oh*	kilogramo
kipper	*a-ren-kay ah-oo-mah-doh*	arenque ahumado
kitchen	*koh-see-nah*	cocina
kiwi fruit	*ki-wee*	kiwi
knife	*koo-chil-yoh*	cuchillo

L
label	*et-ee-ket-ah*	etiqueta
lager	*ser-veh-sah*	cerveza
lamb	*kor-deh-roh*	cordero
leg (of lamb)	*man-ee-tas (de kor-deh-roh)*	manitas (de cordero)
lemon	*li-mon*	limón
lemonade	*gas-ee-oh-sah/lim-on-ah-dah*	gaseosa/limonada
lentil	*len-tek-ah*	lenteja
lettuce	*le-choo-gah*	lechuga
lid	*ta-pa-dehr-ah*	tapadera
lime	*li-mah*	lima
litre	*lee-troh*	litro
liver	*ee-gah-doh*	hígado
lobster	*bo-gah-van-teh*	bogavante
local	*del pay-ihs*	del país
–cheese	*ke-soh del pay-ihs*	queso del país
–specialities	*es-pes-ee-al-ee-dah-des loh-kal-es*	especialidades locales
–wine	*vee-noh de lah tee-air-ra; vee-noh del pay-ihs*	vino de la tierra; vino del país
long-grain (rice)	*gra-noh lahr-goh*	grano largo
low-fat	*de bak-oh kon-ten-ee-doh gra-soh*	de bajo contenido graso

lunch	*all-mwer-thoh/koh-mee-dah*	almuerzo/comida
(Basque)	*baz-kah-ree*	bazkari
(Catalan)	*dee-nahr*	dinar
(Galician)	*shan-tahr*	xantar

M

mackerel	*kah-bal-yah*	caballa
main course	*seg-oon-doh plat-oh*	segundo plato
mandarin	*man-da-ree-nah*	mandarina
margarine	*mahr-gah-ree-nah*	margarina
marinade	*ah-doh-boh*	adobo
market	*mer-kah-doh*	mercado
marmalade	*mer-mel-ah-dah*	mermelada
marzipan	*maz-ah-pan*	mazapán
mature	*ahn-yeh-ko*	añejo
mayonnaise	*may-on-ay-sah*	mayonesa
meal	*koh-mee-dah*	comida
meat	*kar-nay*	carne
meatballs	*al-bohn-di-gas*	albóndigas
melon	*me-lon*	melón
menu	*kahr-tah*	carta
meringue	*mer-en-gay*	merengue
metre	*met-roh*	metro
mild	*swah-vay*	suave
milk	*le-chay*	leche
milkshake	*bat-ee-doh*	batido
minced meat	*kar-nay pee-kah-dah*	carne picada
mineral water	*ag-wah min-er-al*	agua mineral
(sparkling)	*–kon gas*	–con gas
(still)	*–sin gas*	–sin gas
mint	*ee-er-bah bway-nah*	hierba buena
mixed herbs	*ee-er-bas fee-nas*	hierbas finas
mortar		
& pestle	*al-mee-reth*	almirez
muesli	*moos-lee*	muesli
mushrooms	*tor-til-yah de sham-pin-yon-es*	champiñones
mussel	*mek-il-yon*	mejillón
mustard	*mos-tath-ah*	mostaza

N

napkin	*ser-vil-yet-ah*	servilleta
neat (alcohol)	*sol-oh*	solo
nut/nuts	*noo-eth/noo-eh-sehs*	nuez/nueces
nutmeg	*noo-eth mos-kah-dah*	nuez moscada

O

oats/oatmeal	*av-ay-nah*	avena
octopus	*pul-poh*	pulpo
oil	*a-say-tay*	aceite
olive	*a-say-too-nah*	aceituna
–oil	*a-say-tay de ol-ee-vah*	aceite de oliva
omelette	*tor-til-yah*	tortilla
onion	*se-bol-yah*	cebolla
orange	*na-ran-kah*	naranja
–juice	*soo-moh de na-ran-kah*	zumo de naranja
oregano	*or-ee-ga-noh*	orégano
organic	*or-gan-ik-oh*	orgánico
outdoors	*al fres-koh*	al fresco
oven	*orr-noh*	horno
oyster	*os-trah*	ostra

P

packet	*pa-ket-eh*	paquete
paprika	*pee-men-ton*	pimentón
parsley	*per-ek-il*	perejil
parsnip	*chir-iv-ee-ah*	chirivía
party	*fee-es-tah*	fiesta
pasta	*pah-stah*	pasta
pastry (dough)	*mas-ah*	masa
pastry (such as Danish)	*pas-tel-ee-toh*	pastelito
pea	*gwee-san-tay*	guisante
peach	*mel-o-ko-tohn*	melocotón
peanut	*ka-kah-weh-teh*	cacahuete
pear	*peh-rah*	pera
pecan	*pak-an-ah*	pacana
pepper	*pi-mee-en-tah*	pimienta
–mill	*mol-in-il-yo de pi-mee-en-tah*	molinillo de pimienta
peppermint	*men-tah*	menta
pheasant	*fai-san*	faisán
pickles	*en-kür-tee-dos*	encurtidos
picnic	*pik-nik*	picnic
pie	*tor-tah*	torta
pike	*loo-cee-oh*	lucio
pineapple	*pee-nyah*	piña
–juice	*hoo-goh de pin-yah*	jugo de piña
pine nut	*peen-yon*	piñón
pinto bean	*peen-tah*	pinta
pistachio	*pis-tach-oh*	pistacho
pita bread	*pan ah-ra-bay*	pan árabe
plaice	*plat-ee-kah; sol-yah*	platija; solla

plate	*plat-oh*	plato
plum	*si-roo-el-ah*	ciruela
plum tomato	*to-mah-tay (de) peh-rah*	tomate (de) pera
poached egg	*hway-voh es-kal-fah-doh*	huevo escalfado
popcorn	*pa-lom-ee-tas*	palomitas
pork	*ser-doh/pwer-koh*	cerdo/puerco
port	*o-por-toh*	oporto
pot (for cooking)	*kal-deh-ret-ah/mar-mee-tah*	caldereta/marmita
potato	*pat-at-ah*	patata
–chips/crisps	*pat-at-as free-tas*	patatas fritas
–croquette	*krok-et-ah de pat-at-ah*	croqueta de patata
–omelette	*tor-til-yah de pat-at-as*	tortilla de patatas
–salad	*en-sah-lah-dah de pat-at-as*	ensalada de patatas
prawn	*gam-bah*	gamba
price	*preth-ee-oh*	precio
–list	*lis-tah de pres-ee-os*	lista de precios
protein	*pro-tay-ee-nah*	proteína
prune	*si-roo-el-ah pa-sah*	ciruela pasa
pudding (dessert)	*po-stray*	postre
pudding (dish of)	*poo-din*	pudin
pulses	*leg-oom-brays*	legumbres
pumpkin	*ka-lab-ah-sah*	calabaza

Q

quality	*kahlidahd*	calidad
quarter	*kwah-toh*	cuarto
quince	*mem-bril-yoh*	membrillo

R

rabbit	*kon-eh-kho*	conejo
radish	*ra-ban-oh*	rábano
raisin	*pa-sah*	pasa
rare (barely cooked)	*po-koh ech-oh*	poco hecho
raspberry	*fram-bway-sah*	frambuesa
raw	*kroo-doh*	crudo
receipt	*re-see-boh*	recibo
recipe	*re-set-ah*	receta
red cabbage	*kol lom-bah-dah*	col lombarda
red capsicum	*pi-mee-en-toh roh-koh*	pimiento rojo
refrigerator	*nev-ehr-ah/free-goh*	nevera/frigo
restaurant	*res-tor-an-tay*	restaurante
rhubarb	*rwee-bar-boh*	ruibarbo
ribs	*kos-til-yas*	costillas
rice	*ah-rroth*	arroz
–pudding	*ah-rroth kon le-chay*	arroz con leche

ripe — *mad-oo-roh* — maduro
roast beef — *re-dohn-doh al orr-noh* — redondo al horno
roast chicken — *pohl-yoh a-sah-doh* — pollo asado
roast meats — *a-sah-dos* — asados
rosemary — *roh-mehr-oh* — romero
rum — *ron* — ron
runner bean — *hoo-dee-ah ver-day* — judía verde

S

sachet — *bol-see-tah* — bolsita
saffron — *az-ah-fran* — azafrán
sage — *sal-vee-ah* — salvia
salad — *en-sah-lah-dah* — ensalada
salt — *sal* — sal
 –cellar — *sal-eh-roh* — salero
salted/salty — *sah-lah-doh* — salado
sandwich — *sand-gwich* — sándwich
sauce — *sal-sah* — salsa
saucepan — *ka-soh* — cazo
savoury — *sah-lah-doh* — salado
scallop — *ven-er-ah/vee-eh-rah* — venera/vieira
scissors — *tik-ehr-as* — tijeras
seafood — *prod-uk-tos del mahr; mar-is-kos* — productos del mar; mariscos
seasonal — *del tee-em-poh* — del tiempo
selection — *sur-tee-doh* — surtido
semi-skimmed milk — *le-chay sem-ee-des-nah-tah-dah* — leche semi-desnatada
service — *ser-vith-ee-oh* — servicio
 –included — *ser-vith-ee-oh in-cloo-ee-doh* — servicio incluido
set menu — *men-oo* — menú
shandy — *kla-rah* — clara
shell — *ka-par-a-son* — caparazón
shellfish — *mar-is-kos* — mariscos
sherry — *he-reth* — Jerez
shrimp — *gam-bar-oh* — gámbaro
sieve — *kol-a-dor* — colador
skimmed milk — *le-chay des-nah-tah-dah* — leche desnatada
smoked — *a-oo-mah-doh* — ahumado
 –salmon — *sal-mon a-oo-mah-doh* — salmón ahumado
soda water — *soh-dah* — soda
soft — *blan-doh* — blando
soft drink — *re-fres-koh* — refresco
sole — *len-goo-ah-doh* — lenguado
soup — *so-pah* — sopa
 –of the day — *so-pah del dee-ah* — sopa del día
 –plate — *plat-oh sop-ehr-oh* — plato sopero
 –spoon — *koo-chah-rah de so-pah* — cuchara de sopa

sour	*ag-ree-oh*	agrio
sour cream	*nat-ah ag-ree-ah*	nata agria
soy (milk)	*le-chay de soh-kah*	(leche) de soja
spaghetti	*es-pag-et-ees*	espaguetis
Spanish omelette	*tor-til-yah es-pan-yoh-lah*	tortilla española
sparkling	*es-poo-moh-soh*	espumoso
–wine	*kav-ah*	cava
speciality	*es-pes-ee-al-ee-dah*	especialidad
spices	*es-pes-ee-as*	especias
spicy	*pee-kahn-te*	picante
spinach	*es-pee-na-ka(s)*	espinaca(s)
sponge cake	*bis-ko-choh*	bizcocho
spoon	*koo-chah-rah*	cuchara
spring onion	*se-bol-yet-ah*	cebolleta
squid	*chok-os*	chocos
stale	*pa-sa-doh; ran-see-oh*	pasado; rancio
steak	*bis-tek*	bistec
stew	*koh-cee-doh*	cocido
stove	*es-too-fah*	estufa
straight (alcohol)	*sol-oh*	solo
strawberry	*fres-ah*	fresa
strong	*fwer-teh*	fuerte
stuffed	*rel-ye-noh*	relleno
sturgeon	*es-too-ree-on*	esturión
sugar	*as-oo-kah*	azúcar
sultana	*pa-sah sül-tan-ah*	pasa sultana
sun-dried	*sek-ah-doh al sol*	secado al sol
sunflower oil	*a-say-tay de hi-ra-sohl*	aceite de girasol
sunflower seeds	*pee-pah de hi-ra-sohl*	pipa de girasol
supermarket	*su-per-mer-kah-doh*	supermercado
supper (dinner)	*se-nah*	cena
(Basque)	*a-fah-ree*	afari
(Catalan)	*soo-pahr*	sopar
(Galician)	*say-ah*	cea
sweet	*dul-say*	dulce
sweets (candy)	*kara-mel-os*	caramelos

T

table	*mes-ah*	mesa
–wine	*vee-noh de may-sah*	vino de mesa
tablecloth	*man-tel*	mantel
tablespoonful	*koo-chah-rah-dah*	cucharada
tap water	*ag-wah del gr-ee-fo;*	agua del grifo;
	ag-wah nat-u-ral	agua natural
taste	*gus-toh/sah-bor*	gusto/sabor
tea	*teh*	té

teaspoon	*koo-chah-ree-tah*	cucharita
teaspoonful	*koo-chah-rah-dee-tah*	cucharadita
tin opener	*a-bray-lah-tas*	abrelatas
tip	*prop-ee-nah*	propina
toast (bread)	*tos-tah-dah*	tostada
toast (tribute)	*brin-dis*	brindis
toaster	*tos-tah-dor-ah*	tostadora
tofu	*to-foo*	tofu
tomato	*to-mah-tay*	tomate
tomato juice	*hoo-goh de to-mah-tay*	jugo de tomate
tonic water	*(ag-wah) ton-ee-kah*	(agua) tónica
toothpick	*pal-il-yoh*	palillo
tripe	*kal-yos*	callos
trolley	*kar-roh*	carro
trout	*troo-chah*	trucha
tuna	*a-tun*	atún
turkey	*pa-voh*	pavo

U

| used by ... | *kon-soo-mir an-tes de ...* | consumir antes de ... |

V

vanilla	*vay-nil-yah*	vainilla
veal	*ter-neh-rah*	ternera
vegan	*veg-et-ar-ee-ah-noh es-trik-toh*	vegetariano estricto
vegetables	*ver-doo-ras*	verduras
vegetarian	*veg-et-ar-ee-ah-noh*	vegetariano
venison	*ven-ad-oh*	venado
vinegar	*vin-ag-reh*	vinagre
vintage	*ko-sech-ah*	cosecha
vodka	*vod-kah*	vodka

W

waiter (m/f)	*kam-a-rehr-oh/ah*	camarero/a
water	*ag-wah*	agua
watermelon	*san-dee-ah*	sandía
well done (cooked)	*bee-en ech-oh*	bien hecho
wheat	*tree-goh*	trigo
wheat flour	*aree-nah de tree-goh*	harina de trigo
wheatgerm	*ger-men de tree-goh*	germen de trigo
whisk	*bat-ee-dor-ah*	batidora
whisky	*gwis-kee*	güisqui
white	*blan-koh*	blanco

English	Pronunciation	Spanish
whitebait	*bo-keh-ron*	boquerón
white bread	*pan blan-koh*	pan blanco
whiting	*pes-kah-dil-yah*	pescadilla
wholemeal bread	*pan in-teg-ral*	pan integral
wild	*sil-ves-tray*	silvestre
wild mushrooms	*se-tas*	setas
wild rice	*ah-rroth sal-vak-hay*	arroz salvaje
wine	*vee-noh*	vino
wine list	*kar-tah de vee-nos*	carta de vinos
wineskin	*bor-rach-ah*	borracha

Y

| yoghurt | *yog-ür* | yogur |

Z

| zucchini | *ka-lab-ah-sihn* | calabacín |

Spanish Culinary Dictionary

In Spanish, nouns always have a feminine or masculine form. With some exceptions, there are some ways to tell which form a word should take. Generally speaking, feminine forms end in -a and are preceded by the definite article la (the), or the indefinite article una (a). Masculine forms generally end in -o and are preceded by the definite article el (the) or the indefinite article un (a).

A

abadejo *a-ba-deh-kho* pollack (fish)

abajá de Algeciras *aba-kha de al-ge-cir-as* fish soup (Algeciras)

ablandar *ab-lan-dahr* to tenderise (meat)

abocado *abo-kar-doh* smooth, slightly sweet (of wine)

adobo *(see* **dejar en adobo**)

abrebocas *a-bray-boh-kas* appetiser

abrebotellas *a-bray-boh-tel-yas* bottle opener

abrelatas *a-bray-lah-tas* can/tin opener

acebuche *a-say-boo-chay* wild olive

acedera *a-say-der-ra* sorrel

acedía *a-say-dee-ya* plaice/flounder

aceitar *a-say-tahr* to grease

aceite *a-say-tay* oil
–de girasol *de hi-ra-sohl* sunflower oil
–de maíz *de may-iz* corn oil
–de oliva *de ol-ee-vah* olive oil
–de oliva virgen *de ol-ee-vah vir-khen* virgin olive oil
–de oliva virgen extra *de ol-ee-vah vir-khen ex-trah* extra virgin olive oil

aceitera *a-say-ter-rah* cruet

aceitoso *a-say-toh-soh* oily

aceituna *a-say-too-nah* olive
–gordal *gor-dal* queen olive
–negra *neg-rah* black olive
–sin hueso *sin weh-soh* pitted olive
–verde *ver-day* green olive

aceitunas aliñadas *a-say-too-nas a-li-nya-das* marinated olives

aceitunas rellenas *a-say-too-nas rel-ye-nas* olives stuffed with red capsicums or anchovies

aceituno *a-say-too-noh* olive tree

acelgas *a-sel-gas* Swiss chard

achicoria *a-chi-ko-ria* chicory
–roja *ro-khah* radicchio

Achuche *a-choo-che* type of cheese

ácido *ah-si-do* tart (of fruit)

aclarar *a-kla-rahr* to thin (a sauce)

aderezar *a-dehr-e-thar* to dress (a salad)

aditivo *a-dit-ih-vo* additive

adobo *ah-doh-boh* marinade

afilador *a-fil-ah-dor* knife sharpener

afrecho *a-fray-cho* bran

afrutado *a-froo-tah-doh* fruity

Afuega'l Pitu *a-fway-gal pee-too* dry cow's milk cheese (Oviedo)

agarrador *a-garr-ah-daw* pot holder; also oven glove

agriar *ag-ree-ahr* to turn sour

agridulce *ag-ree-dul-say* bittersweet

agrio *ag-ree-oh* sour; sharp

agrios *ag-ree-os* citrus fruits

agua *ag-wah* water
–del grifo *del gr-ee-fo* tap water
–mineral *min-er-al* mineral water
–mineral con gas *min-er-al kon gas* mineral water (sparkling)
–mineral sin gas *min-er-al sin gas* mineral water (still)
–natural *nat-u-ral* tap water
–potable *pot-ab-lay* drinking water

(agua) tónica *(ag-wah) ton-ee-kah* tonic water

aguacate *ag-wah-ka-te* avocado

aguardiente *ag-wah-di-ente* eau de vie; strong spirit
–de sidra *del see-drah* cider brandy
–valle del hjerte *val-ya del hr-teh* cherry-flavoured liqueur

aguaturma *ag-wah-tür-ma* Jerusalem artichoke

aguja *ag-oo-kha* needle fish

ahumado *a-oo-mah-doh* smoked

Ahumado de Aliva *a-oo-mah-doh de al-e-va* smoked cheese (Aliva)

ahumados *a-oo-mah-dos* smoked

ahumar *a-oo-mahr* to smoke (meat etc)

ajada *a-kha-dah* garlic, paprika, vinegar and olive oil sauce (Galicia)

ajenjo *a-khen-koh* absinth

ajiaco *a-khi-akoh* spicy potato dish

ajo *ah-khoh* garlic
  −**blanco** *blan-koh* almond, garlic and sherry soup
  −**de peces del río** *de pe-says del ree-yoh* river fish with garlic

ajoaceite *ah-khoh-ah-say-tay* garlic and oil sauce; garlic mayonnaise

ajoarriero (*see* **bacalao al ajoarriero**)

ajoblanco de Málaga *ah-khoh-blan-ko de mal-ah-gah* garlic soup served with grapes (Málaga)

ajoharina *ah-khoh-ah-ree-nah* potatoes stewed in garlic sauce

ajonjolí *ah-khohn-khol-i* sesame seeds

a la aragonesa *ah lah ar-ah-gon-ay-sah* cooked in a tomato and red capsicum sauce, typical of the Aragón region

a la asturiana *ah lah as-too-ri-ah-nah* cooked in a cider sauce (Asturias)

a la catalana *ah lah kat-ah-lah-nah* cooked in a tomato and green capsicum sauce (Catalunya)

a la madrileña *ah lah mad-ri-len-yah* cooked in a tomato and chilli sauce (Madrid)

a la marinera *ah lah mah-rin-ehr-ah* cooked or served in a white wine sauce

a la navarra *ah lah nah-va-rra* cooked with tomatoes, chorizo and capsicums (Navarra)

a la panadera *ah lah pan-a-deh-rah* cooked in a baker's oven

a la parrilla *ah lah par-ril-yah* grilled

a la plancha *ah lah plahn-chah* grilled

a la riojana *ah lah rio-kha-nah* cooked in a paprika & red chilli sauce (La Rioja)

a la sevillana *ah lah sev-il-yah-nah* cooked in orange or saffron (Seville)

a la sidra *ah lah see-drah* cooked in a cider sauce (Asturias)

a la vasca *ah lah bas-kah* cooked in a parsley and garlic sauce (País Vasco)

a la vizcaína *ah lah biz-kay-ee-nah* cooked in a spicy onion, garlic and paprika sauce (Bizkaia, País Vasco)

al ajoarriero *al ah-khoh-arr-ee-ye-roh* cooked in a sauce of onions, garlic and chilli ('mule-driver's garlic', referring to the drivers who brought this dish from León to Aragón, La Rioja and the Basque Country)

al andaluz *al an-dah-luth* usually refers to a vegetable sauce (Andalucía)

al chilindrón *al chil-in-drohn* cooked in a tomato and red pepper sauce

al fresco *al fres-koh* outdoors

al horno *al orr-noh* baked

al jerez *al he-reth* in a sherry sauce

al pil pil *al pil pil* in a garlic and olive oil sauce

al vapor (*see* **cocido al vapor**)

ala *ah-la* (chicken) wing

alacena *ah-la-say-na* larder

alajú *ah-la-khoo* honey and almond cake

albahaca *al-ba-aka* basil

albaricoque *al-bari-ko-ke* apricot
  −**seco** *say-ko* dried apricot

albariño *al-ba-rin-yo* wine (Galicia)

Albarracín *al-barr-a-sin* type of cheese

albérchigo *alber-chi-go* clingstone peach

albóndigas *al-bohn-di-gas* meatballs
  −**con jerez** *kon he-reth* in sherry sauce
  −**de pescado** *de pes-kah-doh* fish balls

alcachofas *al-ka-choh-fas* artichokes
  −**a la andaluz** *ah lah an-dah-luth* artichokes with bacon and ham
  −**a la cussy** *ah lah koo-sy* artichokes stuffed with chicken livers
  −**a la sevillana** *ah lah sev-il-ya-nah* artichokes & potatoes in saffron sauce
  −**a la vinagreta** *ah lah vin-ag-ret-ah* artichokes in vinaigrette

–guisadas a la española *gwee-sah-das ah lah es-pan-yoh-lah* in wine

–rellenas *rel-ye-nas* stuffed artichokes

alcaparra *al-kah-pah-rrah* caper

alcaucil *al-kah-oo-sil* artichoke

Alella *al-el-yah* wine region (DO) in Catalunya

aleta *al-eh-tah* fin (of a fish)

alfajor *al-fah-kor* honey nut and cinnamon biscuit coated with syrup

alfalfa *al-fal-fah* alfalfa

Algeciras (*see* **abajá de Algeciras**)

Alhama de Granada *al-ah-ma de gra-na-dah* type of cheese

ali-pebre *al-ee-peb-ray* garlic and paprika sauce

Alicante *al-ee-kan-tay* wine region (DO) in València (*see* **queso de Alicante**)

alifara *al-ee-fah-rah* picnic

aliñar *al-in-yahr* to dress (a salad); also to season (meat)

alioli *al-ee-ol-ee* garlic mayonnaise

almacén *al-mah-sen* grocery/general store

Almansa *al-man-sah* wine region (DO) in Castilla

almejas *al-meh-kas* clams – superb eaten raw, and sometimes no larger than a thumbnail

–a la marinera *ah lah mah-rin-ehr-ah* clams in white wine

–a la valenciana *ah lah bal-en-see-ah-nah* clams in white wine

–al horno *al orr-noh* baked clams

–con arroz *kon ah-rroth* clams with rice and onions

–en salsa verde *en sal-sah ver-day* clams in parsley sauce

almendrado *al-men-drah-doh* almond biscuit or cake; chocolate covered ice cream bar

almendras *al-men-dras* almonds

–fritas *free-tas* fried almonds

–saladas *sah-lah-das* salted almonds

almirez *al-mee-reth* mortar and pestle

almuerzo *al-mwer-thoh* brunch; light lunch

–de negocios *de neg-oh-see-os* business lunch

alubia *ah-loo-bee-ah* (haricot) bean

amargo *ah-mahr-goh* bitter

amasado *ah-mah-sah-doh* kneading

amasar *ah-mah-sahr* to knead/mix

amontillado *ah-mon-til-yah-doh* pale, dry sherry with a hazelnut flavour

amoroso *ah-moh-roh-soh* medium-dry sherry

Ampurdán-Costa Brava *ahm-pur-dahn-koh-sta brah-vah* wine region (DO) in Catalunya

anacardo *ah-nah-karh-doh* cashew nut

anca de rana *ahn-kah de rah-nah* frog's leg

anchoas *ahn-cho-as* anchovies – mostly eaten fresh, grilled or fried

–a la barquera *ah lah bahr-keh-rah* marinated anchovies and capers

–en conserva *en kon-serv-ah* tinned anchovies

–fritas a la catalana *free-tas ah lah kat-ah-lah-nah* deep-fried anchovies

andaluz *an-dah-luth* from Andalucía (*see* **callos a la andaluz; cocido andaluz; gazpacho andaluz**)

añejado por *ahn-yeh-kah-doh por* aged by

añejo *ahn-yeh-ko* old/mature

angélica *ahn-khel-ee-kah* angelica

angelote *ahn-khel-oh-tay* monkfish

angostura *ahn-khos-too-rah* bitters

anguila *ahn-gwee-lah* adult eel

anguilas a la vasca *ahn-gwee-las ah lah bas-kah* eels with chillies and garlic

angulas *an-goo-las* baby eels – prized as a delicacy, they resemble vermicelli

–al ajillo *al a-kil-yoh* baby eels with garlic

–en all i pebre *en al-iy ee peb-ray* baby eels with pepper and garlic

anís *ah-nees* aniseed liqueur; anise

–dulce *dul-say* sweet aniseed liqueur

–seco *sek-oh* dry aniseed liqueur

año *an-yoh* year/vintage

Ansó-Hecho *an-soh-ech-oh* creamy white cheese (Huesca)

aparato *a-pahr-ah-toh* appliance

aperitivo *a-per-ee-tee-voh* aperitif

apio *a-pee-oh* celery

Aracena *a-rah-see-nah* type of cheese

aragonesa *(see* **chuletas de cerdo a la aragonesa)**

arándano *a-rahn-ah-doh* blueberry/ cranberry

arenque *a-ren-kay* herring

–ahumado *ah-oo-mah-doh* kipper

arenques frescos *a-ren-kays fres-kos* fresh herrings

la Armada *lah ahr-ma-dah* hard, sharp cow's cheese (León)

arnadi *ah-nah-dee* a gourd sweet

arròs amb fesols i naps *ah-rros amb fe-sols ee naps* rice with turnips and broad beans (Catalunya)

arroz *ah-rroth* rice

–a la Alcireña *ah lah al-see-ren-yah* baked rice dish

–a la cassola *ah lah kas-soh-lah* rice with spicy sausage, pork and seafood

–a la pamplonesa *ah lah pam-plon-ay-sah* cod and tomato rice dish

–a la santanderina *ah lah san-tan-de-ree-nah* rice with salmon

–abanda (de València) *a-ban-dah (de val-en-see-ah)* fish paella

–al caldero *al kal-deh-roh* rice & fish

–azafrán *ah-thah-fran* saffron rice

–Calasparra *kal-ah-spar-rah* medium to short-grain rice used in paella (DO, Murcia)

–catalana *kat-ah-lah-nah* rice with spicy sausage, pork and seafood

–con almejas *kon al-meh-kas* clams and cod with rice

–con costra *kon kos-trah* baked rice dish with meat and beans

–con leche *kon le-chay* rice pudding

–con pollo *kon pohl-yoh* chicken and rice dish

–de Arzak *de ahr-zak* rice dish from the famous Basque restaurant Arzac, made with **koskeras**

–del Delta del Ebro *del del-tah del ee-broh* type of rice (DO)

–empedrado *em-pah-red-ah-doh* rice with tomatoes, cod and white beans

–en oros y bastos *ah-rroth en o-ros ee bas-tos* Valencian rice dish

–estilo barcelonés *es-tee-loh bah-see-loh-nes* paella with peas and ham

–integral *in-teg-ral* brown rice

–marinera *mah-rin-ehr-ah* rice with seafood

–negro *neg-rah* squid in its ink

–rosetxat *ros-et-shat* baked rice dish

–salvaje *sal-vak-hay* wild rice

Arzak *(see* **arroz de Arzak)**

Arzúa *ahr-zoo-ah* type of cheese

asadillo *a-sah-dil-yoh* roasted red capsicums

asados *a-sah-dos* roast meats

asadurilla *a-sah-doo-ril-yah* offal stew

–de cordero *de kor-deh-roh* lamb's liver stew

asar *ah-sahr* to roast

–a la brasa *ah lah bras-ahr* to barbecue

asturiano *as-too-ri-ah-noh* from Asturias

atascaburros *at-as-kah-boo-rros* rabbit casserole

atún *a-tun* tuna – often served marinated and raw *(see* **budín de atún; bull de atún; buñuelo de atún)**

–al horno *al orr-noh* baked tuna

–en escabeche *en es-kah-bay-chay* marinated tuna

ave de corral *av-e de kor-ral* fowl

avellana *av-el-yah-nah* hazelnut

avena *av-ay-nah* oats/oatmeal

aves *av-es* poultry

azafrán *az-ah-fran* saffron *(see also* **arroz azafrán)**

azúcar *as-oo-kah* sugar

–glasé *glas-ay* icing sugar

–moreno *mor-en-oh* brown sugar

B

babero *bab-ehr-oh* bib

Babia y Laciana *bab-ee-ah ee la-see-ah-nah* type of cheese

bacalao *bak-al-ow* cod – usually salted and dried *(see also* **buñuelo de bacalao; croqueta de bacalao**)
  –a la catalana *ah lah kat-ah-lah-nah* roast cod with almond, ham & sherry
  –a la llauna *ah lah yah-oo-nah* roast cod with almond, ham & sherry
  –a la vizcaína *ah lah biz-kay-ee-nah* cod with chillies and capsicums
  –al ajoarriero *al ah-khoh-arr-ee-ye-roh* cod with garlic, parsley and chilli
  –al Club Ranero *al klub ran-eh-roh* cod dish from the famous Basque gastronomic society
  –al pil pil *al pil pil* salted cod in garlic and oil
  –del convento *del kon-ven-toh* cod, potatoes and spinach in broth
  –en salsa verde *en sal-sah ver-day* salted cod in parsley sauce
bacón *ba-kon* bacon
Baena *by-en-ah* olive oil producing region (DO) near Córdoba
bajoques farcides *ba-kho-kes fahr-si-des* capsicums stuffed with rice, pork, tomatoes and spices
Bakio *bak-ee-oh* Txakolí (Bizkaia)
balanza *bal-an-sah* scales (weighing)
bandeja *ban-de-khah* (baking) tray
banderilla *ban-deh-ril-yah* mini tapa skewered on a toothpick
bar *bahr* bar
barbacoa *bahr-bak-ow-a* barbecue
barbo *bahr-boh* red mullet
  –encebollado *en-seb-ol-yah-doh* red mullet with onion
barra *bar-rah* long stick of bread
barricas *bar-ree-kas* 225-litre oak barrels used for maturing Rioja wine
barril *bar-ril* barrel/cask
batata *bat-at-ah* sweet potato
batido *bat-ee-doh* milkshake
batidora *bat-ee-dor-ah* blender/whisk
batir *bat-eer* to cream/whisk
bebida caliente *beb-ee-dah kal-ee-en-tay* hot drink
bebida fresca *beb-ee-dah fres-kah* cold drink

bebidas *beb-ee-das* drinks
  –espirituosas tradicionales de Alicante *es-pir-it-oo-oh-sas trad-is-ee-on-al-es de al-ee-kan-tay* traditional spirits from Alicante (DO)
becada *bek-ah-dah* woodcock
  –con nabos *kon nab-os* with turnips
beicon *beh-kon* streaky bacon rashers
Benasque *ben-as-kay* type of cheese
berberechos *ber-ber-ech-os* cockles
  –en vinagre *en vin-ag-reh* in vinegar
bercianos *ber-see-ah-nos* tomatoes from El Bierzo
berenjenas *be-ren-khen-as* eggplants *(see also* **ensala da de berenjena; gratinado de berenjenas**)
  –a la mallorquina *ah lah mal-yor-kin-ah* with garlic mayonnaise
  –con setas *kon se-tas* with mushrooms
  –de Almagro *de al-mag-roh* from Almagro (DO)
  –salteadas *sal-te-ah-das* sauteed
berro *ber-roh* watercress
berza *ber-sah* cabbage
  –a la andaluz *ah lah an-dah-luth* cabbage and meat hotpot
besugo *be-soo-goh* red bream
  –a la Donostiarra *ah lah don-os-ti-ah-rrah* barbecued with garlic & paprika
  –a la madrileña *ah lah mad-ri-len-yah* baked with tomato sauce
  –estilo San Sebastián *es-tee-loh san seb-as-tee-an* barbecued red bream with garlic and paprika
Beyos *beh-yos* smoked cheese (Asturia)
biberón *bi-ber-ohn* feeding bottle
bicarbonato de sosa *bi-kahr-bon-ah-toh de so-sah* baking soda
bien hecho *bee-en ech-oh* well done (cooked)
bienmesabe *bee-en-mes-ah-beh* sponge cake, egg & almond confection
Bierzo *bee-ehr-soh* wine region (Castilla y León)
Binissalem-Mallorca *bin-is-sal-em-mal-yor-kah* wine region (DO) in the Islas Baleares

biológico *(see* **productos biológicos)**

bisbe *bis-beh* black & white blood sausage

bistec *bis-tek* steak

—con patatas *kon pat-at-as* with chips

bizcocha manchega *bis-ko-choh man-cheh-goh* cake soaked in milk, sugar, vanilla and cinnamon

bizcocho *bis-ko-choh* sponge cake *(see also* **empanadas de bizcocho)**

—de almendra *de al-men-drah* almond cake

—de avellana *de av-el-yah-nah* hazelnut cake

bizcochos borrachos *bis-ko-choh bor-ra-chos* cake soaked in liqueur

Bizkaiko Txakolia *bis-keh-ee-koh chak-ol-ee-ah* Txakolí wine region (DO) of Vizcaya in the País Vasco

blanco *blan-koh* white

blando *blan-doh* soft

blanquear *blan-kee-ahr* to blanch

bocadillo *bok-ah-dil-yoh* bread roll with a filling

bocas de la isla *bo-kas de lah ees-lah* large crab claws

boda *(see* **pastel de boda)**

bodega *bo-deh-gah* wine producer/cellar/shop

bodeguero *bo-deg-weh-roh* wine company

bodigo *bo-dee-goh* bread roll taken to church as an offering

bogavante *bo-gah-van-teh* lobster

bol *bol* bowl

bolet *bol-et* type of mushroom

bollo *bol-yoh* crusty bread roll
—de chicharrones *de chi-chahr-roh-nes* confection from Extremadura

bollos de aceite *bol-yos de a-say-tay* buns made with oil

bollos de leche *bol-yos de le-chay* confection (Extremadura)

bolsita *bol-see-tah* sachet/bag

bonito *bon-ee-toh* white fleshy tuna

boquerón *bo-keh-ron* whitebait

boquerones *bo-keh-roh-nes* anchovies marinated in wine vinegar

—en vinagre *en vin-ag-reh* anchovies in vinaigrette

—fritos *free-tos* fried anchovies

boraja *bo-ra-khah* borage

Borja *(see* **Campo de Borja)**

borracha *bor-rach-ah* wineskin

borracho/a *bor-rach-oh/ah* drunk; soaked in liqueur

bosque *bos-keh* woods/forest

bota *bo-tah* small leather bag used to hold wine

botella *bo-tel-yah* bottle

botellín *bo-tel-yin* small bottle of beer (250 ml)

brama *bra-mah* sea bream

brandy de Jerez *bran-dee de he-reth* Spanish brandy made in Jerez (DO)

brazo de gitano *bra-soh* filled sponge roll

breva *breh-vah* early fig

brindis *brin-dis* toast (tribute)

brócoli *bro-ko-leh* broccoli

brut *brüt* dry (sparkling wine)

brut natur *brüt nat-ür* extra-dry (sparkling wine)

budín de atún *boo-din de a-tun* baked tuna pudding

Buelles *boo-wel-yes* type of cheese

buey *boo-ay* ox *(see* **chuletas de buey; estofado de buey)**

bull de atún *bu-ye de a-tun* rabbit with garlic and tuna boiled with potatoes

Bullas *bul-yas* wine region (DO) in València

buñuelitos *bun-yoo-el-ee-tos* small cheese or ham fritters

—de San José *de san ho-say* lemon and vanilla crepes

buñuelo *bun-yoo-el-oh* fried pastry

—de atún *de a-tun* tuna pastry

—de bacalao *de bak-al-ow* cod pastry

—de chorizo *de choh-ree-thoh* chorizo pastry

—de jamón y queso *de ha-mon ee ke-soh* cheese and ham pastry

—de queso *de ke-soh* cheese pastry

burbuja *bur-boo-khah* bubble

la Bureba *lah bu-ray-bah* type of cheese

Burgos (see **queso de Burgos**)
burrida de ratjada *bür-ree-dah de rat-khah-dah* fish soup with almonds
butifarra (blanca) *boo-tee-far-rah (blahn-kah)* cured pork sausage
  –con setas *kon se-tas* Catalan sausage with mushrooms
  –dolça *dol-sah* cured pork sausage with sugar and cinnamon
  –negra *neg-rah* black pudding

C

caballa *kah-bal-yah* mackerel
caballo de ángel *kah-bal-yoh de ahn-khel* 'angel hair' – pumpkin jam
cabeza *kab-eh-sah* bulb (of garlic)
  –de ternera *de ter-neh-rah* calf's head, split – served boiled and skinned
cabra *ka-bra* goat
cabracho *ka-bra-choh* scorpion fish; mullet
cabrales *ka-bra-les* blue vein mountain cheese aged in caves (DO)
cabrito *kab-ree-toh* kid
  –asado *a-sah-doh* roast kid
cacahuete *ka-kah-weh-teh* peanut
cacao *ka-kow* cocoa
cáceres *kah-ceh-rehs* variety of cheese
cachelos *ka-cheh-los* potatoes with spicy sausage and pork
cadera *ka-deh-rah* rump
cádiz *kah-dis* fresh goat's milk cheese
café *ka-fay* coffee (see **molinillo de café**)
  –con leche *kon le-chay* with milk
  –cortado *kor-tah-doh* small, with milk
  –descafeinado *des-kaf-ay-in-ah-doh* decaffeinated
  –doble *doh-blay* long black
  –en grano *en gra-noh* whole coffee beans
  –escocés *es-koh-thes* with Scotch whisky
  –exprés *ex-pres* espresso
  –instantáneo *in-stan-tah-nay-oh* instant
  –molido *mol-ee-doh* ground
  –solo *soh-loh* black
  –vienés *vee-en-es* with whipped cream

cafetera *ka-fay-teh-rah* coffee pot/maker
cafetería *ka-fay-teh-ree-yah* cafe
caja *ka-khah* box
calabacín *ka-lab-ah-sihn* zucchini (courgette)
calabacines al horno *ka-lab-ah-see-nes al orr-noh* baked zucchini (courgette)
calabaza *ka-lab-ah-sah* pumpkin
el Calado *el ka-lah-doh* famous underground cellar in La Rioja
calamares *kal-a-mah-res* calamari – popular fried or stuffed
  –a la bilbaína *ah lah bil-bay-ee-nah* squid cooked in its ink
  –en su tinta *en su tin-tah* squid cooked in its ink
  –fritos a la romana *free-tos ah lah roh-mah-nah* squid rings fried in batter
  –rellenos *rel-ye-nos* stuffed squid
Calasparra (see **arroz Calasparra**)
Calatayud *kal-at-ai-ud* wine region (DO) in Aragón
calçots *kal-sots* spring onion-like vegetables chargrilled and eaten with a romesco dipping sauce in Spring
caldeirada *kal-day-ee-rah-dah* salted cod and potatoes in a paprika sauce; also fish soup
caldereta *kal-deh-ret-ah* small boiling pot (for cooking); also stew
  –asturiana *kal-deh-ret-ah as-too-ri-ah-nah* fish stew
  –de cordero *kal-deh-ret-ah de kor-deh-roh* lamb stew
  –de cordero a la pastora *de kor-deh-roh ah lah pas-tor-ah* lamb & vegetable stew
  –de langosta *de lan-gos-tah* lobster stew
  –de pescado *de pes-kah-doh* fish stew
  –de pescado y mariscos *de pes-kah-doh ee mar-is-kos* fish & shellfish stew
  –gallega *gal-yeh-gah* vegetable stew
caldero (see **arroz al caldero**)
caldillo de perro *kal-dil-yoh de per-rho* 'puppydog soup' – stew of onions, fresh fish and orange juice
caldo *kal-doh* broth; clear soup; stock

–al estilo del Mar Menor *al es-tee-loh del mahr men-or* fish stew from the Mar Menor

–gallego *gal-yeh-goh* broth with haricot beans, ham and sausage

–guanche *gwoo-an-chay* vegetable soup (Canary islands)

caldoso *kal-doh-soh* soggy/watery/runny

calidad *kah-li-dahd* quality

caliente *kal-ee-en-tay* hot (temperature)

callos *kal-yos* tripe

–a la andaluz *ah lah al an-dah-luth* tripe casserole with chickpeas

–a la gallega *ah lah gal-yeh-gah* tripe casserole with chickpeas and ham

–a la madrileña *ah lah mad-ri-len-yah* tripe casserole with chorizo & chillies

–a la montañesa *ah lah mon-tan-yeh-sah* tripe with capsicums and wine

–a la riojana *ah lah ree-oh-khah-nah* tripe cooked with paprika

–a la vizcaína *ah lah biz-kay-ee-nah* tripe with onion, garlic and paprika

–de bacalao *de bak-al-ow* salted cod tripe

camarero/a *kam-a-rehr-oh/ah* waiter

camarones fritos *kam-ah-roh-nes free-tos* deep-fried prawns

cambio *kam-bee-oh* change

Camerano *kam-er-ah-noh* fresh goat's cheese (Logroño)

Campo de Borja *kam-poh de bor-kha* wine region (DO, Aragón)

Campurriano (see **pollo Campurriano**)

Can Pujol *can poo-jol* soft goat's cheese (Catalunya)

caña *kan-yah* glass of beer (250 ml)

canagroc *kan-ah-grok* mushroom

cañaillas de la Isla *kan-yah-il-yas de lah ees-lah* boiled sea-snails

canalones *kan-al-oh-nes* squares of pasta for making cannelloni

–con espinaca *kon es-pee-na-ka* cannelloni with spinach, anchovies and bechamel

–con jamón *kon ha-mon* cannelloni with ham, onion, tomato and eggs

–con pescado **kon pes-kah-doh** cannelloni with cod, eggs and mushrooms

canapés de fiambres *kan-ap-ehs de flam-brehs* mini hors d'oeuvres with ham, anchovies or cheese

canela *kan-el-ah* cinnamon

cangrejo *kan-gre-khoh* large-clawed crab usually eaten steamed or boiled

cangrejos de coña *kan-gre-khos de kon-yah* crab sticks

cangrejos de río al estilo de Burgos *kan-gre-khos de ree-yoh al es-tee-loh de bür-gos* freshwater crabs in brandy and tomato sauce

Cantabria (see **queso de Cantabria**)

cantalupo *kan-tal-oo-poh* cantaloupe

canutillos *kan-oo-til-yos* cream biscuits

caparazón *ka-par-a-son* shell

capones de Villalba *ka-pon-es de vil-yal-bah* dish of chicken marinated in brandy – eaten at Christmas

caqui *ka-kwee* persimmon

caracoles *kara-koh-les* snails

–a la riojana *ah lah ree-oh-khah-nah* snails in paprika sauce

carajillo *kara-khil-yoh* black coffee with brandy

–de ron *de ron* black coffee with rum

carajitos del profesor *kara-khee-tos del pro-fes-or* Asturian dessert

caramelos *kara-mel-os* caramels/confection

cardamomo *kahr-dah-moh-moh* cardamom

cardo *kahr-doh* cardoon

cardos fritos *kahr-dos free-tos* fried thistles

Cariñena *kar-in-yen-ah* wine region (DO) in Aragón

carn d'olla (see **escudella i carn d'olla**)

carne *kar-nay* meat (see also **empanada de carne**)

–de membrillo *de mem-bril-yoh* quince 'cheese'

–molida *mol-ee-dah* minced meat

–picada *pee-kah-dah* minced meat

carnero *kar-neh-roh* mutton

carnicería *kahr-nee-seh-ree-ah* butcher's shop/stall

carpa *kahr-pah* carp

carro *kar-roh* trolley

carta *kahr-tah* menu
 –de vinos *de vee-nos* wine list

carvi *kahr-vee* caraway seed

casa *(see* **especialidades de la casa***)*

casadielles *ka-sah-dee-el-yes* dessert (Asturia)

cascanueces *ka-sah-noo-eh-sehs* nutcracker

casero *ka-seh-roh* home-made

Casín *ka-seen* type of cheese

Casoleta *ka-sol-et-ah* type of cheese

cassolada *kas-sol-ah-dah* potato and vegetable stew with bacon and ribs

castaña *kas-tan-yah* chestnut

castellana *(see also* **chanfaina castellana***)*

castellano *(see* **cocido castellano; queso Castellano***)*

catador *kah-tah-dor* wine-taster

catalana *(see* **a la catalana; arroz catalana; crema catalana***)*

cava *kah-vah* sparkling wine

caviar *kav-ee-ah* caviar

Cayena *kay-en-ah* cayenne

caza *ka-sah* game

cazo *ka-soh* saucepan

cazón *ka-sohn* dogfish/shark – this fish feeds on shellfish giving it a sweet scallop-like flavour

cazuela (de barro) *kath-way-lah (de bar-roh)* earthenware cooking dish
 –de fideos *de fi-day-os* noodle dish with beans and cod
 –de hígado *de ee-gah-doh* liver casserole
 –de mariscos *de mar-is-kos* seafood casserole
 –de pescado *de pes-kah-doh* fish casserole

cazuelitas de langostinos San Rafael *kath-whel-ee-tas de lan-gos-tee-nos san raph-ay-el* baked rice with seafood

cebada *se-bah-dah* barley

cebolla/s *se-bol-yah/s* onion/s

 –con miel *kon mee-el* onions in honey
 –en adobo *se-bol-yas en ah-doh-boh* pickled onions

cebolleta *se-bol-yet-ah* chive

cebollita *se-bol-yi-tah* baby onion

cebollitas al horno *se-bol-yi-tas al orr-noh* baked baby onion

cebollitas con pasas *se-bol-yee-tas kon pah-sas* baked baby onion with raisins

Cebreiro *se-breh-ee-roh* mild and tangy cow's cheese (Cebreiro mountains)

cecina *se-see-nah* cured meat

cecina de León *se-see-nah de lay-on* cured meats (DO, León)

cena *se-nah* formal dinner; dinner party; supper

cenicero *se-ni-seh-roh* ashtray

centeno *sen-ten-oh* rye

centímetro *sen-tee-met-roh* centimetre

centollo *sen-tol-yoh* spider crab

centro comercial *sen-troh koh-mer-see-al* shopping centre

cep *sep* type of mushroom

cerdo *ser-doh* pork *(see* **escalope de cerdo***)*

cereales *ser-ee-al-es* cereal

cereza *se-ray-sah* cherry
 –silvestre *sil-ves-tray* wild cherry

cerezas de la montaña de Alicante *se-ray-sas de lah mon-tan-yah de al-ee-kan-tay* wild cherries (DO, Alicante)

cervecería *ser-ves-eh-ree-ah* beer bar

Cervera *ser-veh-rah* fresh white cheese (València)

cerveza *ser-veh-sah* beer
 –de barril *de bar-ril* draught beer
 –negra *neg-rah* dark beer
 –rubia *roo-bee-ah* light beer

chacinería *chak-in-eh-ree-ah* stall or shop selling cured meats

chacolí *chak-oh-lee* light, sharp white wine (Basque Country, also **txakolí***)*

chafar *cha-fahr* to mash

chalota/e *cha-lot-ah/eh* shallot

champaña *sham-pan-yah* champagne

champiñones *sham-pin-yon-es* cultivated white mushrooms

–al ajillo *al a-khil-yoh* garlic mushrooms

–en adobo *en ah-doh-boh* marinated mushrooms

–rellenos de jamón *rel-ye-nos de ha-mon* mushrooms stuffed with ham

–rellenos de revuelto *rel-ye-nos de rev-wel-toh* mushrooms stuffed with scrambled egg

–rellenos y fritos *rel-ye-nos ee free-tos* fried stuffed mushrooms

–salteados *sal-tee-ah-dos* sautéed mushrooms

chanfaina castellana *chan-fay-ee-nah kas-tel-yah-nah* rice and offal stew

chanfaina salmantina *chan-fay-ee-nah sal-man-tee-nah* rice and offal stew

chanquetes *chan-keh-tehs* whitebait; baby anchovies

chanquetes fritos *chan-keh-tes free-tos* whitebait or baby anchovies fried in oil

chapata *cha-pat-ah* ciabatta

charcutería *char-koo-teh-ree-ah* delicatessen

chateo *chat-eh-oh* bar-hopping, to have a wine or two in a succession of bars

chato *chat-oh* glass of red wine

chef *chef* chef

chicharrones *(see **bollo de chicharrones**)*

chicle *chic-leh* chewing gum

chigre *chig-reh* bar serving food and cider in northern Spain

chilindrón *(see **al chilindrón**)*

Chinchón *chin-chon* alcoholic drink from Madrid (DO)

chipirón *chip-ee-ron* baby squid – very popular in the Basque Country

chipirones en su tinta *chip-ee-ron-es en soo tin-tah* baby squid served in its ink

chiquito *chik-whee-toh* small glass of wine; small portion

chirimoya *chir-ee-moy-ah* custard apple

chirivía *chir-iv-ee-ah* parsnip

chistorra *chis-tor-rah* sausage cooked over charcoal (Navarra)

chocolate *chok-oh-lah-tay* chocolate *(see also **mus de chocolate; natillas de chocolate; pastel de chocolate**)*

–(caliente) *(kal-ee-en-tay)* thick hot chocolate

chocos *chok-os* squid

chorizo *choh-ree-thoh* spicy red cooked sausage, similar to salami *(see also **buñuelo de chorizo**)*

–al vino *al vee-noh* chorizo in wine

–de Pamplona *de pam-plo-nah* fine-textured, hard chorizo

–de Salamanca *de sal-ah-man-kah* chunky chorizo from Salamanca

–en hojaldre *en hoh-khal-dray* chorizo in pastry

–extra *ex-trah* with 30% meat to 57% fat

–primera *pree-mer-ah* with 26% meat to 60% fat

–segunda *seg-oon-dah* with 24% meat to 65% fat

–tercera *ter-sair-ah* with 20% meat to 70% fat

choto *choh-toh* baby kid

–al ajillo *al a-khil-yoh* in garlic sauce

chufa *choo-fáh* tiger nut

chuletas *choo-let-as* chops/cutlets

–al sarmiento *al sahr-mee-en-toh* chops prepared over wood from vines

–de buey *de boo-ay* beef chops

–de cerdo a la aragonesa *de ser-soh ah lah ar-ah-gon-ay-sah* baked pork chops with wine and onion

–de cerdo a la madrileña *ah lah mad-ri-len-yah* baked pork chops

–de cordero vilareal *de kor-deh-roh vil-ah-ree-al* lamb chops with bacon

–de ternera a la castellana *de ter-neh-rah ah lah kas-tel-yah-nah* veal chops with mashed garlic

–de ternera a la zingara *de ter-neh-rah ah lah sin-gar-ah* veal cutlets in ham with a sherry sauce

–de tocino con salsa de tomate *de toh-see-noh kon sal-sah de to-mah-tay* chops in tomato sauce

chupete *choo-pet-eh* dummy/pacifier

chupito *choo-pee-toh* shot of spirits

churrasco *choo-ras-coh* grilled meat in a tangy sauce; Galician meat dish

churros *choo-ros* fried doughnut strips bought from street-sellers or in cafés

cierva *(see* **pastel de cierva**)

ciervo *si-er-voh* deer

cigala *si-gah-lah* crayfish

ciruela *si-roo-el-ah* plum
   –pasa *pa-sah* prune

ciruelas rellenas *si-roo-ay-las rel-ye-nas* stuffed prunes

civet de llebre *si-vet de yeb-ray* hare stew

clara *kla-rah* shandy

clavo *kla-voh* clove

Club Ranero *klub ran-eh-roh* famous Basque gastronomic society *(see also* **bacalao al Club Ranero**)

coca *koh-kah* dense cake from Mallorca

cochifrito de cordero *koh-chi-free-toh de kor-deh-roh* lamb fried with garlic and lemon

cochinillo *koh-chi-neel-yoh* suckling pig
   –asado *a-sah-doh* roast suckling pig
   –asado a feira *a-sah-doh ah fay-ee-rah* roast suckling pig stuffed with sausage
   –a la madrileña *ah lah mad-ri-len-yah* stew made with meat and chickpeas
   –a la sevillana *ah lah sev-il-yah-nah* stew of meat fried with beaten eggs
   –al vapor *al vay-poo-a* steamed
   –andaluz *an-dah-luth* meat and chickpea stew
   –castellano *kas-tel-yah-noh* meat and chickpea stew
   –de lentejas *de len-te-khas* lentil and chorizo casserole
   –de pelotas *de pel-oh-tas* meatball stew
   –maragato *mahr-ah-gah-toh* stew (La Maragatería, León)

cocido *koh-cee-doh* cooked; also chickpea, pork and chorizo stew

cocina *koh-see-nah* kitchen

coco *koh-koh* coconut

cóctel *kok-tel* cocktail

codillo *kod-il-yoh* knuckle (of pork)

codoñate *kod-on-yah-tay* quince cake

codornices a la plancha *kod-or-nee-says ah lah plan-chah* grilled quail

codornices con hoja de parra *kod-or-nee-says kon oh-khah de par-rah* quail with vine leaves

codornices estofadas *kod-or-nee-says es-to-fah-das* braised quail

codorniz *kod-or-nis* quail
   –con pimientos *kon pi-mee-en-tos* capsicums stuffed with quail

cojonudo *ko-khoh-noo-doh* **tapa** (Burgos)

col *kol* cabbage
   –con butifarra negra y alubias *kon boo-tee-far-rah neg-rah ee ah-loo-bee-as* cabbage with **butifarra** and beans
   –lombarda *lom-bah-dah* red cabbage

cola *koh-lah* tail

colador *kol-a-dor* sieve

coles de bruselas *kol-es-de broo-sel-as* Brussels sprouts

coliflor *kol-i-flor* cauliflower

collá *kol-yah* yoghurt cheese (València)

colmenilla *kol-men-il-yah* morel

colza *(see* **aceite de colza**)

comarcas vinícolas *ko-mah-kas vin-ee-koh-las* small wine-growing areas without **DO** status

combinado *com-bin-ah-doh* cocktail

comedor *kom-e-dohr* dining room

comida *koh-mee-dah* lunch/meal
   –de bebé *de beb-ay* baby food
   –infantil *in-fan-til* baby food

comino *koh-mee-noh* cumin

con hielo *kon ee-el-oh* with ice

coñac *kon-yak* brandy
   –de Jerez *de he-reth* Spanish brandy (DO, Jerez)

Conca de Barbera *kon-kah de bah-ber-ah* wine region (DO) in Catalunya

Condado de Huelva *kon-dah-doh de wel-vah* wine region (DO) in Andalucía

Conejero *kon-eh-kheh-roh* type of cheese

conejo *kon-eh-kho* rabbit (*see also* **guiso de conejo estilo canario**)

–al ajillo *al a-khil-yoh* rabbit with garlic

–con castañas *kon kas-tan-yas* rabbit with chestnuts

–con peras *kon peh-ras* rabbit & pears

–de monte *de mon-tay* wild rabbit

–estofado *es-to-fah-das* braised rabbit

confitat *kon-fit-at* seasoned pork conserved in lard

confitería *kon-fit-er-ee-ah* cake shop (also selling confectionery)

confituras *kon-fit-oo-ras* conserves

congelado *kon-gel-ah-doh* frozen

congrio *kon-gree-oh* conger eel

conill i pollastre *kon-il ee pol-yas-treh* rabbit and chicken dish (València)

con leche (*see* **café con leche**)

conservante *kon-ser-van-teh* preservative

consomé *kon-som-ay* consomme

consumir antes de … *kon-soo-mir an-tes de …* best before …

convento *kon-ven-toh* convent – a good source of traditional confectionery & cakes (*see also* **bacalao del convento**)

convite *kon-vee-teh* a get-together

copa *koh-pah* glass (of wine/sprirrits)

copita *koh-pee-tah* sherry glass

copos de avena *kop-os de av-en-ah* rolled oats

coquina *ko-kwin-ah* large clam

coquito del Brasil *kok-wee-toh de bra-sil* Brazil nut

corazón *ko-ra-thon* heart

cordero *kor-deh-roh* lamb (*see* **asaduril-la de cordero; guisado de cordero**)

–al chilindrón *al chil-in-drohn* lamb in tomato and capsicum sauce

–con almendras *kon al-men-dras* lamb in almond sauce

–en salsa picante *en sal-sah pee-kahn-te* lamb in spicy sauce

–lechal *le-chal* baby lamb

–lechal al estilo de Murcia *le-chal al es-tee-loh de mur-see-ah* stuffed legs of baby lamb

–manchego *man-cheh-goh* lamb from la Mancha (DO)

–pascual *pas-kwahl* spring lamb

corral (*see* **de corral**)

cortado (*see* **café cortado**)

cortadillo *kor-tah-dil-yoh* small confection with a pumpkin filling

corto (de cerveza) *kor-toh (de ser-vay-sah)* small glass of beer (125 ml)

corvina *kor-vee-nah* maigre; sea bass

–a la vasca *ah lah bas-kah* vinegared maigre (soup) with potatoes

corzo *kor-zoh* roe deer

cosecha *ko-sech-ah* vintage/harvest

Costers del Segre *kos-tehs del seg-ray* wine region (DO) in Catalunya

costillas *kos-til-yas* ribs

costra (*see* **arroz con costra**)

crema *kre-mah* cream (*see* **queso crema**)

–al ron *al ron* rum cream

–catalana *kat-ah-lan-ah* creme brulee

–de coco *de koh-koh* sponge with a coconut and egg sauce

–de espinacas *de es-pee-na-kas* cream of spinach soup

–de Málaga *de mal-ah-gah* zabaglione (dessert) made with Málaga wine

–de naranja *de na-ran-khah* orange cream dessert

–de San José *de san ho-say* egg custard flavoured with cinnamon

–de verduras *de de ver-doo-ras* cream of vegetable soup

criadilla de tierra *kree-ah-dil-yah de tee-air-ra* truffle

criadillas *kree-ah-dil-yas* testicles

criado *kree-ah-doh* matured

–por *por* matured by

crianza *kree-an-thah* wine aged for at least one year in vats, & one in bottles

crocante *krok-an-tay* ice cream with chopped nuts and chocolate

croissant *kra-sont* croissant

croqueta *krok-et-ah* croquette

–de bacalao *de bak-al-ow* cod

–de huevo *de hway-voh* egg

–de jamón *de ha-mon* ham

–de patata *de pat-at-ah* potato

crudo *kroo-doh* raw

cuajada *kwah-khah-dah* milk junket with honey

cuarto *kwah-toh* quarter

cubalibre *koo-bah-lee-bray* rum or gin mixed with cola

cubata *koo-bah-tah* a mixed spirit

cubiertos *koo-bee-ehr-tos* cutlery

cubito de hielo *koo-be-toh de ee-el-oh* ice cube

cuchara *koo-chah-rah* spoon
  –de postre *de pos-tray* dessert spoon
  –de sopa *de so-pah* soup spoon

cucharita *koo-chah-ree-tah* teaspoon

cucharón *koo-chah-ron* ladle

cuchillo *koo-chil-yoh* knife

cuello *kwel-yoh* neck

cuenta *kwen-tah* bill (check)

cuerpo *(see* **de cuerpo***)*

culantro *koo-lan-troh* coriander/cilantro

cumpleaños *kum-ple-an-yos* birthday *(see also* **pastel de cumpleaños***)*

curado *koo-rah-doh* cured

curar *koo-rahr* to cure

cúrcuma *kür-koo-mah* turmeric

curry *kü-rri* curry (powder)

D

dátil *dat-il* date

de bajo contenido graso *de bah-khoh kon-ten-ee-doh gra-soh* low-fat

de corral *de kor-ral* free-range (chicken)

de cuerpo *de kwer-poh* full-bodied

de granja *de gran-khah* free-range (eggs)

de soja *de so-khah* soya

degustación *de-gus-tas-ee-on* tasting

dehesa de Extremadura *de-ye-sah de ex-trem-a-doo-rah* ham (DO, Extremadura)

dejar en adobo *de-khahr en ah-doh-boh* to marinate

del país *del pay-ihs* local

del tiempo *del tee-em-poh* seasonal

denominación de origen (DO) *de-nom-ee-nath-ee-on de or-ee-khen* a guarantee of high standards and regional origin used on the labelling of wines and certain foods

desayuno *des-ai-yoo-noh* breakfast

descafeinado *(see* **café descafeinado***)*

descongelar *des-kon-khel-ah* to thaw

despojos *des-poh-khos* offal

destornillador *des-tor-nil-yah-dor* screwdriver cocktail (vodka and orange)

diente *dee-en-tay* clove (of garlic)

(DO) *(see* **denominación de origen***)*

doble *doh-blay* double (shot of spirits) – *see also* **café doble**

dorada *dor-ah-dah* gilthead bream

dorada a la sal *dor-ah-dah ah lah sal* salted sea beam

dulce *dul-say* sweet
  –de batata *e bat at-ah* sweet potato pudding from Málaga

dulces *dul-ses* sweets

dulces de las monjas *dul-ses de las mon-khas* confectionery made by nuns and sold in convents or cake shops

duro *doo-roh* hard

E

ebullición *(see* **punto de ebullición***)*

elaborado por *e-lab-or-ah-doh por* produced by

embeber *em-beb-er* to soak

embotellado por *em-bot-el-yah-doh por* bottled by

embutidos *em-boo-tee-dos* generic name for cured sausages

empanada *em-pan-ah-dah* savoury pie
  –de carne *de kar-nay* spicy meat
  –de espinaca *de es-pee-na-ka* spinach
  –de vieiras *de vee-eh-ras* scallop
  –santiaguesa *san-ti-ah-gwes-ah* scallop
  –valenciana *val-en-see-ah-nah* with tomato, ham, eggs, leek & garlic

empanadas de bizcocho *em-pan-ah-das de bis-ko-choh* sweet (Extremadura)

empanadilla *em-pan-nah-deel-ya* small pie, either sweet or savoury

empanado *em-pan-ah-doh* coated in bread crumbs

empanar *em-pa-nah* to coat in bread crumbs

emparedado *em-pah-red-ah-doh* sandwich

–de jamón y espárragos *de ha-mon ee es-parr-ah-goh* fried ham and asparagus rolls

–de patata y espinaca *de pat-at-ah ee es-pee-na-ka* potato slices stuffed with spinach

empedrado *(see* **arroz empedrado***)*

empiñonado *em-pin-yon-ah-doh* small marzipan-filled pastry with pinenuts

en escabeche *en es-kah-bay-chay* marinated

en pepitoria *en pep-ee-tor-ee-ah* in an almond and saffron sauce

en salazón *en sal-a-thon* cured

en salsa verde *en sal-sah ver-day* in a parsley and garlic sauce

encurtidos *en-kur-tee-dos* pickles

endibia *en-dib-ee-ah* endive

endibias con jamón ibérico *en-dib-ee-as kon ha-mon ee-ber-ee-ko* endives with ham

enebrina *eneb-ree-nah* juniper

eneldo *e-nel-doh* dill

enfriar *en-free-ahr* to chill

ensaimada mallorquina *en-sai-mah-dah mal-yor-kin-ah* spiral-shaped bun made with lard

ensalada *en-sah-lah-dah* salad

–a la vasca *ah lah bas-kah* salad made with olive, capsicum and tomato

–de arroz *de ah-rroth* rice salad

–de berenjena *de ber-en-khay-nah* eggplant salad

–de frutas *de froo-tas* fruit salad

–de habas *de ab-as* broad bean salad

–de hortelano *de or-tel-ah-doh* mixed vegetable salad

–de judías blancas *de hoo-dee-as blan-kas* bean salad

–de langosta *de lan-gos-tah* lobster salad

–de patatas *de pat-at-as* potato salad

–de perdiz *de per-dees* marinated partridge salad

–del tiempo *del tee-em-poh* seasonal salad

–madrileña *ah lah mad-ri-len-yah* lettuce, tomatoes, olives, anchovy, vinegar and hard-boiled eggs

–mixta *mix-tah* mixed salad

–rusa *roo-sah* Russian salad (potato and tuna in mayonnaise)

–sevillana *sev-il-yah-nah* chicory and endive leaves with olives and herbs

–valenciana *val-en-see-ah-nah* green capsicums, lettuce and oranges

ensaladera *en-sah-lah-deh-rah* salad bowl

ensaladilla de tomates y pimientos verdes *en-sah-lah-dil-yah de to-mah-tes ee pi-mee-en-tos ver-days* tomato and green capsicum salad

entrada *en-trah-dah* entree/starter

entrante *en-tran-tay* entree/starter

entremés *en-tray-mes* starter; mixed platter similar to antipasto which includes salads, cold cuts and pickles

erizo de mar *er-ee-tho de mahr* sea urchin

escaldadillas *es-kal-dah-dil-yas* dough soaked in orange juice and fried

escalfar *es-kal-fahr* to poach

escalivada *es-kal-ee-vah-dah* roasted red capsicums in olive oil

escalope *es-kal-oh-pay* escalope

–Cordon Bleu *kor-dohn bloo* with ham and cheese

–de cerdo *de ser-doh* pork

–de ternera *de ter-neh-rah* veal

escalopes de ternera rellenas *es-kal-oh-pes de ter-neh-rah rel-ye-nas* deep fried veal cutlets stuffed with egg and cheese

escama *es-kam-ah* scale (on fish)

escarcho *es-kar-choh* roach

escarola *es-kahr-oh-lah* endive

escocés *(see* **café escocés***)*

escudella a la catalana *es-coo-del-ya ah lah kat-ah-lah-nah* potato, rice and bacon stew (Catalunya) escudella i carn d'olla *es-coo-del-ya ee karn dol-yah* potato, rice and bacon stew (Catalunya)

escurridor *es-koo-rree-dor* colander

espaguetis *es-pag-et-ees* spaghetti

espárrago de Navarra *es-parr-ah-goh de Nah-va-rra* asparagus (DO, Navarra)

espárragos *es-parr-ah-gos* asparagus
  –con dos salsas *kon dos sal-sahs* asparagus & tomato or paprika mayonnaise
  –en vinagreta *en vin-ag-ret-ah* asparagus in vinaigrette
  –mimosa *mee-moh-sah* asparagus and egg salad
  –montañeses *mon-tan-yes-es* calve's tails stewed in tomato and asparagus
  –sevillanos *sev-il-yah-nos* asparagus with garlic

especialidad *es-pes-ee-al-ee-dah* speciality

especialidades de la casa *es-pes-ee-al-ee-dah-des de lah ka-sah* house specialities

especialidades locales *es-pes-ee-al-ee-dah-des loh-kal-es* local specialities

especias *es-pes-ee-as* spices

espina *es-pee-nah* fish bone

espinaca(s) *es-pee-na-ka(s)* spinach (see also **crema de espinacas; empanada de espinaca**)
  –a la catalana *ah lah kat-ah-lah-nah* spinach with pinenuts and raisins

espumante *es-poo-man-tay* sparkling wine

espumar *es-poo-mahr* to skim

espumoso *es-poo-moh-soh* sparkling

esqueixada *es-kwesh-ah-dah* cod dressed with olives, tomato and onion

estofado *es-to-fah-doh* stew/stewed
  –de buey (a la asturiana) *de boo-ay (ah lah as-too-ri-ah-nah)* braised ox with vegetables
  –de rabo de toro *de rah-boh de to-roh* stewed bull's tail with vegetable sauce
  –de vaca a la catalana *de ba-kah ah lah kat-ah-lah-nah* Catalan beef stew
  –montañesa *mon-tan-yeh-sah* beef and vegetable stew
  –venado *ven-ah-doh* venison stew

estofar *es-to-fahr* to braise

estragón *es-tra-gon* tarragon

estufa *es-too-fah* stove

esturión *es-too-ree-on* sturgeon

etiqueta *et-ee-ket-ah* label

etxeko kopa *et-shek-oh koh-pah* ice cream dessert

exprés (see **café exprés**)

exprimidor *ex-prim-i-dor* juicer

exquisito *ex-kwis-ee-toh* exquisite

F

faba asturiana *fah-bah as-too-ri-ah-nah* Asturian white bean (DO), similar to a lima bean and used in **fabada**

fabada asturiana *fah-bah-dah as-too-ri-ah-nah* stew made with pork, blood sausage and white beans

faisán *fai-san* pheasant

fardalejo *fahr-da-le-khoh* Riojan sweet

farinato *fahr-in-at-oh* fried sausage served with eggs (Salamanca)

fariñes *fahr-in-yes* corn pudding

farmacia *fahr-mas-ee-ah* chemist/pharmacy

faves a la catalana *fah-ves ah lah kat-ah-lah-nah* broad beans with ham

fayules *fay-oo-les* Asturian dessert

fermentado en barrica *fer-men-tah-doh en bar-ree-kah* wine fermented in oak

fiambre de jamón *fee-am-bray de ha-mon* pressed luncheon meat

fiambres *fee-am-brays* cold meats
  –surtidos *sür-tee-dos* selection of cold meats

fideos *fi-day-os* pasta noodles (see also **cazuela de fideos**)
  –a la cazuela *ah lah kath-way-lah* sausage and noodle stew
  –con almejas *kon al-meh-khas* noodles with baby clams

fideua *fid-way-ah* rice or noodles with fish and shellfish

fideus a la cassola *fi-day-us ah lah kas-soh-lah* Catalan noodle dish

fiesta *fee-es-tah* party

filete *fil-et-ay* steak; any boneless slice of meat

–a la parrilla *ah lah par-ril-yah* grilled beef steak

–de ternera *de ter-neh-rah* veal steak

–empanado *em-pan-ah-dah* crumbed pork fillets with ham & cheese

filetes de rodaballo a la andaluz *fil-et-es de roh-dah-bal-yoh ah lah an-dah-luth* turbot fillets with vegetables

filloas *fil-yoh-as* Galician pancakes filled with cream

fino *fee-noh* pale & fragrant dry sherry

flan *flan* creme caramel

–catalán *kat-ah-lahn* creme brulee

–con nata *kon nat-ah* creme caramel with whipped cream

–de Pascuas *de pas-kwas* Easter cheese flan (Mallorca)

flaó *flow-a* sweet cheese flan

Flor de Guía *flor de gee-ah* type of cheese

flor manchego *flor man-cheh-goh* deep-fried sweet wafers

floristería *flor-is-teh-ree-ah* flower shop

Fondillón *fon-dil-yon* aged wine liqueur (Alicante)

frambuesa *fram-bway-sah* raspberry

frangellos *fran-gel-yos* sweet made from cornmeal, milk and honey

freidurías *fray-e-doo-ree-as* fried fish shops common in Andalucía

freir *fray-ir* to fry/saute

fresa *fres-ah* strawberry

fresco *fres-koh* fresh (see also **al fresco**)

fricandó de langostinos *free-kan-doh de lan-gos-tee-nos* shrimp in almond sauce

frigo *free-goh* fridge

frío *free-oh* cold

fritangas *free-tan-gas* fried gofio

frite *free-teh* lamb stew, served on festive occasions

frito *free-toh* fried

fritos *free-tos* fritters

–con miel *kon mee-el* honey-roasted

fritura *free-too-rah* mixed fried fish

frixuelos *frix-hwel-os* Asturian dessert

fruta *froo-tah* fruit (see **ensalada de frutas**)

–variada *var-ee-ah-dah* selection of fresh fruit

frutas en almíbar *froo-tas en al-mee-bah* fruit in syrup

frutería *froo-teh-ree-ah* fruit shop/stall

frutos secos *froo-tos sek-os* nuts and dried fruit

fuego *fweh-goh* heat/flame

–lento *len-toh* low heat

fuerte *fwer-teh* strong

fuet *fu-et* thin pork sausage

G

gachas *ga-chas* dish from Extremadura

gachas manchegas *ga-chas man-cheh-gas* flavoured porridge

gaditano *ga-dee-ta-noh* from Cádiz

gallega (see **callos a la gallega**)

gal(l)ego *gal-yeh-goh* from Galicia (see also **queso gallego**)

galianos *gal-ee-an-os* gravy-soaked dough in **gazpacho manchego**

galleta *gal-yet-ah* biscuit

gallina *gal-yee-nah* hen

–en pepitoria *en pep-e-taw-ree-ah* chicken in almond sauce

gamba *gam-bah* shrimp/prawn

gámbaro *gam-bar-oh* shrimp (prawn)

gambas *gam-bas* shrimps (prawns)

–a la plancha *ah lah plan-chah* grilled shrimp

–al ajillo *al a-khil-yoh* garlic shrimps

–al jerez *al he-reth* shrimp in sherry

–en gabardina *en ga-bar-dee-nah* shrimp in batter

–rebozadas *re-both-ah-das* shrimps fried in batter

Gamonedo *ga-mon-ay-doh* sharp tasting cheese, smoked and cured

ganso *gan-soh* goose

–adobo *ah-doh-boh* preserved goose

garbanzos *gar-bahn-thos* chickpeas

–a la madrileña *ah lah mad-ri-len-yah* chickpeas with **chorizo** and garlic

–con cebolla *kon se-bol-yah* chickpeas in onion sauce

–con espinacas *kon es-pee-na-kas* chickpeas with spinach

–tostados *tos-tah-dos* roasted chickpeas (sold as a snack)

garbure *gah-boo-ray* green vegetable soup; also pork and ham dish

garrafa *gar-raf-ah* carafe

Garrotxa *gar-rot-cha* cheese; also a region in Northern Catalunya

garúm *gar-oom* olive and anchovy dip

gaseosa *gas-ee-oh-sah* lemonade

Gata-Hurdes *gat-ah-hur-des* cheese

gazpacho *gas-pa-choh* cold tomato soup

–andaluz *an-dah-luth* with chopped salad vegetables

–extremeño *ex-trem-en-yoh* with onions or raw eggs (Extremadura)

–pastoril *pas-toh-ril* rabbit stew with tomato and garlic

gazpachos manchegos *gas-pa-chos man-cheh-gos* game and vegetable hotpot

Gaztazarra *gaz-taz-ahr-rah* cheese

gelatina *gel-at-ee-nah* gelatin

Genestoso *gen-es-tos-oh* type of cheese

germen de trigo *ger-men de tree-goh* wheatgerm

Getariako Txakolina *get-ar-ee-ak-oh chak-ol-ee-nah* Txakolí region (DO) of Guipúzcoa

ginebra *hin-eb-rah* gin

girasol (*see* **aceite de girasol**)

gitano *git-ah-noh* Andalucían chickpea and tripe stew (*see* **menudo gaditano**)

glasé (*see* **azúcar glasé**)

gofio *goh-fee-oh* toasted cornmeal or barley

Gomera *gom-eh-rah* type of cheese

Gorbea *gor-bay-ah* sheep's milk cheese

gramos *gram-os* grams

gran almacén *gran al-mah-sen* department store

granada *gra-na-dah* pomegranate (*see also* **Alhama de Granada**)

granadilla *gra-na-dil-yah* passion fruit

granizados *gra-nee-zah-dos* iced drinks

granja (*see* **de granja**)

grano *gra-noh* grain

–largo *lahr-goh* long-grain (rice)

gran reserva *grahn re-serv-ah* best-quality wine aged for at least three years in oak barrels and one in bottles

grasa *gra-sah* fat (*see also* **de bajo contenido graso**)

gratinado de berenjenas *gra-tin-ah-doh de ber-en-khe-nas* eggplant gratin

Grazalema *graz-a-lem-ah* type of semi-cured sheep's milk cheese

grelos *gre-los* turnip greens

grifo m *grif-oh* tap

grosella espinosa *grow-sel-yah es-pee-noh-sah* gooseberry

grosella negra *grow-sel-yah neg-rah* blackcurrant

grosella roja *grow-sel-yah ro-khah* redcurrant

grosella silvestre *grow-sel-yah sil-ves-tray* gooseberry

guanche *gwan-chay* from the Canary islands

Guía (*see* **Flor de Guía**)

guijuelo *gwi-hwe-loh* ham (DO, Salamanca)

guinda *gwin-dah* black cherry

guindilla *gwin-dil-yah* mild green chilli

guisado de cordero *gwee-sah-doh de kor-deh-roh* lamb ragout

guisado de ternera *gwee-sah-doh de ter-neh-rah* veal ragout

guisado de trigo *gwee-sah-doh de tree-goh* corn and chickpea soup

guisante *gwee-san-tay* pea

–seco *sek-oh* split pea

guisantes con jamón a la española *gwee-san-tes kon ha-mon ah lah es-pan-yoh-lah* pea and ham dish

guisat de marisco *gwee-sat de mar-is-koh* stew made with fish and seafood

guiso de conejo estilo canario *gwee-soh de kon-eh-kho es-tee-loh kan-ah-ree-oh* rabbit stew guiso de rabo de toro *gwee-soh de rah-boh de to-roh* stewed bull's tail with potatoes

güisqui *gwis-kee* whisky

gusto *gus-toh* taste (*see also* **sabor**)

H

habas *ab-as* broad beans (*see also* **ensalada de habas**)
  –a la catalana *ah lah kat-ah-lah-nah* broad bean stew with **butifarra**
  –a la granadina *ah lah gra-na-dee-nah* broad beans with eggs and ham
  –con salchichas *kon sal-chee-chas* broad beans with sausages
  –fritas *free-tas* fried broad beans (sold as a snack)

habichuela *ab-ee-choo-el-ah* white bean

hacer compota de *ath-er kom-pot-ah de* to stew (fruit)

hamburguesa *am-bur-gway-sah* hamburger

harina *ah-ree-nah* flour
  –de maíz *de may-iz* cornmeal
  –de trigo *de tree-goh* wheat flour
  –integral *in-teg-ral* wholemeal flour
  –para fritos y rebozados *pa-rah free-tos ee re-both-ah-dos* flour used to coat food for frying
  –para pan *pa-rah pan* durum wheat flour used in breadmaking
  –para repostería *pa-rah re-pos-teh-ree-ah* fine-milled soft wheat flour for baking cakes

helado *el-ah-doh* ice cream

helar *el-ahr* to chill

hermejo *er-me-khoh* roux (sauce base)

Herreño *er-ren-yoh* type of cheese

hervido *er-vee-doh* boiled/poached

hervir *er-vear* to boil

hidrato de carbono *ee-drah-toh de kahr-bon-oh* carbohydrate

hielo *ee-el-oh* ice (*see* **cubito de hielo**)

hierba buena *ee-er-bah bway-nah* mint

hierbas *ee-er-bas* herbs
  –finas *fee-nas* mixed herbs

higaditos *ee-ga-dee-tos* fried liver

hígado *ee-gah-doh* liver (*see also* **cazuela de hígado**)
  –a la favorita *ah lah fav-or-ee-tah* liver stew
  –con arroz *kon ah-rroth* liver and rice dish
  –de ternera esto fada *de ter-neh-rah es-to-fah-dah* braised calve's liver

higo *ee-goh* fig
  –seco *sek-oh* dried fig

higos con dulce de Málaga *ee-gos kon dul-say de mal-ah-gah* figs in Málaga wine

higos con miel *ee-gos kon mee-el* figs in honey

hinojo *in-o-khoh* fennel

hipermercado *ee-per-mer-kah-doh* hypermarket

hogaza *og-ath-ah* a dense, thick-crusted bread

hoja de laurel *oh-khah de lo-rel* bay leaf

hoja de parra vine leaf

hojaldre (*see* **chorizo en hojaldre**)

hojaldres *oh-khahl-drays* small flaky pastries covered in sugar

hojas verdes *oh-khas ver-days* green vegetables

holandesa (*see* **salsa de holandesa**)

hongos *on-gos* fungi

hora de comer *or-ah de kom-er* lunchtime

horchata *or-chat-ah* tiger nut or almond milk-drink (Valencia)

hornazo *orr-nath-oh* bread stuffed with sausage

horno *orr-noh* oven (*see also* **al horno**)
  –de leña *de lenyah* wood-fired oven

hortalizas *or-tal-ee-thahs* vegetables

hortelano (*see* **ensalada de hortelano**)

hueso *weh-soh* bone

huevillos *hway-vil-yos* confection (Extremadura)

huevo *hway-voh* egg (*see also* **croqueta de huevo**)
  –cocido *koh-cee-doh* boiled egg
  –de chocolate *de chok-oh-lah-tay* chocolate egg

–de codorniz *de koh-dohr-nis* quail's egg
–de granja *de gran-khah* free-range egg
–frito *free-toh* fried egg
–relleno *rel-ye-noh* stuffed egg
huevos *hway-vos* egg dishes
–a la flamenca *ah lah flah-men-kah* baked vegetables with egg and ham
–al estilo Sóller *al es-tee-loh sohl-yer* fried eggs on **sobresada**, served with a milk and vegetable sauce
–al trote *al troh-tay* boiled eggs filled with tuna and mayonnaise
–con espárragos trigueros *kon es-parr-ah-gos tri-goo-e-ros* poached eggs with asparagus
–en salsa agria *en sal-sah ag-ree-ah* boiled eggs in wine and vinegar
–escalfados *es-kal-fah-dos* poached eggs
–escondidos *es-kon-dee-dos* scrambled eggs and ham wrapped in a pancake
–presidencia *pres-ee-den-see-ah* boiled eggs stuffed with liver pâté, served on spinach with bechamel
–revueltos *rev-wel-tos* scrambled eggs
humo *oo-moh* smoke

I

ibérico *ee-ber-ee-koh* native Spanish pig
ibicenco *i-bee-sen-coh* from Ibiza
Ibores *ee-bor-es* type of cheese
Idiazábal *id-ee-ath-ah-bal* semisoft smoky sheep's cheese (DO, Basque Country)
INDO *in-doh* Instituto Nacional de Denominaciones de Origen (wine and food classification board)
infantil (*see* **menú infantil**)
información nutricional *in-for-mas-ee-on noo-tris-ee-on-al* nutritional analysis (on food packaging)
infusión *in-foo-see-on* herbal tea

inglesa (*see* **salsa inglesa**)
ingrediente *in-gred-ee-en-tay* ingredient
instantáneo (*see* **café instantáneo**)
integral *in-teg-ral* wholewheat/wholemeal
intxaursalsa *int-shaur-sal-sah* Christmas walnut dessert (Basque Country)
invierno *in-vee-er-noh* winter

J

jabalí *ha-bah-lee* wild boar
–con salsa de castaños *kon sal-sah de kas-tan-yos* wild boar in chestnut sauce
jamón *ha-mon* ham
–al jerez *al he-reth* ham baked with dried fruit and sherry
–al jerez con espinacas *al he-reth kon es-pee-na-kas* boiled ham and spinach with a sherry sauce
–cocido *koh-see-doh* cooked ham
–de Huelva *de wel-vah* ham (DO, Huelva)
–de Jabugo *de ha-boo-goh* Jamón Ibérico said to be the best in Spain (Jabugo, Huelva)
–de Teruel *de ter-oo-el* ham (DO, Teruel)
–de Trévelez *de trev-el-eth* Jamón Ibérico (Trévelez, Granada)
–Dehesa de Extremadura *day-eh-sah de ex-trem-ah-doo-rah* ham (DO, Extremadura)
–dulce *dul-say* boiled ham
–Guijuelo *gwi-hwe-loh* ham from Salamanca (DO)
–Ibérico *ee-ber-ee-ko* cured Spanish ham from native black pigs
–serrano *se-rrah-noh* cured mountain ham
–York *york* boiled ham
jarra (de vino) *ha-rrah (de vee-noh)* jug of wine
jengibre *hen-ee-bray* ginger
Jerez *he-reth* (*see also* **al jerez**) sherry; also a sherry region (DO, Andalucía)

joven *(see* **vino joven**)

judía *hoo-dee-ah* when fresh, a green bean; also when dried, a kidney bean
  –verde *ver-day* green/runner bean

judías blancas *(see* **ensalada de judías blancas**)

judias del tío Lucas *hoo-dee-as del tee-oh loo-kas* bean stew with garlic and bacon

judias verdes a la castellana *hoo-dee-as ver-days ah lah kas-tel-yah-nah* fried capsicums, garlic and green beans

judias verdes a la leonesa *hoo-dee-as ver-days ah lah lay-on-es-ah* green beans with ham

judias verdes con jamón *hoo-dee-as ver-days kon ha-mon* green beans with ham

judión *hoo-dee-on* kidney bean

judiones de la granja *hoo-dee-on-es de lah gran-khah* pork and bean stew

jugo *hoo-goh* juice
  –de lima *de lee-mah* lime juice
  –de naranja *de na-ran-khah* orange juice
  –de piña *de pin-yah* pineapple juice
  –de tomate *de to-mah-tay* tomato juice

Jumilla *hoo-mil-yah* wine region (DO) in Murcia

K

kilogramo *ki-loh-gram-oh* kilogram

kiskilla *kis-kil-yah* shrimp (**also spelled quisquilla**)

kiwi *ki-wee* kiwi fruit

kokotxas *koh-kot-shas* fleshy filaments from a fish's throat

L

lacón *la-kon* cured shoulder of pork served with beans, greens & potatoes
  –con grelos *kon gre-los* shoulder of pork with turnip greens

lácteo *(see* **productos lácteos**)

lágrima *lag-ree-mah* sweet dark Málaga wine

langosta *lan-gos-tah* lobster *(see also* **ensalada de langosta**)
  –a la ibicenca *ah lah i-bee-sen-cah* lobster with stuffed squid

langostinos *lan-gos-tee-nos* king prawns *(see also* **fricandó de langostinos**)
  –a la plancha *ah lah plan-chah* grilled king prawns

Lanzarote *lan-za-rot-ay* wine region (DO) in the Canary Islands

lata *lat-ah* can

lavanco *lav-an-koh* wild duck

lechazo *le-cha-thoh* baby lamb
  –al horno *al orr-noh* roast baby lamb

leche *le-chay* milk
  –de cabra *de ka-bra* goat's milk
  –de soja *de soh-khah* soy milk
  –desnatada *des-nah-tah-dah* skimmed milk
  –frita *free-tah* dessert made from milk and flour fried in egg
  –merengada *mer-en-ga-dah* iced milk dessert with egg whites, cinnamon and sugar
  –semi-desnatada *sem-ee-des-nah-tah-dah* semi-skimmed milk

lechón *le-chon* suckling pig

lechuga *le-choo-gah* lettuce

legumbres *leg-oom-brays* pulses; also vegetables; also vegetable dishes
  –secas *sek-as* dried pulses

leguminosas *leg-oom-in-oh-sas* legumes

lengua *len-gwah* tongue
  –a la aragonesa *ah lah ar-ah-gon-ay-sah* tongue in tomato and capsicum sauce
  –escarlata *es-kar-lah-tah* tongue in spicy paprika sauce

lenguado *len-gwah-ah-doh* sole
  –a la plancha *ah lah plan-chah* grilled sole
  –a la romana *ah lah roh-mah-nah* sole in batter
  –al chacolí con hongos *al chak-oh-lee kon on-gos* sole with white wine and mushrooms
  –frito *free-toh* fried sole

lenguados al plato *len-gwah-dos al plat-oh* sole and mushroom casserole

lenguas con salsa de almendras *len-gwas kon sal-sah de al-men-dras* tongue in almond sauce

lenguas de obispo *len-gwas de oh-bis-poh* 'bishop's tongues' – confection from Andalucía

lentejas *len-tek-as* lentils (*see also* **cocido de lentejas; potaje de lentejas**)

–de la Armuña *de lah ar-moon-ya* lentils from Armuña (DO)

–aliñadas *ah-lin-ya-das* lentils in vinaigrette

–con chorizo *kon choh-ree-thoh* lentil and chorizo casserole

–con sobrasada *kon so-bra-sah-dah* lentils with sobrassada sausage

–onubenses *on-oo-ben-says* lentils with spicy sausage and onion

Les Garrigues *les garr-ee-gwes* olive-oil producing area (DO)

levar *lev-ahr* to prove

lichi *li-che* lychee

licor *li-kor* liquor/liqueur

–de avellana *de av-el-yah-nah* hazelnut liqueur

–de huevo *de hway-voh* advocaat

–de manzana *de man-tha-nah* apple liqueur

–de melocotón *de mel-o-ko-tohn* peach liqueur

–de melón *de me-lon* melon liqueur

liebre *lee-eb-ray* hare

–con castañas *kon kas-tan-yas* hare with chestnuts

–estofada *es-to-fah-dah* stewed hare

lima *li-mah* lime

limón *li-mon* lemon

limonada *lim-on-ah-dah* lemonade – carbonated soda

lista de precios *lis-tah de pres-ee-os* price list

litro *lee-troh* litre

litrona *lee-tron-ah* litre bottle of beer

llagostí a l'allioli *yag-os-tee ah la-lee-ol-ee* grilled prawns in garlic mayonnaise

llano *yan-oh* type of mushroom

llauna (*see* **bacalao a la llauna**)

llenguado a la nyoca *yen-gwah-doh ah lah nee-ok-ah* sole with pine nuts and raisins

locales (*see* **especialidades locales**)

lomo *loh-moh* fillet/loin/sirloin

–curado *koo-rah-doh* cured pork sausage

–de cerdo *de ser-doh* loin of pork

–de cerdo a la Baturra *de ser-doh ah lah bat-oo-rrah* pork fillets in ham and olive sauce

–de cerdo envuelto en col *de ser-doh en-vwel-toh en kol* pork and cabbage rolls

–de cerdo relleno *de ser-doh rel-ye-noh* stuffed & deep fried pork cutlets

–embuchado *em-boo-chah-doh* pork loin stuffed into a sausage and cured

–frito con alubias *free-toh kon ah-loo-bee-as* fried pork loin & broad beans

longaniza *lon-gan-ee-sah* long, skinny **chorizo**

lubina *loo-bee-nah* sea bass

–a la marinera *ah lah mah-rin-ehr-ah* sea bass in parsley sauce

lucio *loo-cee-oh* pike

M

macedonia de frutas *mal-ed-oh-nee-ah de froo-tas* fruit salad

macedonia de verduras *math-ee-do-nee-ah de ver-doo-ras* mixed vegetables

macis *ma-sis* mace

Madeira *ma-deh-rah* Madeira

madrileña (*see* **a la madrileña; callos a la madrileña; chuletas de cerdo a la madrileña; ensalada madrileña**)

madurar *mad-oo-rahr* to ripen

maduro *mad-oo-roh* ripe

magdalena *mag-dal-en-ah* small fairy cake to dunk in coffee

magras *mag-ras* fried eggs, ham, cheese and tomato

–al estilo de Aragón *al es-tee-loh de ar-ah-gohn* sliced ham in tomato sauce

Mahón *ma-hon* cow's cheese (DO)

maíz *may-iz* maize/corn

–tierno *ti-er-noh* sweetcorn

Málaga *mal-ah-gah* strong sweet sherry (*see also* **crema de Málaga**)

mallorquina (*see* **ensaimada mallorquina**)

Mancha *man-chah* wine region (DO)

Manchego *man-cheh-goh* hard sheep's milk cheese, available semi-cured, ripe and aged (DO, La Mancha)

mandarina *man-da-ree-nah* tangerine/mandarin

mango *man-goh* mango

manitas (de cerdo) *man-ee-tas (de ser-doh)* (pig's) trotters

–de cerdo a la vizcaína *de ser-doh ah lah biz-kay-ee-nah* trotters in sauce

–(de cordero) *(de kor-deh-roh)* leg (of lamb)

–de cordero a la catalana *de kor-deh-roh ah lah kat-ah-lah-nah* fried leg of lamb

manteca *man-tek-ah* lard

mantecado *man-tek-ah-doh* a soft lard biscuit; also dairy ice cream

mantel *man-tel* tablecloth

mantequilla *man-tek-il-yah* butter
–sin sal *sin sal* unsalted butter

manzana *man-tha-nah* apple

manzanas asadas *man-tha-nas a-sah-das* baked apples

manzanilla *man-thah-nil-ya* chamomile tea; also dry sherry; also Seville olive

maragato (*see* **cocido maragato**)

margarina *mahr-gah-ree-nah* margarine

marinera (*see* **a la marinera**)

mariscos *mar-is-kos* shellfish/seafood (*see also* **cazuela de mariscos**; **guisat de marisco**; **paella de marisco**)

marisquería *mar-is-keh-ree-yah* stall or shop specialising in shellfish

marmita *mar-mee-tah* pot (for cooking); also stew

marmitako *mar-mee-tak-oh* fresh tuna fish and potato casserole

marrano *mar-ran-oh* pork

martini *mar-tee-nee* martini

mar y cel *mahr ee sel* dish of sausages, rabbit, shrimp and angler fish

masa *mas-ah* pastry (dough)

mastuerzo *mas-ter-zoh* cress

Mato *mat-oh* type of cheese

mayonesa *may-on-ay-sah* mayonnaise

mazapán *maz-ah-pan* marzipan
–de Toledo *de tol-ay-doh* marzipan (Toledo)

medallones de merluza *med-al-yon-es de mer-loo-thah* hake steaks

mediana *med-ee-ah-nah* bottle of beer (300 ml)

medio *med-ee-oh* half

medio litro *med-ee-oh li-troh* half a litre

mejillones *me-khi-yon-es* mussels
–a la marinera *ah lah mah-rin-ehr-ah* mussels in white wine
–a la vinagreta *ah lah vin-ag-ret-ah* mussels vinaigrette
–al vapor *al vah-por* steamed mussels
–al vino blanco *al vee-noh blan-koh* mussels in white wine
–Cantabria *kan-tah-bri-ah* mussels in mustard sauce
–con salsa *kon sal-sah* mussels with tomato sauce

mejorana *me-khor-ah-nah* marjoram

mel i mató *mel ee mat-oh* a dessert of curd cheese with honey

melisa *me-lee-sah* lemon balm

melocotón *mel-o-ko-tohn* peach

melocotones al vino *mel-o-ko-toh-nes al vee-noh* peaches in red wine

melocotones en almíbar *mel-o-ko-toh-nes en al-mih-bahr* peaches in syrup

melón *me-lon* melon

membrillo *mem-bril-yoh* quince

Memia *me-mee-ah* sheep's milk curd cheese (Basque)

menestra *men-eh-strah* mixed vegetable stew
–de pollo *de pohl-yoh* chicken and vegetable stew

–de Riaño *de ree-ahn-yoh* vegetable stew from León

–tudelana *too-del-ah-nah* Tudela bean and vegetable stew

menta *men-tah* mint/peppermint

Méntrida *men-tree-dah* wine region (DO) in La Mancha

menú *men-oo* set menu

–de la casa *de lah ka-sah* fixed price menu

–del día *del dee-ah* the set menu of the day

–infantil *in-fan-til* children's menu

menudillos *men-oo-dil-yos* giblets

menudo gaditano *men-oo-doh ga-dee-ta-noh* Andalucían chickpea and tripe stew *(see* **gitano***)*

mercado *mer-kah-doh* market

mercado de abastos *mer-kah-doh de ab-as-tos* market selling fresh food

merengue *mer-en-gay* meringue

merienda *mer-ee-en-dah* afternoon tea

merlango *mer-lan-goh* hake

merluza *mer-loo-thah* hake

–a la catalana *ah lah kat-ah-lah-nah* hake toasted with tomato sauce

–a la gallega *ah lah gal-yeh-gah* hake and potato casserole

–a la koxkera *ah lah kox-keh-rah* hake in a garlic sauce (Basque Country)

–a la ondarresa *ah lah on-dah-rray-sah* hake dish (Basque Country)

–a la plancha *ah lah plan-chah* fried hake

–a la riojana *ah lah ree-o-khah-nah* hake with chillies

–a la romana *ah lah roh-mah-nah* hake in batter

–a la sidra *ah lah see-drah* hake in cider sauce

–a la vasca *ah lah bas-kah* hake in green sauce

–al ajoarriero *al ah-khoh-arr-ee-ye-roh* hake wirh garlic, parsley and chilli

–al cava *al kah-vah* hake in champagne sauce

–al coñac *al kon-yak* hake in brandy sauce

–al pil pil *al pil pil* hake in garlic

–con romesco *kon roh-mes-koh* hake in romesco sauce

–en salsa verde *en sal-sah ver-day* hake in parsley sauce

–encebollada *en-seb-ol-yah-dah* hake with onion sauce

–frita *free-tah* fried hake

mermelada *mer-mel-ah-dah* marmalade

mero *mer-oh* halibut; grouper; sea bass

mesa *mes-ah* table

mesón *mes-on* bar serving food and wine

método tradicional *met-oh-doh trad-is-ee-on-al* traditional method

mezcla *meth-klah* blend – also coffee blend usually 80% normal roast and 20% **torrefacto**, or dark roast

michirones *mich-ee-ron-es* bean dish (Murcia)

miel *mee-el* honey

miel de azahar *mee-el de ah-zah-ah* orange blossom honey

–de caña *de kan-yah* treacle

–de la Alcarria *de lah al-kar-ree-ah* honey from the Alcarria region (DO)

migas *mee-gas* fried cubes of bread with capsicums

–a la aragonesa *ah lah ar-ah-gon-ay-sah* fried bread with bacon rashers in tomato sauce

–canas *kan-as* cubes of bread soaked in milk and fried

–de pastor *de pas-tor* bread cubes fried in garlic, served with egg and sausage

–mulatas *moo-lat-as* cubes of bread soaked in chocolate and fried

mijo *mee-kho* millet

milhojas *mil-o-khas* millefeuille (flaky pastry stuffed with cream)

mojarra *mokh-ahr-rah* type of sea bream

moje manchego *moh-khay man-cheh-goh* cold broth with black olives

mojete *mo-khet-ay* dipping sauce for bread, made from potatoes, garlic, tomatoes and paprika

—murciano *mur-see-ah-noh* fish and capsicum dish
mojo *mo-kho* spicy capsicum sauce
molinillo de café *mol-in-il-yo de ka-fay* coffee grinder
molinillo de pimienta *mol-in-il-yo de pi-mee-en-tah* pepper mill
mollejas *mol-ye-khas* sweetbreads
mollete *mol-yet-ay* soft round bap
monas de pascua *mon-as de pas-kwa* Easter cakes; figures made of chocolate
mongetes seques i butifarra *mon-get-ehs sek-wes ee boo-tee-far-rah* haricot beans with roasted pork sausage
monjas *(see dulces de las monjas)*
montadit *mon-tah-deets* bread-topped **tapa**
montado *mon-tah-doh* small open sandwich, served as a **tapa**
montaña *mon-tan-yah* mountain
Monte Enebro *mon-tay e-neb-roh* soft cheese log (Avila)
Monterrei *mont-er-rai* wine region (DO) in Galicia
Montilla-Moriles *mon-til-yah-mor-il-es* wine/sherry region (DO, Andalucía)
Montsec *mont-sek* type of cheese
mora *mo-rah* mulberry/blackberry
moraga de sardina *moh-rah-gah de sah-din-ah* fresh anchovies on a spit
morcilla *mor-sil-yah* black pudding, often stewed with beans & vegetables
—asturiana *as-too-ri-ah-nah* smoked black pudding used in **fabada**
—blanca *blan-kah* white cured sausage
—de Burgos *de bür-gos* black pudding (Burgos)
morcillo *mor-sil-yoh* knuckle (of veal)
morcón *mor-son* course sausage, large and round (Extremadura)
morel *mor-el* type of mushroom
Morella *mor-el-yah* mild goat's cheese (Castellón)
morro *mor-roh* middle fish fillet
morros (de cerdo) *mor-ros (de ser-doh)* (pig's) cheeks

mortadela *mor-tah-del-ah* mortadella sausage
mortero *mor-teh-roh* mortar
morteruelo *mor-tehr-wel-oh* pate dish containing offal, game and spices
moruno *mor-un-oh* small **tapa** serving on bread or a toothpick
moscatel *mos-kah-tel* sweet **Málaga** wine made with the Muscatel grape
mostachones *mos-tach-on-es* small cakes for dipping in coffee or hot chocolate (*also spelled* **mostatxones**)
mostaza *mos-tath-ah* mustard
—en grano *en gra-noh* mustard seed
mosto *mos-toh* unfermented grape juice
múgil *moo-khil* grey mullet
mujol guisado *moo-khol gwee-sah-doh* red mullet
mujol *moo-khol* grey mullet
Murcia *(see* **queso de Murcia**)
mus de chocolate *mus de chok-oh-lah-tay* chocolate mousse
muslo *mus-loh* (chicken) leg and thigh
muy rico *moy ri-koh* very tasty

N

nabo *nab-oh* root vegetable; turnip
ñame *nya-may* yam & sugar-cane syrup
naranja *na-ran-khah* orange (*see also* **crema de naranja**)
nata *nat-ah* cream
—agria *ag-ree-ah* sour cream
—montada *mon-tah-dah* whipped cream
natillas *na-teel-yas* creamy custard dessert
—de chocolate *de chok-oh-lah-tay* chocolate custard
navaja *nav-a-khah* razor clam
—suiza *swee-thah* Swiss-Army knife
Navarra *nah-va-rra* wine region (DO) *(see* **a la navarra**)
navegante *nav-e-gan-tah* tapa (Burgos)
nécora *nek-or-ah* small crab
negocios *(see* **almuerzo de negocios**)
nevera *nev-ehr-ah* fridge; cool box; eskie

níscalo *nis-kal-oh* type of mushroom

níspero *nis-pe-roh* loquat

ñora *nyo-rah* sweet red capsicum (usually found dried)

la Nucia *lah noo-see-ah* type of cheese

nueces *noo-eh-sehs* nuts

nueva cocina española *noo-eh-vah koh-see-nah es-pan-yoh-lah* new Spanish cuisine, which adapts traditional dishes to modern tastes

nueva cocina vasca *noo-eh-vah koh-see-nah bas-kah* modern Basque cooking

nuez *noo-eth* nut/walnut

–de América *de am-er-ic-ah* pecan nut

–de Brasil *de bra-sil* Brazil nut

–de nogal *de nog-ahl* walnut

–moscada *mos-kah-dah* nutmeg

Nulles *nul-yes* wine region (DO) in València

O

oca *oh-kah* goose

ojo *o-khoh* eye

oliva (*see* **aceite de oliva**)

olla *ol-yah* meat and vegetable stew; also pot (for cooking)

–a presión *ah pres-ee-on* pressure cooker

–exprés *ex-pres* pressure cooker

–freidora *fray-ee-dor-ah* deep fryer

–gitana *git-ah-nah* vegetable & fruit stew

–podrida *pod-rid-ah* 'rotten pot' – meat & vegetable stew

oloroso *ol-oh-roh-soh* sweet, dark sherry with a golden colour

onubense *on-oo-ben-say* from Huelva

oporto *o-por-toh* port

Orduña *oor-dün-yah* strong-tasting sheep's milk cheese (Alava)

orégano *or-ee-ga-noh* oregano

oreja de mar *or-ekh-ah de mahr* abalone

orcjas (de cerdo) *or ekh-as (de ser-doh)* (pig's) ears

orgánico *or-gan-ik-oh* organic

origen (*see* **denominación de origen**)

oronja *or-on-khah* type of mushroom

Oropesa *or-oh-pe-sah* sheep's milk cheese

ortiga de mar *or-tee-gah de mahr* sea anemone

orujo *or-oo-khoh* **aguardiente** (DO, Galicia)

ostión *os-tee-on* giant oyster

ostiones a la gaditana *os-tee-on-es ah lah ga-dee-ta-nah* Cádiz oysters with garlic, parsley and bread crumbs

ostra *os-trah* oyster

otoño *o-ton-yoh* autumn

oveja *o-beh-kha* mutton

P

pá amb oli *pah am o-lee* toasted bread with garlic and olive oil

pá amb tomàquet *pah am tom-ah-ket* **tapa** of toasted bread rubbed with tomatoes, served with garlic & oil

pacana *pak-an-ah* pecan

pacharán navarro *pa-cha-ran nah-va-rra* sloe gin (DO, Navarra)

paella *pai-el-yah* rice dish which has many regional variations

–alicantina *al-ee-kan-tee-nah* with chicken and rabbit

–castellana *kas-tel-yah-nah* with meat

–catalana *kat-ah-lah-nah* paella with pork sausages, squid and chilli

–de marisco *de mar-is-koh* seafood paella

–de pollo *de pohl-yoh* chicken paella

–marinera *mah-rin-ehr-ah* fish and seafood paella

–negre *neg-ray* squid ink paella

–valenciana *val-en-see-ah-nah* paella with seafood and chicken (Valencia)

–zamorana *tham-or-ah-nah* paella with meat

pá i all *pah ee al* (*see* **pá amb oli**)

pajita *pa-khee-tah* straw

pala *pa-lah* spatula (used for serving)

paletilla *pa-let-eel-yah* shank/shoulder

palillo *pal-il-yoh* toothpick

palillos *pal-il-yos* chopsticks

palitos de queso *pal-e-tos de ke-soh* cheese straws

Palma, La *lah pal-mah* wine region (DO) in the Canary Islands

palmera *pal-mer-ah* palm leaf-shaped flaky pastry, often coated in chocolate

Palmero *pal-mer-oh* type of cheese

palo cortado *pa-loh kor-tah-doh* medium-dry sherry

palo de Mallorca *pah-loh de mal-yor-kah* drink from Mallorca (DO)

palomitas *pa-lom-ee-tas* popcorn

Pamplona (*see* **chorizo de Pamplona**)

pan *pan* bread

　–aceite *a-say-tay* flat round bread

　–árabe *ah-ra-bay* pita bread

　–blanco *blan-koh* white bread

　–de Alá *de al-ah* 'Allah's Bread' – dessert

　–de boda *de boh-dah* sculpted bread traditionally made for weddings

　–de centeno *de sen-ten-oh* rye bread

　–de hozizo *de choh-ree-thoh* bread baked with a sausage in it

　–de cuajada *de koo-akh-ah-dah* pastry filled with curd cheese

　–de higos *de ee-gos* fig cake

　–de maíz *de may-iz* cornbread (Galicia)

　–de molde *de mol-day* white sandwich bread

　–dulce *dul-say* sweet buns

　–duro *doo-roh* stale bread, used for toasting and eating with olive oil

　–integral *in-teg-ral* wholemeal bread

panaché *pan-ah-chay* mixed vegetable stew

panadera (*see* **a la panadera**)

panadería *pan-ah-der-ee-ah* bakery

panallets *pan-al-yets* marzipan sweets

panceta *pan-set-ah* salt-cured streaky bacon

panchineta *pan-chee-net-ah* almond tart

panecillo *pan-ee-sil-yoh* small bread roll

panojas malagueñas *pan-oh-khas mal-ah-gwen-yas* sardine dish

papas arrugadas *pa-pas ar-roo-gah-das* potatoes boiled in their jackets

paquete *pa-ket-eh* packet

pardilla *par-dil-yah* type of mushroom

pargo *par-goh* sea bream

parrilla (*see* **a la parrilla**)

parrillada *par-ril-yah-dah* grilled meats

　–de mariscos *de mar-is-kos* seafood grill

pasa *pa-sah* raisin

　–de Corinto *de kor-in-toh* currant

pasa sultana *pa-sah sul-tan-ah* sultana

pasado *pa-sa-doh* stale

pasapurés *pa-sa-poo-res* potato masher

Pasiego *pa-see-ay-goh* creamy white cheese used in **quesada** (Santander)

pasta *pah-stah* pasta

pastel *pas-tel* cake

　–de boda *de bo-dah* wedding cake

　–de chocolate *de chok-oh-lah-tay* chocolate cake

　–de cierva *de si-er-vah* meat pie

　–de cumpleaños *de kum-ple-an-yos* birthday cake

　–de nata *de nat-ah* cream cake

　–de ternera *de ter-neh-rah* veal loaf

pastelería *pas-tel-er-ee-ah* cake shop

pastelito *pas-tel-ee-toh* pastry (such as Danish pastry)

pastelitos de miel *pas-tel-ee-tos de mee-el* honey fritters

pastorejo *pas-tor-ekh-oh* slices from the head of an animal

pataco *pat-ak-oh* tuna and potato stew

patas *pat-as* trotters/feet

patatas *pat-at-as* potatoes (*see also* **croqueta de patata**; **emparedado de patata y espinaca**; **ensalada de patatas**)

　–a la riojana *ah lah ree-okh-ah-nah* potatoes with chorizo and paprika

　–alioli *al-ee-ol-ee* in garlic mayonnaise

　–bravas *brah-vas* in spicy tomato sauce

–con chorizo *kon choh-ree-thoh* with chorizo

–estofadas *es-to-fah-das* boiled

–fritas *free-tas* chips/crisps

pato *pa-toh* duck

–a la andaluz *ah lah an-dah-luth* duck with chickpeas

–a la naranja *ah lah na-ran-khah* duck with orange sauce

–a la sevillana *ah lah sev-il-yah-nah* duck with orange sauce

–alcaparrada *al-ka-par-rah-dah* duck with capers and almonds

–con aceitunas *kon a-say-too-nas* duck with olive sauce

pava *pa-vah* kettle

pavo *pa-voh* turkey

pececillos *pes-e-sil-yos* small fish

pechina *pech-ee-nah* scallop

pecho *pech-oh* breast (of lamb)

pechuga *pech-oo-gah* breast (poultry)

Pedroches *ped-roh-ches* sharp and tangy sheep's milk cheese (Córdoba)

pelapatatas *pe-lah-pat-at-as* peeler

pelar *pel-ahr* to peel

pellofa *pel-yof-ah* gin-based drink (Menorca)

pelotas *(see* **cocido de pelotas***)*

Peñamellera *pen-yah-mel-yer-ah* type of cheese

Penedès *pen-ed-es* wine region (DO) in Catalunya

pepinillo *pep-in-il-yoh* gherkin

pepinillos rellenos *pep-in-il-yos rel-ye-nos* stuffed pickles

pepino *pep-ee-noh* cucumber

pepitoria *pep-it-or-ee-ah* sauce made with egg and almond

pepitos *pep-ee-tos* chocolate eclair cakes filled with custard

pera *peh-rah* pear

la Peral *lah peh-ral* soft cheese

perca *per-sah* perch

percebe *per-seb-ay* goose barnacle

perdices a la manchega *per-dee-says ah lah man-cheh-gah* partridge in red wine and capsicums

perdices con chocolate *per-dee-says kon chok-oh-lah-tay* partridge with chocolate

perdiz *per-dees* partridge *(see also* **ensalada de perdiz***)*

–con coles *kon koh-les* partridge with stuffed cabbage

perechico *per-ech-ee-co* edible fungi from Vitoria *(also spelled* **perretxiku***)*

peregrina *pe-reg-ree-na* scallop

perejil *per-e-khil* parsley

pericana *per-ik-ah-nah* dish of olives, cod oil, capsicums and garlic

perifollo *per-i-fol-yoh* chervil

Perilla *per-il-yah* firm bland type of cheese made from cow's milk

perretxiku *per-ech-ee-cu* edible fungi from Vitoria *(also spelled* **perechico***)*

perrito caliente *per-ree-toh kal-ee-en-tay* hot dog

pescada á galega *pes-kah-dah ah gal-ay-gah* hake fried in olive oil and served with garlic and paprika sauce

pescadería *pes-kah-der-ee-yah* fish shop/stall

pescadilla *pes-kah-dil-yah* whiting; young hake

pescadito frito gaditano *pes-kah-dee-toh free-toh ga-dee-ta-noh* fish dish (Cádiz)

pescaditos rebozadas *pes-kah-dee-tos re-both-ah-das* small fish fried in batter

pescado *pes-kah-doh* fish

–a l'all cremat *ah lal kre-mat* fish in burnt garlic

pescaíto frito *pes-kay-ee-toh free-toh* tiny fried fish

pestiños *pes-tin-yos* honey-coated aniseed pastries; also fried filled pancakes

pez espada *peth es-pa-dah* swordfish

–frito *free-toh* fried swordfish steaks on a skewer

picada *pee-kah-dah* a mixture of garlic, parsley, toasted almonds and nuts, often used to thicken sauces

picadillo *pee-kah-dil-yoh* salad consisting of diced vegetables
–de atún *de a-tun* salad made with diced tuna and capsicums
–de cerdo *de ser-doh* spiced minced pork dish
–de ternera *de ter-neh-rah* minced veal
picadora *pee-kah-door-ah* mincer
picante *pee-kahn-te* spicy
picar *pee-kahr* to chop/mince
pichón *pee-chon* pigeon
pichones a la abulense *pee-cho-nes ah lah ab-oo-len-say* pigeon dish (Avila)
pichones asados *pee-cho-nes a-sah-dos* roast pigeons
Picón *pee-kon* blended blue cheese (DO) made with cow's milk
Picos de Europa *pee-kos de oo-roh-pah* blended blue cow's milk cheese (DO)
Pido *pee-doh* type of cheese
pie de rata *pee-ay de rah-tah* type of mushroom
pierna *pee-er-nah* leg
–de cabrito asado *de kab-ree-toh a-sah-doh* roast leg of kid
–de cordero rellena *de kor-deh-roh rel-ye-nah* stuffed leg of lamb
pil pil (*see* **al pil pil**)
pilotes *pee-loh-tehs* Catalan meatballs
pimentón *pee-men-ton* paprika
–dulce *dul-say* sweet paprika
–picante *pi-kahn-te* spicy paprika
pimienta *pi-mee-en-tah* pepper (*see also* **molinillo de pimienta**)
–blanca *blan-kah* white pepper
–de Jamaica *de ha-may-ka* allspice
–negra *neg-rah* black pepper
pimiento *pi-mee-en-toh* capsicum
–amarillo *am-ah-ril-yo* yellow capsicum
–del Piquillo de lodosa *del pik-wil-yoh* capsicums (DO, Pamplona)
–rojo *roh-khoh* red capsicum
–verde *ver-day* green capsicum

pimientos *pi-mee-en-tos* capsicums from El Bierzo, which are said to be especially good
–a la riojana *ah lah ree-o-khah-nah* roast red capsicum fried in oil and garlic
–al chilindrón *al chil-in-drohn* capsicum casserole
–fritos *free-tos* fried capsicums
–picantes *pi-kahn-tes* spicy red capsicums
–rellenos *rel-ye-nos* *ree-ok-ah-nos* stuffed red capsicums
piña *pee-nyah* pineapple
pinchito moruno *peen-chee-toh* lamb and chicken kebabs
pinch(it)o *peen-(chee)-toh* small tapa served on bread or a toothpick
piñón *peen-yon* pinenut
pinta *peen-tah* pinto bean
pintada *peen-tah-dah* guinea fowl
pintxo *peen-cho* **tapa** (Basque Country)
pipa de girasol *pee-pah de hi-ra-sohl* sunflower seeds
piparrada vasca *pee-par-rah-dah bas-kah* capsicum and ham casserole with egg and tomato
piper muturtxodunak bakailuz beteak *pee-per mut-ur-chod-oo-nak bak-ai-luth bet-e-ak* red capsicums stuffed with cod
pipirrana *pee-peer-ran-ah* capsicum, onion, tomato & marinated fish salad
piquillo *pik-wil-yoh* small red capsicums – sweet and spicy
pistacho *pis-tach-oh* pistachio
pisto manchego *pis-toh man-cheh-goh* fried or stewed zucchini with capsicum and tomatoes
plancha (*see* **a la plancha; codornices a la plancha**)
plátano *plat-an-oh* banana
platera *plat-ehr-ah* type of mushroom
platija *plat-ee-khah* plaice
plato *plat-oh* plate (*see also* **primer plato**)
–combinado *kom-bin-ah-doh* meal served on one plate

–del día *del dee-ah* dish of the day

–sopero *sop-ehr-oh* soup plate

platos típicos *plat-os tip-i-kos* well-known local dishes

playa *plai-yah* beach

pocha *poch-ah* type of bean

pochas a la riojana *poh-chas ah lah ree-o-khah-nah* beans with chorizo in spicy paprika sauce

pochas con almejas *poh-chas kon al-meh-khas* beans with clams

poco hecho *po-koh ech-oh* rare (cooked)

pollería *pol-yehr-ee-ah* chicken shop

pollo *pohl-yoh* chicken (see also **arroz con pollo**; **menestra de pollo**)

–al ajillo *al a-khil-yoh* garlic chicken

–al chilindrón *al chil-in-drohn* chicken in tomato and capsicum sauce

–asado *a-sah-doh* roast chicken

–Campurriano *kam-poo-rree-ah-noh* chicken with rice and capsicums

–con samfaina *kon sam-fay-ee-nah* chicken with mixed vegetables

–de corral *de kor-ral* free-range chicken

–en escabeche *en es-kah-bay-chay* marinated chicken

–en pepitoria *en pep-ee-tor-ee-ah* chicken in an egg and almond sauce

–en salsa de ajo *en sal-sah de ah-khoh* chicken in garlic sauce

–granadina *de gra-na-dee-nah* chicken with wine and ham

–y capón del Prat *ee kah-pon del prat* chicken from Prat de Llobregat (DO)

–y langosta *ee lan-gos-tah* chicken with crayfish

polvo a feira *pohl-voh ah fay-ee-rah* spicy boiled octopus

polvorón *pol-vor-on* almond shortbread, often eaten at Christmas

pomelo *pom-el-oh* grapefruit

ponche *pon-chay* sweet **aguardiente**

porrón *por-ron* wine bottle with a long drinking spout

porru-salda *por-roo-sal-dah* cod and potato stew (see also **purrusalda**)

Porrua *por-roo-ah* type of cheese

postre *pos-tray* dessert

–de naranja *de na-ran-khah* cream-filled oranges

potaje castellano *pot-a-khay kas-tel-yah-noh* broth made with beans and sausages

potaje de garbanzos *pot-a-khay de gar-ban-thos* chickpea broth

potaje de habichuelas alfonsinas *pot-a-khay de ab-ee-choo-el-as al-fon-sin-as* bean and sausage broth

potaje de jaramago *pot-a-khay de har-ah-mah-goh* stew made with a turnip-like vegetable

potaje de lentejas *pot-a-khay de len-tek-as* lentil broth

pote gallego *poh-tay gal-yeh-goh* stew

potito *pot-ee-toh* jar of baby food

precio *preth-ee-oh* price

primavera *pree-mah-ver-ah* spring

primer plato *pree-mer plat-oh* first course

pringada *prin-gah-dah* bread dipped in sauce; a marinated sandwich

Priorato *pri-oh-rah-toh* wine region (DO) in Catalunya

productos biológicos *prod-uk-tos bee-oh-lo-gee-kos* organic produce

productos del mar *prod-uk-tos del mahr* seafood

productos lácteos *prod-uk-tos lak-tay-os* dairy products

puchero *poo-cheh-roh* casserole

–canario *kan-ah-ree-oh* casserole made with chickpeas, corn and meat

pudin *poo-din* pudding

puerco *pwer-koh* pork

puerro *pwer-roh* leek

pulpo *pul-poh* octopus

–a la leonesa *ah lah lay-on-es-ah* octopus cooked with onions

–gallego *gal-yeh-goh* spicy boiled octopus

punta de diamante *pun-tah de dee-ah-man-tay* confection from València

puntillitas *pun-til-yee-tas* baby inkfish fried in batter

purrusalda *poo-rroo-sal-dah* cod and potato stew (*see also* **porru-salda**)

Puzol *pu-thol* fresh ewe's milk cheese from València

PVP *pay-vay-pay* price

Q

queimada *kway-mah-dah* **orujo**, lemon and coffee drink (Galicia)

quesada *ke-sah-dah* cheesecake-type dessert from Cantabria

quesailla *ke-sah-il-yah* type of cheese

queso *ke-soh* cheese
  –azul *a-thul* blue cheese
  –Castellano *kas-tel-yah-noh* type of cheese
  –con membrillo *kon mem-bril-yoh* **manchego** cheese with quince
  –crema *kre-mah* cream cheese
  –de Alicante *de al-ee-kan-tay* goat's cheese
  –de Burgos *de bür-gos* soft but firm white cheese
  –de cabra *de ka-bra* goat's cheese
  –de Cantabria *de kan-tah-bri-ah* creamy cow's milk cheese (DO)
  –de la Serena *de lah se-reh-nah* ewe's milk cheese from Badajoz (DO)
  – de León *de lay-on* cheese from mountain cows
  –de Murcia *de mür-see-ah* type of cheese
  –de ovejà *de o-beh-kha* sheep's milk cheese
  –de vaca *de ba-ka* cow's milk cheese
  –del país *del pay-ihs* local cheese
  –en aceite *en a-say-tay* cheese in olive oil, served as a **tapa**
  –fresco *fres-koh* fresh cheese
  –gallego *gal-yeh-goh* creamy Galician cheese made from cow's milk

  –Majorero *ma-khor-eroh* goat's milk cheese with a strong flavour (DO)
  –Mallorquín *mal-yor-kin* type of cheese

quesucos de Liébana *ke-soo-kos de li-eh-ban-ah* cow's milk cream cheeses (DO)

quinto *kin-toh* very small bottle of beer (200 ml)

quisquilla *kis-kil-yah* shrimp (**also spelled kiskilla**)

quitar la espina *kee-tahr lah es-pee-nah* to fillet (a fish)

quitar las tripas *qee-tahr las trip-as* to gut (a fish)

R

rábano *ra-ban-oh* radish

rabas en salsa verde *rah-bas en sal-sah ver-day* squid in green sauce

rabassola *ra-bas-so-lah* mushroom

rabo (de buey) *rah-boh (de boo-ay)* (ox) tail (*see* **estofado de rabo de toro; guiso de rabo de toro**)

ración *rath-ee-on* a large **tapa** serving

rallador *ral-yah-dor* grater

rallar *ral-yahr* to grate

ramillete albaicinero *ram-il-yet-ay albai-sin-ehr-oh* bunch of herbs including bay leaf, mint and parsley (El Albaícin)

rancio *ran-see-oh* stale

rape *ra-peh* monkfish
  –a la gallega *ah lah gal-yeh-gah* monkfish with potatoes and garlic sauce
  –a la Monistrol *ah lah mon-is-trol* monkfish with bechamel sauce
  –a la plancha *ah lah plan-chah* grilled monkfish
  –al jerez *al he-reth* monkfish in sherry sauce
  –con patatas *kon pat-at-as* monkfish with potatoes

ratafia *ra-tah-fee-ah* Catalan liqueur

raya *rai-yah* coarse **oloroso** sherry; also ray fish

rebozado *re-both-ah-doh* in bread-crumbs or batter

rebozar *re-both-ahr* to coat in batter

receta *re-set-ah* recipe

recetario *re-set-ahr-ee-oh* cookbook

recibo *re-see-boh* receipt

redondo *re-dohn-doh* round (of beef)
–al horno *al orr-noh* roast beef
–de ternera al horno *de ter-neh-rah al orr-noh* roasted round of veal

refresco *re-fres-koh* soft drink

regañaos *re-gan-yows* pastry stuffed with sardines and red capsicum

relleno *rel-ye-noh* stuffed/stuffing

remolacha *re-mol-ach-ah* beetroot

reo *ray-oh* sea trout
–con almejas *kon al-meh-khas* sea trout with clams

repollo *re-pol-yoh* cabbage

repostería *re-pos-teh-ree-ah* confectionery

requesón *rek-wes-on* curd; curd/cottage cheese

reserva *re-serv-ah* vintage wine; also reservation

restaurante *res-tor-an-tay* restaurant

revuelto *rev-wel-toh* scrambled eggs
–de ajos *de ah-khos* with garlic
–de mixto *de mix-toh* with vegetables
–de setas *de se-tas* with mushrooms

Riaño (*see* **menestra de Riaño**)

Rias Baixas *ree-as bash-as* wine region (DO) in Galicia

Ribeiro *rib-ee-ir-oh* wine region (DO) in Galicia

Ribera del Duero *rib-er-ah del dweh-roh* wine region (DO) in Castilla y León

riñón *rin-yon* kidney

riñones al jerez *rin-yon-ehs al he-reth* kidneys in a sherry sauce

Rioja *ree-o-khah* wine from La Rioja

rizada *riz-ah-dah* kale

róbalo *ro-bal-oh* haddock; sea bass

rodaballo *ro-dab-al-yoh* turbot/brill

rollo pastelero *rol-yoh pas-tel-er-oh* rolling pin

romero *roh-mehr-oh* rosemary; also cheese covered in rosemary (Castilla La Mancha)

romesco *roh-mes-koh* sweet red capsicum, almonds and garlic sauce

ron *ron* rum (*see also* **crema al ron**)

Roncal *ron-sal* cured ewe's milk cheese (DO, Pyrenees)

rosado *ro-sah-doh* rosé

rosca de carne *ros-kah de kar-nay* meatloaf wrapped in bacon

rosca/o *ros-kah/koh* small sweet bun

roscón *ros-kon* a large **rosca**
–de pascua/Reyes *de pas-kwa/ray-es* **roscón** for Easter or Christmas, decorated with sugar and glace fruits

rosetxat (*see* **arroz rosetxat**)

rosinoc *ros-in-ok* type of mushroom

rosquilla *ros-kwil-yah* a mini **rosca**

rossejat *ros-se-khat* rice with fish and shellfish

rostit *ros-tit* roast chicken dish (Catalunya)

rovelló *rov-el-yoh* type of mushroom

rovellons a la plancha *roh-bel-yons ah lah plan-chah* garlic mushrooms

rubio *roo-bee-oh* red gurnard fish

Rueda *rway-dah* wine region (DO) in Castilla y León

ruibarbo *rwee-bar-boh* rhubarb

russinyol *roo-sin-yol* type of mushroom

S

sabayon *sab-ay-on* zabaglione – dessert made with egg, sugar and marsala
–de naranja *de na-ran-khah* orange zabaglione

sabor *sa-bor* flavour (*see also* **gusto**)

sacacorchos *sa-ka-kor-chos* corkscrew

sagardotegi *sa-gar-dot-egi* cider house (Basque Country)

sagú *sa-goo* sago

sal *sal* salt

salado *sah-lah-doh* salty/savoury/salted (of peanuts)

salchicha *sal-chee-chah* pork sausage

salchichón *sal-chee-chon* peppery, cured white sausage

salero *sal-eh-roh* salt cellar

salmantino *sal-man-tee-noh* from Salamanca (*see* **chanfaina salmantina**)

salmón *sal-mon* salmon
–a la ribereña *ah lah rib-er-en-yah* salmon in a cider sauce
–ahumado *a-oo-mah-doh* smoked salmon
–al noso estilo *al noh-soh es-tee-loh* Galician salmon, in a mushroom and sherry sauce[*]

salmonete *sal-mon-et-ay* red mullet

salmorejo *sal-mor-e-khoh* thick **gazpacho** made from tomato, bread, olive oil, vinegar, garlic and green capsicum
–de Córdoba *de cor-doh-bah* **gazpacho** made with more vinegar than usual
–de Toledo *de tol-ay-doh* partridge pâté (Toledo)

salpicón *sal-pee-kon* fish or meat salad

salsa *sal-sah* sauce
–alioli *al-ee-ol-ee* garlic and olive oil vinaigrette; garlic mayonnaise
–de holandesa *de ol-an-des-ah* hollandaise sauce
–de mayonesa *de may-on-ay-sah* mayonnaise sauce
–de tomate *de to-mah-tay* tomato sauce
–inglesa *in-glay-sah* Worcestershire sauce
–romesco *roh-mes-koh* dried capsicum & almond sauce (Catalunya)
–tártara *tah-ta-rah* tartar sauce
–verde *ver-day* parsley & garlic sauce

sultana (*see* **pasa sultana**)

salteado *sal-tee-ah-doh* sautéed

saltear *sal-tee-ahr* to sauté

salvado *a-fray-cho* bran

salvaje (*see* **arroz salvaje**)

salvia *sal-vee-ah* sage

samfaina *sam-fay-ee-nah* grilled vegetable sauce

sancocho *san-ko-choh* fish dish served with potatoes

San José (*see* **buñuelitos de San José; crema de San José**)

San Simón *san see-mon* firm bland cheese made from cow's milk

sandía *san-dee-ah* watermelon

sándwich *sand-gwich* sandwich
–mixto *mix-toh* toasted ham and cheese sandwich

sangría *san-gree-ah* punch made with red wine, lemonade and fruit

sanocho canario *san-oh-choh kan-ah-ree-oh* baked monkfish with potatoes

santanderino *san-tan-de-ree-noh* from Santander

santiagués *san-tee-ah-gwes* from Santiago de Compostela

santo *san-toh* saint's day

sardinas *sah-din-as* sardines
–a la asturiana *ah lah as-too-ri-ah-nah* sardines in cider sauce
–a la murciana *ah lah mur-see-ah-nah* sardine and tomato casserole
–a la parrilla *ah lah par-ril-yah* grilled sardines
–en cazuela *en kas-way-lah* sardines served in a clay pot
–en escabeche *en es-kah-bay-chay* marinated sardines
–fritas *ree-tas* deep-fried sardines
–fritas en adobo *free-tas en a-doh-boh* marinated fried sardines

sargo *sahr-goh* bream

sartenek *sahr-ten-ek* Basque feast

secado al sol *sek-ah-doh al sol* sun-dried

seco *se-koh* dry

segundo plato *seg-oon-doh plat-oh* second/main course

la Selva *lah sel-vah* type of cheese

semi-curado *sem-ee-koo-rah-doh* semi-cured

semidulce *sem-ee-dul-say* medium-sweet

semiseco *semi-sek-oh* semi-dry

sémola *sem-ol-ah* semolina

sepia *sep-ee-ah* cuttlefish

Serena (see **queso de la Serena**)

serranías de Málaga *serr-ah-nee-as de mal-ah-gah* goat's milk cheese

serrat *ser-rat* type of cheese

servicio *ser-vith-ee-oh* service
  –incluido *in-cloo-ee-doh* service included

servilleta *ser-vil-yet-ah* napkin

Servilleta *ser-vil-yet-ah* type of cheese

sésamo *ses-amo* sesame

sesos *seh-sos* brains

seta de marzo *se-tah de mah-soh* type of mushroom

setas *se-tas* wild mushrooms
  –a la kashera *ah lah kash-air-ah* sautéed wild mushrooms
  –a la plancha *ah lah plan-chah* grilled mushrooms
  –de Orduña al horno *de or-dun-yah al orr-noh* roasted mushroom (Orduña)
  –rellenas *rel-ye-nas* stuffed mushrooms

sevillana (see **a la sevillana; ensalada sevillana; espárragos sevillanos**)

shangurro al horno *shan-gu-rro al orr-noh* stuffed spider-crab (see also **txangurro relleno**)

la Siberia *lah si-behr-ee-ah* type of cheese

sidra *see-drah* cider (see also **a la sidra**)

sidrería *sid-rehr-ee-ah* cider bar

Sierra de Segura *see-eh-rah de seg-oo-rah* olive oil producing region (DO)

Sierra Morena *see-eh-rah mor-en-ah* type of cheese

silla alta; sillita *sil-yah al-tah; sil-yee-tah* high chair

siluro *sil-oo-roh* eel-like fish

silvestre *sil-ves-tray* wild

sin crianza *sin kree-an-thah* un-aged wine

sitake *sit-ak-ay* type of mushroom

Siurana *see-oo-ran-ah* olive oil (DO, Tarragona)

sobao (pasiego) *soh-bow (pas-ee-ay-goh)* small sponge square

sobrasada de Mallorca *so-bra-sah-dah de mal-yor-kah* a spreadable spicy, red sausage, speciality of Mallorca (DO)

Sociedad Gastronómica *soth-ee-dad gas-tron-om-ee-kah* Basque Gastronomic Society

soda *soh-dah* soda water

sodio *soh-dee-oh* sodium

sofrit pagés *soh-freet pag-hes* vegetable stew

sofrito *soh-free-toh* fried tomato sauce

soja *soh-khah* soya bean

sol y sombra *sol ee som-brah* 'sun and shade' – anise and brandy

soldaditos de Pavía *sol-dad-ee-tos de pav-ee-ah* cod fritters

solla *sol-yah* plaice

solo *sol-oh* straight

solomillo *sol-oh-mil-yoh* fillet

Somontano *so-mon-tan-oh* wine region (DO) in Aragón

sopa *so-pah* soup
  –aragonesa *ar-ah-gon-ay-sah* liver and cheese soup, served with toasted bread
  –burgalesa *bur-gal-ay-sah* crayfish and lamb soup
  –crema de yemas *kre-mah de yem-as* soup made with egg and ham
  –de ajo *de ah-khoh* garlic soup
  –de arroz *de ah-rroth* rice soup
  –de cebolla *de se-bol-yah* onion soup
  –de fideos *de fi-day-os* noodle soup
  –de frutos de mar *de froo-tos de mahr* shellfish soup
  –de gallina *de gal-yee-nah* chicken soup
  –de legumbres *de leg-oom-brays* vegetable soup
  –de lentejas *de len-te-khas* lentil soup
  –de marisco *de mar-is-koh* fish & shellfish soup
  –de ostras *de os-tras* oyster soup
  –de patatas *de pat-at-as* potato soup
  –de pescado *de pes-kah-doh* fish soup
  –de queso *de ke-soh* cheese and onion soup

–de rape *de ra-peh* monkfish soup

–de tortuga *de taw-too-gah* turtle soup

–de verduras *de ver-doo-ras* vegetable soup

–del día *del dee-ah* soup of the day

–mallorquina *mal-yor-kin-ah* meat soup with tomatoes and eggs

–real *ree-al* ham & chicken soup

–seca mallorquina *sek-ah mal-yor-kin-ah* dry soup made with cabbage

sopas de leche *so-pah de le-chay* pieces of bread soaked in milk and cinnamon

sopas engañadas *so-pah en-gan-yah-das* capsicum, onion shoots, vinegar, figs and grapes

sopera *so-pehr-ah* soup tureen

sorbete *sor-bet-ay* sorbet

sorbete de naranja *sor-bay-tay de na-ran-khah* orange sorbet

Soria *so-ree-ah* goat's milk cheese (Soria)

sorroputún *sor-roh-poo-tun* tuna casserole

suave *swah-vay* mild

suizo *swee-thoh* sugared bun

sukaldi *soo-kal-dee* beef stew

supermercado *su-per-mer-kah-doh* supermarket

suquet *soo-ket* clams in almond sauce

suquet de peix *soo-ket de pesh* fish stew

surtido *sur-tee-doh* selection/assortment

suspiros de monja *sus-pee-ros de mon-khah* 'nun's sighs', custard sweet

T

taberna *tab-er-nah* bar

Tacoronte-Acentejo *tak-or-on-tay-a-sen-te-khoh* wine region (DO) in the Canary Islands

tajo *ta-khoh* chopping board

tallarines *tal-yahr-in-es* pasta noodles

talo *tal-oh* corn bread (Bizkaia)

tamiz *ta-mith* sifter

tapadera *ta-pa-dehr-ah* lid

tapa/s *ta-pa/s* small portions of hot or cold food served in a bar

Tarragona *tar-ra-gon-ah* wine region (DO) in Catalunya

tarro *tar-roh* jar

tarta *tahr-tah* cake

–de almendra *de al-men-drah* almond tart

–de cumpleaños *de kum-ple-an-yos* birthday cake

–de manzana *de man-tha-nah* apple tart

–de queso *de ke-soh* cheesecake

–de Santiago *de san-tee-ah-goh* cinnamon and powdered almond tart

–helada *e-lah-dah* ice cream cake

–nupcial *nup-see-al* wedding cake

–valenciana *val-en-see-ah-nah* almond tart

tartaleta *tahr-tah-let-ah* tartlet

tartaletas de cangrejo *tahr-tah-let-as de kan-gre-khoh* crab tartlets

tartaletas de gambas *tahr-tah-let-as de gam-bas* shrimp tartlets

tartaletas de huevos revueltos *tahr-tah-let-as de hway-vos rev-wel-tos* scrambled egg tartlets

tasca *tas-ka* bar

taza *ta-thah* cup

tazón *ta-thon* (mixing) bowl

té *teh* tea

tenacillas *ten-ah-sil-yas* tongs

tenca *ten-kah* tench

tenedor *ten-e-dor* fork

Tenerife *ten-er-ee-fay* type of cheese

ternasco *ter-nas-koh* spit-roasted suckling lamb

ternasco de Aragón *ter-nas-koh de ar-ah-gohn* suckling-lamb from Aragón (DO)

ternera *ter-neh-rah* veal – often more mature *(see also* **escalope de ternera; escalopes de ternera rellenas; guisado de ternera)**

–la condesita *ah lah kon-des-ee-tah* veal in almond and sherry sauce

–a la sevillana *ah lah sev-il-yah-nah* veal served with wine and olives

–asada *a-sah-dah* roast veal

–en cazuela con berenjenas *en kath-way-lah kon ber-en-khen-as* veal and eggplant casserole

–encebollada *en-seb-ol-yah-dah* veal and onion stew

–gallega *gal-yeh-gah* veal (DO, Galicia)

Terra Alta *ter-rah al-tah* wine producing region (DO) in Catalunya

Tetilla *tet-il-yah* creamy and pungent cow's milk cheese (DO, Galicia)

tiempo (see **del tiempo**)

tienda de alimentación *tee-en-dah de al-ee-men-tath-ee-on* local food store

tienda de comestibles *tee-en-dah de kom-es-tee-blays* local food store

tienda de vinos *tee-en-dah de vee-nos* wine shop

tierra (see **criadilla de tierra**)

Tietar *tee-et-ar* mozarella-like cheese (Avila)

tigra *tig-rah* **tapa** (Burgos)

tijeras *tikh-er-as* scissors

tila *tee-lah* lime tea

tinta ink (see **chipirones en su tinta**)

tinto *tin-toh* red

tirijaras *tir-i-khah-ras* confection from the Canary Islands

tiznao *tith-now* shredded cod baked with vegetables

tocino *toh-see-noh* salt pork; bacon

–del cielo *del si-el-oh* creamy dessert made with egg yolk and sugar, with a caramel topping

tocrudo *to-kroo-doh* 'everything raw' – salad made with meat, garlic, onion and green capsicum

tojunto *to-khoon-toh* mountain rabbit, onion & green capsicum stew

tomate *to-mah-tay* tomato

–(de) pera *(de) peh-rah* plum tomato

–frito *free-toh* tinned tomato sauce

tomates enteros y pelados *to-mah-tes en-tehr-os ee pe-lah-dos* (tinned) whole tomatoes

tomates rellenos de atún *to-mah-tes rel-ye-nos de a-tun* tomatoes stuffed with tuna

tomates triturados *to-mah-tes trit-oo-rah-dos* (tinned) puréed tomatoes

tomillo *to-mil-yoh* thyme

tonel *ton-el* barrel

tónica con ginebra *ton-ee-kah kon hin-eb-rah* gin and tonic

toro *to-roh* bull meat

Toro *to-roh* wine producing region (DO) in Castilla y León

torrefacto *tor-ray-fak-toh* dark-roasted coffee beans

torrija *tor-ree-khah* French toast

torta *tor-tah* pie/tart; also flat bread

–de aceite *de a-say-tay* sweet, flat cake or biscuit made with oil

–de anchoas *de ahn-choh-as* anchovy pie

–de miel y nueces *de mee-el ee noo-eh-sehs* pastry strips with honey and nuts

–de morcillas *de mor-sil-yah* black pudding pie

–del casar *del ka-sar* type of cheese

–imperial *im-per-e-al* nougat-like confection

–manchega *man-cheh-gah* large round unleavened bread from La Mancha, eaten with **gazpacho manchego**

–pascualina *pas-kwal-ee-nah* spinach and egg pie eaten at Easter

tortell *tor-tel* ring cake (Catalunya)

tortilla *tor-til-yah* omelette

–a la murciana *ah lah mür-see-ah-nah* vegetable

–de bacalao *de bak-a-low* cod

–de champiñones *de sham-pin-yon-es* mushroom (see also **tortilla de setas**)

–de chorizo *de choh-ree-thoh* spicy sausage

–de espinaca *de es-pee-na-ka* spinach

–de gambas *de gam-bas* shrimp

–de patatas *de pat-at-as* potato

–de setas *de se-tas* mushroom (see also **tortilla de champiñones**)

–española *es-pan-yoh-lah* potato and onion omelette

–francesa *fran-say-sah* plain

–gallega *gal-yeh-gah* potato with chilli, ham and peas

–sacramente *sak-rah-men-tay* with offal, potatoes, red capsicum and peas

tortillas de camarones *tor-til-yah de kam-ah-roh-nes* shrimp fritters

tortita *tor-tee-tah* waffle

tostada *tos-tah-dah* toasted bread

tostadora *tos-tah-dor-ah* toaster

tostar *tos-tahr* to roast

tostón *tos-ton* roast suckling pig

Tresviso *tres-vee-soh* cheese-making region

trigo *tree-goh* wheat (see **guisado de trigo**)

–sarraceno *sar-rah-sen-oh* buckwheat

trinchante *trin-chan-tay* carving knife

trinxat amb rosta *trin-shat am ros-tah* pork, cabbage and potato dish

tripas *trip-as* intestines/guts

tripasai *trip-as-ai* gourmet

triturador de ajos *try-too-rah-dohr de ah-khos* garlic press

trompero *trom-ehr-oh* type of mushroom

Tronchón *tron-chon* mild ewe's milk cheese (Teruel)

tronco de merluza *tron-koh de mer-loo-thah* hake with clams

trucha *troo-chah* trout

–a la marinera *ah lah mah-rin-ehr-ah* trout in a white wine sauce

–ahumada *ah-oo-mah-dah* smoked trout

–en escabeche *en es-kah-bay-chay* marinated trout

truchas a la montañesa *troo-chas ah lah mon-tan-yeh-sah* trout with capsicums and wine

truchas a la navarra *troo-chas ah lah nah-va-rra* trout with ham

truchas con vino y romero *troo-chas kon vee-noh ee roh-mehr-oh* trout with red wine and rosemary

truchas escabechadas *troo-chah es-kah-bay-cha-das* marinated trout

trufa *troo-fah* truffle

–tarta *tah-tah* chocolate truffle cake

tubo *too-boh* glass of beer (250 ml)

tudelana (see **menestra tudelana**)

tumbet (de peix) *tum-bet (de pesh)* vegetable soufflé, sometimes containing fish (see also **tombet de peix**)

Tupi *too-pee* type of cheese

turrón *too-rron* Spanish nougat

–de Alicante *too-rron de al-ee-kan-tay* chunky **turrón** from Alicante (DO)

–de fruta *too-rron de froo-tah* **turrón** covered in glacé fruit

–de gofio *too-rron de goh-fee-oh* nougat made with a cornmeal or barley dough (Canary Islands)

–de Jijona *too-rron de hi-khoh-nah* soft fine **turrón** (DO, Jijona)

–guirlache *gweer-lah-chay* almond and caramel **turrón**

txakolí *chak-oh-lee* also spelled **chacolí** – light, sharp white wine (Basque Country; Navarra)

txacoliñ gorri *chak-oh-lin gor-ree* red grape **txakolí**

txacoliñ zuri *chak-oh-lin zoo-ree* white grape **txakolí**

txangurro (relleno) **chan-gu-rro (rel-ye-noh)** stuffed spider-crab (see also **shangurro al horno**)

txarriboda *char-ree-bo-dah* Basque feast

txipirones *chip-ee-ron-es* baby squid in their own ink

txitxardiñak *chit-shahr-din-yak* baby eels with garlic

U

Ulloa *ul-yoh-ah* soft cow's milk cheese

Urbies *ur-be-yes* type of cheese

Utiel-Requena *ut-ee-el-rek-en-yah* wine region (DO) in València

uva *oo-bah* grape

–de corinto *de kor-in-toh* currant

–pasa *pas-ah* raisin

–sultana *sul-tah-nah* sultana

V

vaca *ba-ka* beef (*see also* **queso de vaca**)

vacuno *va-koo-noh* beef

vainilla *vay-nil-yah* vanilla

vajilla *va-khil-yah* crockery/dishes

Valdeorres *val-de-or-res* wine region (DO) in Galicia

Valdepeñas *val-de-pen-yas* wine region (DO) in La Mancha

Valdeteja *val-det-e-khah* type of cheese

Valencia *val-en-see-ah* wine-producing region (DO)

valenciana (*see* **almejas a la valenciana; empanada valenciana; ensalada valenciana**)

Valle de Arán *val-yay de a-ran* type of cheese

vapor *va-poo-ar* steam (*see also* **al vapor**)

vaporera *va-poo-ar-ehr-ah* steamer

vasca (*see* **a la vasca; ensalada a la vasca**)

vaso *bah-soh* glass; glass of wine

vegetariano *veg-et-ar-ee-ah-noh* vegetarian
　–estricto *es-trik-toh* vegan

vela *vel-ah* candle

venado *ven-ad-oh* venison (*see also* **estofado venado**)

vendimia *ven-dim-ee-ah* vintage/harvest

venera *ven-er-ah* scallop

la Vera *lah ver-ah* type of cheese

verano *ve-rah-noh* summer

verdulería *ver-dul-ehr-ee-ah* greengrocer

verduras *ver-doo-ras* vegetables (*see also* **crema de verduras**)

vermut *ver-moot* vermouth

Vidiago *vid-ee-ah-goh* type of cheese

vieira *vee-eh-rah* scallop
　(*see also* **empanada de vieiras**)

vieiras al vino blanco *vee-eh-ras al vee-noh blan-koh* scallops in white wine

vieiras con col *vee-eh-ras kon kol* scallops with white cabbage

vieiras estofadas *vee-eh-ras es-to-fah-das* stewed scallops

viejas *vee-e-khas* grouper

viejo *vee-e-khoh* aged (of cheese etc)

vilareal (*see* **chuletas de cordero vilareal**)

villagodio *vil-yah-god-ee-oh* large steak

Villalón *vil-yal-on* curd cheese from ewe's milk

vinagre *vin-ag-reh* vinegar
　–de Jeréz *de he-reth* sherry based vinegar

vinícolas (*see* **comarcas vinícolas**)

vino *vee-noh* wine; glass of wine (*see also* **batalla del vino**)
　–corriente *korr-ee-en-te* house wine
　–de la casa *de lah ka-sah* house wine
　–de la tierra *de lah tee-air-ra* local wine
　–de mesa *de may-sah* table wine
　–de pasto *de pah-stoh* table wine
　–de reserva *de re-serv-ah* wine aged for at least two years in vats and one year in the bottle
　–del país *del pay-ihs* local wine
　–joven *hoh-ven* unaged wine
　–peleón *pel-ee-on* plonk; cheap wine

visita *vis-ee-tah* almond cake

vizcaína (*see* **a la vizcaína**)

vuelco *vwel-koh* each of the three stages in the serving of a traditional **cocido**

W

whisky de centeno *gwis-kee de sen-ten-oh* rye whisky

X

xato *shat-oh* chicory salad

xoli *shol-ee* sausage (Lérida)

Y

Yecla *yek-lah* wine region (DO) in Murcia
yemas *yeh-mas* small round cakes
yogur *yog-ur* yoghurt

Z

zamorano *tham-or-ah-noh* cheese made with sheep's milk (DO)
zanahoria *zan-a-or-ee-ah* carrot
zarangollo *tha-ran-gol-yoh* fried zucchini
zarzamora *zar-zam-or-ah* blackberry
zarzuela de mariscos *thar-thway-lah de mar-is-kos* spicy shellfish stew
zarzuela de pescado *thar-thway-lah de pes-kah-doh* fish in almond sauce

zonas de crianza *tho-nas de kree-an-thah* the three 'authorised' Rioja-producing regions, Rioja Alta, Rioja Alavesa and Rioja Baja
zumo *soo-moh* juice
–de lima *de lee-mah* lime juice
–de naranja *de na-ran-khah* orange juice
–de piña *de peen-yah* pineapple juice
–de tomate *de to-mah-tay* tomato juice
zurito *zoo-ree-toh* small glass of beer (125 ml)
zurracapote *thoor-rah-kah-poh-tay* mulled wine
zurrukutano *zoo-rroo-koo-tah-noh* cod and green capsicum soup

A

alcohol, *see also* wine, sherry, beer
    aguardientes 102-3
    anís 102
    cider 97
    Licor 43 103
    orujo 103
    Ponche Caballero 103
    sangría 101
Alella 84
All Saint's Day 126
Almería 51
Andalucía 24-5, 30, 51, 54, 57, 94, 206
Aragón 84, 173
Arbeca 55
Art Nouveau 161
Artíes 174
Arzak Restaurant 164
Asturias 145

B

Bar Antillano 205
Bar Boquería 180
Bar Clemen's 180
Bar Kisoco 180
Bar Pinotxo 180
Bar Sant Josep 180
Barcelona 42, 161-63, 201
Barrio de la Viña 121
Basque Country 164-73
beer 97-9
    Cruzcampo 97-8
    Damn 99
    Mahou 99
    San Miguel 99
Benissano 61
Bermuda Triangle 31
bread 24-5, 152
Byass 93

C

Cádiz 33, 51, 121, 140-2
Camino de Santiago 164
Cantabria 145, 149, 154

Carnavale 121
Casa Irene 174
Castilla-La Mancha 51
Castillo San Sebastián 142
Castro, Fidel 143
Castro, Rosalia de 85
Catalunya 25, 51, 81, 155, 159-63
Catedral del Apóstol 151
Catherine of Aragón 93
Cato the Elder 42
cava, *see* wine
Cervantes 30
Charlemagne 164
cheese 26, 122, 223
    Ahumado de Aliva 154
    garrotxa 159
    Idiazábal 171
    La Peral 154
    Mahón 159
    Manchego 26
    San Simón 153
    Tetilla 154, 162
children 231
chocolate 16, 105
Chocolatería de San Ginés 137
Christians 90
Christmas 122-3
Cibeles 137
coffee 106
Columbus 159
cooking 109-16
Córdoba 51
culture 9-22

D

Damm, Auguste Kuentzmann 99
Denominations of Origin and
    Specificity 15
desserts 70-2
    adoquines 173
    alfajor 123
    almendrado 123-4
    bienmesabe 123
    bizcochos borrachos 123
    cabello de angel 123
    churros 16

INDEX

Compota de Peras 221, 223
crema Catalana 214
galletas 184-5
hojaldres 123
huessos santos 122, 126
intxaursalsa 123
mantecado 123
mazapán 123
membrillo 123
monas de Pascua 121
mostachones 123
pestiño 123
polvorón 123
roscón de Reyes 122-3
turrón 122-4
yema 123
diabetics 232
dinner 19
Drake, Sir Frances 93
drinks 77-108

E
Easter 121
eating habits 19, 228
Ebro Valley 51
eggs 27
El Levante 57-8, 112, 155
El Palmar 125
Elizabeth I 93
etiquette 21-2
Extremadura 126

F
Falstaff, Sir John 93
festivals
    All Saint's Day 126
    Carnavale 121
    Christmas 122-3
    Easter 121
    Running of the Bulls in Pamplona 125
    San Fermín 125
    Tomatina, The 126
    Wine War, The 121
Franco, Francisco 143

fruit 32-3
    apples 147
    figs 44
    oranges 33
    pears 221

G
Galicia 85, 145, 154, 183
Garduña Restaurante 181
Gaudí, Antoni 159, 161, 163
Gerona 57
goblins 143
Goya, Francisco 136
Granada 51
grapes 32, *see also* wine
Gypsies 30

H
health 225-34
Hemingway, Ernest 164
Henry I 93
herbs 46-7
history 15
Holy Trinity 12
Hondarribia 44
horchata 105
horno asador, *see* places to eat & drink
hors d'oeuvres, *see* tapas
Huelva 51
hunting 43

I
influences
    Celtic 143
    French 164
    German 164
    Moorish 70, 131, 164
    Roman 12, 40, 131, 141, 161, 164
inquisition 140
Irízar, Louis 166-7

J
Jabugo 35
Jaén 51, 54
James the Apostle 151

K
Kiosco Moderno 180
Kiosco Universal 180

L
La Boquería (market) 159, 177-81
La Coruña 143, 147-8
La Mancha 26, 30, 161
La Sagrada Família 161, 163
Lent 121
leprechauns 143
Lérida 55
Liebana 154
López, Cándido 131
Luis Bertrán, San 126

M
Madrid 33, 133-9, 205
Magaña, Antonio 181
Málaga 51, 54
Mallorca 57
markets 177-81
meat
    beef 44
    bull 43
    carne de lidia 43
    cecina 42, 187, 224
    chicken 44
    duck 33, 44
    game 43
    goat 42
    ham 34-9, 122, 214
    lamb 44, 121, 173
    partridge 44
    pigeon 44
    pork 44, 145
    rabbit 44, 173, 218-9
    salchichón 224
    sausages 40-1
    tripe 133
    turkey 122
    venison 42
Menorca 159
menus
    a la carte 215
    set 211-4
    wine list 216
Mercado Central 33, 142
Miño 88
Montilla 94
Museum of Gallego Breads 152
mushrooms 168

N
Napoleon 58
New Year's Eve 121

O
olive oil 49-55, 140, 187, 224, 227
olives 25, 32, 44, 179, 223
    Arbequina 55
    Cornicabra 55
    Hojiblanco 54
    Picual 54
Osborne, Roberto & Tomas 93, 97

P
paella 59-61, 213, 218, 219
País Vasco, see Basque Country
Palace Hotel 205
Pamplona 125
Parc Güell 163
pasta 159
Pego 57
Penedès 81-4
Petit Bar 180
picnics 141-2, 151-2, 161-3, 173
places to eat & drink 180, 189-208
    casa de comidas 195
    chocolatería 208
    horchatería 208
    horno asador 192
    jamónería 199
    restaurante 194
    sidrería 207
    taberna 206
    tasca 196-8
    terraza 193
Playa de la Caleta 142

Plaza de las Cortes 137
Plaza de Santa Ana 136
Plaza de Topete 141
Plaza Mayor 136
Praza da Inmaculada 152
Praza de Cervantes 152
Priorato 84

R

Raventós, Jose 83
regions 127-74
    Atlantic Spain 143-54
    Heart of Spain 128-42
    Mediterranean Spain 155-63
    Pyrenees 165-74
Restaurants, *see* places to eat & drink
Rías Baixas 87
Ribeiro 88
rice 57-61
Rioja 84, 89-91
Running of the Bulls 125

S

saffron 59-60, 161, 187
salad 33, 213, 221
Salamanca 35
San Fermín Festival 125
San Sebastián 164
Sandeman 93
Sandvitxeria Central 180
Santiago de Compostela 151-4
sauces
    garlic 64
    green 66
    marinades 65
    mayonnaise 66
    nut 65
    onion 148
    paprika 64
    pimentón 64
    Salsa Romesco 63
    sherry wine 132
    sofrito 64
    wine 65

seafood 29
    anchovies 29, 177, 223
    bream 122
    clams 177
    cod 29-31, 122, 170, 173, 178
    crab 173
    eel 31
    eels 223
    goose barnacles 149
    hake 147, 148
    mussels 148, 177, 223
    octopus 143-4, 223
    prawns 29
    sardines 29, 223
    shellfish 122, 157, 177
    shrimp 177
    squid 223
    trout 174
    tuna 29, 173, 177-8, 223
seaweed 177
Segovia 131-2
Sevilla 33, 51, 54
sherry 93-6
    Amontillado 95
    Fino 95
    Manzanilla 95
shopping 175-88
Sierra de Huelva 35
siesta 19
Sobrino de Botín 191
soft drinks 106
solera system 93
Soriano, Andres 99
soups 67-9
    caldo gallego 149, 211
    gazpacho 68-9, 211
    salmorejo 24
speciality shops
    bodega 183
    carnicería 183
    charcutería 183
    confitería 183
    frutería 33, 183
    panadería 183
    pastelería 183

pescadería 183
polería 183
tienda 183
verdulería 183
spices 46-7
staples 23-76
supermarkets 184-5

T

tapas, 26, 73-76, 128-31, 223
tea 105
Teruel 35
tipping 194
Toledo 30
Tomatina, The 126
tortilla 27

U

utensils
adobe horno 214
calderetas 114
cazuela 113, 114, 131, 187, 214
chupitos 188
hornos asadores 131
jarras 188
maquina 38
mortero y mano 115
ollas 113
paellera 113, 187
parrillada 113
porrón 113
queimada 188

V

Valdeorras 88
Valencia 47
Vega, Samuel de 115
vegetables 155

asparagus 213
beans 155
broccoli 33
capsicums 172
eggplant 33
spinach 220
tomatoes 33, 126
turnips 44
vegetarian 201-3, 214

W

water 107-8, 227
mineral 108
wine 79-91
Albariño 85, 87-8, 147
cava 83-4, 122
Garnacha 84, 91
Garnacha Blanca 84, 91
Godello 88
Graciano 91
Lado 88
L'Ermita 84
Loureira 88
Macabeo 84
Malvasia 91
Manzuelo 91
Mencía 88
Palomino 94
Pansá Blanca 84
Pansá Rosada 84
Parellada 81, 84
Tempranillo 90, 91
Torrontés 88
Treixadura 88
Viña Sol 81
Vi Novell 91
Viura 91
Xarel-lo 84
Wine War, The 121

302

INDEX

Boxed Text

A Galician Cheese Tasting 154
Anguilas (Eels) 31
Antonio Magaña – Faces of Gastronomy 181
Basket of Basque 173
Certified Olive Oil Areas 54
Choose Your Brew 106
Closed for Lunch 195
Creating Cava 83
Denominations of Origin and Specificity 15
Don't Miss
    Heart of Spain 129
    Mediterranean Spain 159
    Pyrenees, The 164
Dress Your Salad 33
Essential Oil, The 53
Faces of Gastronomy - Jose Grimaldi 18
Food on the Runs 230
For the Love of Guts 45
Grape Varieties of Rioja 91
Grazing Hell - Tips For The Transient Herbivore 202-3

Ham in Montefrio 38
I'll Have the Vegetable Version, Please 201
Joke's on Me, The 169
Loving Lard 140
Mineral Water Classifications 108
Mortero Y Mano (Mortar & Pestle) 115
Mushroom Mania 168
Navidad (Christmas) 122-3
Nocturnal Madrileños 135-7
Nothing on the Side 215
Oil Overload 227
Olive Oils 51
Paella Man 61
Saints' Days 118
Solera System, The 96
Stranger in a Strange Land 166
Tabasco 47
Tascas and Kids 76
Test Your Ham Knowledge 35
Test Your Tomatina Knowledge 126
Unseen Hand, The 184-5
Water Rights 57
Wisdom in Wine 89

Maps

Barcelona 162
Cádiz 141
Hondaribia 170
La Coruña 143
Madrid 138

regions 128
San Sebastián (Donostia) 170
Santiago de Compostela 151
Sevilla 129
Valencia 156

Recipes

Ajo Blanco (White Gazpacho) 69
Almendrados (Almond Biscuits) 124
Callos a la Madrileña (Tripe Casserole with Chorizo and Chillies) 133
Churros con Chocolate (Fried Doughnut Strips with Chocolate) 16
Compota de Peras (Pear Compote) 221
Ensalada de Arroz (Rice Salad) 125
Fabada Asturiana (Stew made with Pork, Blood Sausage and White Beans) 145
Garbanzos con Espinacas (Chickpeas with Spinach) 220
Gazpacho Andaluz (Andalucían

Gazpacho) 68
High Mountain Trucha (Trout) 174
Merluza Encebollada (Hake with Onion Sauce) 148
Paella de La Huerta (Paella with Rabbit and Vegetables) 218-9
Pimientos Rellenos (Stuffed Red Capsicums) 172
Salsa Romesco 63
Sangria 101
Tortillas de Camarones (Shrimp Fritters) 18
Zarzuela De Mariscos (Spicy Shellfish Stew) 157

More World Food Titles

Brimming with cultural insight, the World Food series takes the guesswork out of new cuisines and provide the ideal guides to your own culinary adventures. The books cover everything to do with food and drink in each country – the history and evolution of the cuisine, its staples & specialities, and the kitchen philosophy of the people. You'll find definitive two-way dictionaries, menu readers and useful phrases for shopping, drunken apologies and much more.

The essential guides for travelling and non-travelling food lovers around the world, look out for the full range of World Food titles including:

Italy,
Morocco,
Mexico,
Thailand,
Turkey,
Vietnam,
Deep South (USA),
France,
Ireland &
Hong Kong.

Out to Eat Series

Lonely Planet's Out to Eat series takes its food seriously but offers a fresh approach with independent, unstuffy opinion on hundreds of hand-picked restaurants, bars and cafes in each city. Along with reviews, Out to Eat identifies the best culinary cul-de-sacs, describes cultural contexts of ethnic cuisines, and explains menu terms and ingredients.

Updated annually, new Out to Eat titles include:
Melbourne, Paris, Sydney, London and San Francisco.

Planet Talk

Our FREE quarterly printed newsletter is full of tips from travellers and anecdotes from Lonely Planet guidebook authors. Every issue is packed with up-to-date travel news and advice, and includes:

- a postcard from Lonely Planet co-founder Tony Wheeler
- a swag of mail from travellers
- a look at life on the road through the eyes of a Lonely Planet author
- topical health advice
- prizes for the best travel yarn
- news about forthcoming Lonely Planet events
- a complete list of Lonely Planet books and other titles

To join our mailing list, residents of the UK, Europe and Africa can email us at go@lonelyplanet.co.uk; residents of North and South America can do so at info@lonelyplanet.com; the rest of the world can email talk2us@lonelyplanet.com.au, or contact any Lonely Planet office.

The Lonely Planet Story

Lonely Planet published its first book in 1973 in response to the numerous 'How did you do it?' questions Maureen and Tony Wheeler were asked after driving, bussing, hitching, sailing and railing their way from England to Australia. Written at a kitchen table and hand collated, trimmed and stapled, *Across Asia on the Cheap* became an instant local bestseller.

Eighteen months in South-East Asia resulted in their second guide, *South-East Asia on a Shoestring*, which they put together in a backstreet Chinese hotel in Singapore in 1975. The 'yellow bible', as it quickly became known to backpackers around the world, soon became the guide to the region. It has sold well over ¾ million copies and is now in its 10th edition, still retaining its familiar yellow cover.

Today there are over 400 titles, including travel guides, walking guides, language kits & phrasebooks, travel atlases & maps, diving guides, restaurant guides, first time travel guides, condensed guides, illustrated pictorials and travel literature. The company is the largest independent travel publisher in the world.

The emphasis continues to be on travel for independent travellers. Tony and Maureen still travel for several months of each year and play an active part in the writing, updating and quality control of Lonely Planet's guides.

They have been joined by over 120 authors and over 400 staff at our offices in Melbourne (Australia), Oakland (USA), London (UK) and Paris (France). Travellers themselves also make a valuable contribution to the guides through the feedback we receive in thousands of letters each year and on our web site.

The people at Lonely Planet strongly believe that travellers can make a positive contribution to the countries they visit, both through their appreciation of the countries' culture, wildlife and natural features, and through the money they spend. In addition, the company makes a direct contribution to the countries and regions it covers. Since 1986 a percentage of the income from each book has been donated to ventures such as famine relief in Africa; aid projects in India; agricultural projects in Central America; Greenpeace's efforts to halt French nuclear testing in the Pacific.

Lonely Planet Offices

Australia
PO Box 617, Hawthorn, Victoria 3122
☎ 03-9819 1877
fax 03-9819 6459
email:talk2us@lonelyplanet.com.au

USA
150 Linden St, Oakland, CA 94607
☎ 510-893 8555 TOLL FREE: 800 275 8555
fax 510-893 8572
email: info@lonelyplanet.com

UK
10a Spring Place, London NW5 3BH
☎ 020-7428 4800
fax 020-7428 4828
email: go@lonelyplanet.co.uk

France
1 rue du Dahomey, 75011 Paris
☎ 01 55 25 33 00
fax 01 55 25 33 01
email: bip@lonelyplanet.fr